THE TOP
10
OF SPORT

THE TOP
10
OF SPORT

Russell Ash
and Ian Morrison

CONTENTS

London, New York, Munich, Melbourne, Delhi

A PENGUIN COMPANY

Senior Editor Nicki Lampon
Senior Art Editor Anna Benjamin
DTP Designers Sonia Charbonnier, Rajen Shah
Production Heather Hughes
Managing Editor Sharon Lucas
Managing Art Editor Marianne Markham
Category Publisher Stephanie Jackson

Produced for Dorling Kindersley by
Design Revolution Ltd,
Queens Park Villa,
30 West Drive,
Brighton BN2 0QW

Senior Designer Becky Willis
Designer Michael Lebihan
Project Editor Julie Whitaker

Published in Great Britain in 2002 by
Dorling Kindersley Ltd,
80 Strand, London WC2R 0RL

2 4 6 8 10 9 7 5 3 1

A CIP catalogue record of this book is available from
the British Library

ISBN 07513 4642 X

Reproduction by Colourscan, Singapore

Printed and bound in Slovakia by Neografia

See our complete catalogue at
www.dk.com

INTRODUCTION

Top 10 lists

There are certain subjects that naturally benefit from being presented in the form of lists. Sport, with its focus firmly on winning, and hence comparison between the relative success of one individual or a team against another, is among the most fitting. Indeed, there are some sports – most notably cricket in the United Kingdom and baseball in the United States – whose statistics captivate their followers almost as much as the sports themselves.

Sports coverage

The Top 10 of Sport presents the 10 (or sometimes, in view of the presence of several of equal standing, more than 10) leaders in innumerable aspects of every major sport, including national and international competitions, and major divisions within each, as well as those that attract fewer followers. We have tried to be even-handed about what to include and what to omit, but if you are passionate about one of the more minority sports and distressed by its absence, please accept our apologies.

▼ Golfing superstar Tiger Woods. His appearance on more than one list in this book emphasizes his status as one of the top golfers of all time.

Made to measure

The Top 10 of Sport contains a mixture of hard statistical facts and trivia, while the "At the Start" entries briefly detail the origins and developments of each sport. Quotations by and about sportspeople provide the only detour into personal opinion, since all the Top 10 lists that follow are entirely quantifiable – highest scorers, leading award- or money-winners, and so on – or rank the 10 first achievers in a particular area of sporting endeavour. Cut-off dates in most instances are as of the end of the latest season, but inevitably some seasons were in progress as we went to press. Equal entries are generally listed alphabetically, unless a goal differential or similar offers some distinction between those of otherwise equal standing.

Sporting superstars

One of the things Top 10 lists do is to highlight just how far ahead of their competitors certain superstars of sport are. When we see exponents such as Tiger Woods in golf or Wayne Gretzky in ice hockey appear so prominently in so many lists, it further emphasizes their status within their respective fields.

World class

The many Olympic lists offer country comparisons, while those within sports indicate national skills and enthusiasms. While large countries – especially the former Soviet Union and the USA – dominate many sports, it is notable that small countries such as Hungary figure prominently in sports like fencing and table tennis, while, perhaps surprisingly, Cuba matches Japan in women's judo.

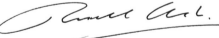

Record-breakers

Top 10 lists provide a perspective where the achievements of individuals can be seen alongside those of their rivals, so we can see at a glance just how unassailable their leads appear to be. However, even though so many are hard acts to follow, it would be short-sighted to say that they will never be beaten: the once "impossible" four-minute-mile record now stands at 3 minutes 43.13 seconds, and although there are world records that have stood for almost 20 years, they are in the minority as new sporting generations challenge the records of their predecessors.

Contact us

If you have any comments or corrections, or ideas for new lists for a future edition of The Top 10 of Sport, please contact us at: ash@pavilion.co.uk (Russell Ash) or igm@atlas-iap.es (Ian Morrison).

ATHLETICS

At the Start

The origin of running competitions can be dated back to 3800 BC in Egypt. At the first Olympic Games, the athletes (from the Greek, *athlos*, a contest) competed in running, jumping, discus and javelin throwing, wrestling, and boxing. The earliest-recorded winner of an athletics competition was Coroebus of Elis, who won the stadium-length sprint race at the Olympics in 776 BC. His prize was an apple. Modern additions to track and field events include the Marathon, which commemorates the run of Pheidippides from Marathon to Athens in 490 BC, bringing news of a victory over the invading Persians. After breaking the news, he dropped dead.

- Longest-standing current Olympic records
- Most track & field gold medals in men's events
- Most track & field gold medals in women's events
- Countries with track & field golds in men's events
- Track & field medal winners at one Olympics
- Countries with track & field golds in women's events

> Perhaps there's no such thing as an unbeatable performance, but for a reasonable facsimile thereof, Beamon's leap of 29 feet 2½ inches at the Mexico City Olympics, October 1968 does nicely.
> **Red Smith,** sportswriter

OLYMPIC CHAMPIONS

Top 10 Longest-standing current Olympic records

	Event	Athlete/country	Winning distance/time/score	Date
1	Men's long jump	Bob Beamon, USA	8.90 m	18 Oct 1968
2	Women's shot	Ilona Slupianek, East Germany	22.41 m	24 July 1980
3	Women's 800 metres	Nadezhda Olizarenko, USSR	1 min 53.42 sec	27 July 1980
4	Women's 4 x 100 metres	East Germany	41.60 sec	1 Aug 1980
5	Decathlon	Daley Thompson, UK	8,847 points	9 Aug 1984
6	Men's 5,000 metres	Saïd Aouita, Morocco	13 min 5.59 sec	11 Aug 1984
7	Men's marathon	Carlos Lopes, Portugal	2 hr 9 min 21 sec	12 Aug 1984
8	Men's shot	Ulf Timmermann, East Germany	22.47 m	23 Sep 1988
9 =	Women's 100 metres	Florence Griffith-Joyner, USA	10.54 sec	24 Sep 1988
=	Women's heptathlon	Jackie Joyner-Kersee, USA	7,291 points	24 Sep 1988

Bob Beamon's record-breaking jump in 1968 is regarded as one of the greatest achievements in athletics. He was aided by Mexico City's rarefied atmosphere, but to add a staggering 55 cm (22½ in) to the old world record and win the competition by 71 cm (28 in) was no mean feat. At 29 ft 2½ in, Beamon's jump was the first to exceed 28 feet, let alone 29 feet. The next jump to exceed 28 feet in the Olympics was not until 1980, 12 years after Beamon's leap.

Top 10 Most track & field gold medals in men's events*

	Athlete/country	Golds
1	Ray Ewry, USA	10
2 =	Carl Lewis, USA	9
=	Paavo Nurmi, Finland	9
4 =	Michael Johnson, USA	5
=	Ville Ritola, Finland	5
=	Martin Sheridan, USA	5
7 =	Harrison Dillard, USA	4
=	Archie Hahn, USA	4
=	Hannes Kolehmainen, Finland	4
=	Alvin Kraenzlein, USA	4
=	Eric Lemming, Sweden	4
=	Jim Lightbody, USA	4
=	Al Oerter, USA	4
=	Jesse Owens, USA	4
=	Myer Prinstein, USA	4
=	Mel Sheppard, USA	4
=	Lasse Viren, Finland	4
=	Emil Zatopek, Czechoslovakia	4

* Including relays

Top 10 Most track & field gold medals in women's events*

	Athlete/country	Golds
1 =	Evelyn Ashford, USA	4
=	Fanny Blankers-Koen, Netherlands	4
=	Betty Cuthbert, Australia	4
=	Bärbel Wockel (née Eckert), East Germany	4
5 =	Valerie Brisco-Hooks, USA	3
=	Olga Bryzgina, USSR/Unified Team	3
=	Shirley de la Hunty-Strickland, Australia	3
=	Gail Devers, USA	3
=	Florence Griffith-Joyner, USA	3
=	Marion Jones, USA	3
=	Jackie Joyner-Kersee, USA	3
=	Tatyana Kazankina, USSR	3
=	Marie-Josè Perèc, France	3
=	Tamara Press, USSR	3
=	Wilma Rudolph, USA	3
=	Renate Stecher, East Germany	3
=	Irena Szewinska-Kirzenstein, Poland	3
=	Gwen Torrence, USA	3
=	Wyomia Tyus, USA	3

* Including relays

DID YOU KNOW? Bob Beamon nearly didn't make the 1968 Olympic long jump final. His first two qualifying jumps were "no jumps" – one more and he would have been out.

Top 10 Countries with track & field golds in men's events

	Country	Golds
1	USA	265
2	Finland	48
3	UK	43
4	USSR/Unified Team/Russia	38
5	Sweden	17
6	Kenya	15
7 =	East Germany	14
=	Germany/West Germany	14
9	Italy	13
10 =	Canada	12
=	Poland	12

Top 10 Track & field medal winners at one Olympics

	Athlete/country	Year	Gold medals	Silver medals	Bronze medals	Total
1	Ville Ritola, Finland	1924	4	2	0	6
2 =	Irving Baxter, USA	1900	2	3	0	5
=	Marion Jones, USA	2000	3	0	2	5
=	Paavo Nurmi, Finland	1924	5	0	0	5
=	Martin Sheridan, USA	1906	2	3	0	5
6 =	Erik Backman, Sweden	1920	0	1	3	4
=	Fanny Blankers-Koen, Netherlands	1948	4	0	0	4
=	Florence Griffith-Joyner, USA	1988	3	1	0	4
=	Hannes Kolehmainen, Finland	1912	1	0	3	4
=	Alvin Kraenzlein, USA	1900	4	0	0	4
=	Eric Leeming, Sweden	1906	1	0	3	4
=	Carl Lewis, USA	1984	4	0	0	4
=	Jim Lightbody, USA	1904	3	1	0	4
=	Paavo Nurmi, Finland	1920	3	1	0	4
=	Jesse Owens, USA	1936	4	0	0	4
=	Stanley Rowley, Australia	1900	1	0	3	4

Ritola's medals of 1924 were as follows: Gold: 10,000 metres, 3,000 metres steeplechase, 3,000 metres track team race, cross-country (team). Silver: 5,000 metres, cross-country (individual).

Top 10 Countries with track & field golds in women's events

	Country	Golds
1	USA	44
2	USSR/Unified Team/Russia	39
3	East Germany	25
4	Germany/West Germany	17
5	Australia	11
6	Romania	10
7	Poland	7
8 =	France	6
=	Netherlands	6
=	UK	6

◀ Bob Beamon on the way to his world record leap at the 1968 Mexico Olympics. It was his first jump of the competition.

FASTEST MEN & WOMEN

- ▷● Fastest women's 400-metre runners of all time
- ● Fastest men's 400-metre runners of all time
- ● Fastest women's 200-metre runners of all time
- ● Fastest women's 100-metre runners of all time
- ● Fastest men's 200-metre runners of all time
- ● Fastest men's 100-metre runners of all time

> The ones who believed in themselves the most were the ones who won.
> **Florence Griffith-Joyner**

Top 10 Fastest women's 400-metre runners of all time*

Athlete/country	Date	Time (sec)
1 Marita Koch, East Germany	6 Oct 1985	47.60
2 Jarmilla Kratochvilova, Czechoslovakia	10 Aug 1983	47.99
3 Marie-Josè Perèc, France	29 July 1996	48.25
4 Olga Vladykina-Bryzgina, USSR	6 Oct 1985	48.27
5 Tatyana Kocembova, Czechoslovakia	10 Aug 1983	48.59
6 Cathy Freeman, Australia	29 July 1996	48.63
7 Valerie Brisco-Hooks, USA	6 Aug 1984	48.83
8 Chandra Cheeseborough, USA	6 Aug 1984	49.05
9 Falilat Ogunkoya, Nigeria	29 July 1996	49.10
10 Olga Nazarova, USSR	25 Sep 1988	49.11

* Outdoor performances; only the best performance for each athlete is included

Source: IAAF

Marita Koch set her world-best mark during the 1985 IAAF World Cup in Canberra. Since then, only one woman has come within a second of her record time.

Top 10 Fastest men's 400-metre runners of all time*

Athlete#	Date	Time (sec)
1 Michael Johnson	26 Aug 1999	43.18
2 Harry Reynolds	17 Aug 1988	43.29
3 Quincy Watts	5 Aug 1992	43.50
4 Danny Everett	26 June 1992	43.81
5 Lee Evans	18 Oct 1968	43.86
6 Steve Lewis	28 Sep 1988	43.87
7 Larry James	18 Oct 1968	43.97
8 = Alvin Harrison	19 June 1996	44.09
= Jerome Young	21 June 1998	44.09
10 Derek Mills	4 June 1995	44.13

* Outdoor performances; only the best performance for each athlete is included

\# All USA

Source: IAAF

The fastest 400 metres by a non-USA athlete is 44.14 seconds by Cuba's Roberto Hernandez at Seville on 30 May 1990.

◄ The 2000 Sydney Olympics 100-metre champion Maurice Green of the USA proudly celebrates his win.

Top 10 Fastest women's 200-metre runners of all time*

	Athlete/country	Date	Time (sec)
1	Florence Griffith-Joyner, USA	29 Sep 1988	21.34
2	Marion Jones, USA	11 Sep 1998	21.62
3	Merlene Ottey, Jamaica	13 Sep 1991	21.64
4 =	Heike Drechsler, East Germany	29 June 1986	
		29 Aug 1986	21.71
=	Marita Koch, East Germany	10 June 1979	
		21 July 1984	21.71
6 =	Grace Jackson, Jamaica	29 Sep 1988	21.72
=	Gwen Torrence, USA	5 Aug 1992	21.72
8 =	Silke Gladisch-Möller, East Germany	3 Sep 1987	21.74
=	Marlies Oelsner-Göhr, East Germany	3 June 1984	21.74
10	Juliet Cuthbert, Jamaica	5 Aug 1992	21.75

* Outdoor performances; only the best performance for each athlete is included

Source: IAAF

Top 10 Fastest women's 100-metre runners of all time*

	Athlete/country	Date	Time (sec)
1	Florence Griffith-Joyner, USA	16 July 1988	10.49
2	Marion Jones, USA	12 Sep 1998	10.65
3	Christine Arron, France	19 Aug 1998	10.73
4	Merlene Ottey, Jamaica	7 Sep 1996	10.74
5	Evelyn Ashford, USA	22 Aug 1984	10.76
6	Irina Privalova, Russia	6 July 1994	10.77
7	Dawn Sowell, USA	3 June 1989	10.78
8 =	Xuemei Li, China	18 Oct 1997	10.79
=	Inger Miller, USA	22 Aug 1999	10.79
10	Marlies Oelsner-Göhr, East Germany	8 June 1983	10.81

* Outdoor performances; only the best performance for each athlete is included

Source: IAAF

Since "Flo-Jo" became the first woman under 10.50 seconds, no other woman has gone below 10.60 for the 100 metres. Her record time was set in the quarter-finals of the 1988 Seoul Olympics.

Top 10 Fastest men's 200-metre runners of all time*

	Athlete/country	Date	Time (sec)
1	Michael Johnson, USA	1 Aug 1996	19.32
2	Frank Fredericks, Namibia	1 Aug 1996	19.68
3	Pietro Mennea, Italy	12 Sep 1979	19.72
4	Michael Marsh, USA	5 Aug 1992	19.73
5 =	Joe DeLoach, USA	28 Sep 1988	19.75
=	Carl Lewis, USA	19 June 1983	19.75
7	Ato Boldon, Trinidad	13 July 1997	19.77
8	Tommie Smith, USA	16 Oct 1968	19.83
9	Francis Obikwelu, Nigeria	25 Aug 1999	19.84
10	John Capel, USA	23 July 2000	19.85

* Outdoor performances; only the best performance for each athlete is included

Source: IAAF

Pietro Mennea's world record stood for nearly 17 years. When it was broken, two men went under his mark on the same day.

Top 10 Fastest men's 100-metre runners of all time*

	Athlete/country	Date	Time (sec)
1	Maurice Green, USA	16 June 1999	9.79
2 =	Donovan Bailey, Canada	27 July 1996	9.84
=	Tim Montgomery, USA	13 July 2001	9.84
=	Bruny Surin, Canada	22 Aug 1999	9.84
5	Leroy Burrell, USA	6 July 1994	9.85
6 =	Ato Boldon, Trinidad	19 Apr 1998, 17 June 1998	
		16 June 1999, 2 July 1999	9.86
=	Frank Fredericks, Namibia	3 July 1996	9.86
=	Carl Lewis, USA	25 Aug 1991	9.86
9 =	Linford Christie, UK	15 Aug 1993	9.87
=	Obadele Thompson, Barbados	11 Sep 1998	9.87

* Outdoor performances; only the best performance for each athlete is included

Source: IAAF

At the age of 16, Canadian-born Donovan Bailey ran 100 metres in 10.65 seconds. Before turning his attention full-time to athletics, he had worked as a stockbroker.

◄ The world's fastest woman, Florence Griffith-Joyner, who died of heart failure in September 1998 at the age of just 38.

- Women's high jumpers of all time
- Men's high jumpers of all time
- Men's triple jumpers of all time
- Women's long jumpers of all time
- Men's long jumpers of all time

JUMPING GIANTS

Top 10 Women's high jumpers of all time*

	Athlete/country	Date	Height (metres)
1	Stefka Kostadinova, Bulgaria	30 Aug 1987	2.09
2	Lyudmila Andonova, Bulgaria	20 July 1984	2.07
3 =	Inha Babakova, Ukraine	15 Sep 1995	2.05
=	Tamara Bykova, USSR	22 June 1984	2.05
=	Heike Redetzky-Henkel, Germany	31 Aug 1991	2.05
6 =	Hestrie Cloete, South Africa	4 Aug 1999	2.04
=	Silvia Costa, Cuba	9 Sep 1989	2.04
=	Venelina Veneva, Bulgaria	2 June 2001	2.04
9 =	Tatyana Babashkina, Russia	30 May 1995	2.03
=	Ulrike Meyfarth, West Germany	21 Aug 1983	2.03
=	Louise Ritter, USA	7 Aug 1988	2.03
=	Niki Bakoyiánni, Greece	3 Aug 1996	2.03

* Outdoor performances; only the best performance for each athlete is included

Source: IAAF

> It's only jumping into a sandpit.
> **Jonathan Edwards,** after breaking the triple jump world record, 1995.

◀ Javier Sotomayor of Cuba, the high jump world record holder.

Top 10 Men's high jumpers of all time*

	Athlete/country	Date	Height (metres)
1	Javier Sotomayor, Cuba	27 July 1993	2.45
2	Patrik Sjöberg, Sweden	30 June 1987	2.42
3	Igor Paklin, USSR	4 Sep 1985	2.41
4 =	Charles Austin, USA	7 Aug 1991	2.40
=	Sorin Matei, Romania	20 June 1990	2.40
=	Rudolf Povarnitsyn, USSR	11 Aug 1985	2.40
=	Vyacheslav Voronin, Russia	5 Aug 2000	2.40
8 =	Hollis Conway, USA	30 July 1989	2.39
=	Jianhua Zhu, China	10 June 1984	2.39
10 =	Gennadiy Avdeyenko, USSR	6 Sep 1987	2.38
=	Sergey Malchenko, USSR	4 Sep 1988	2.38
=	Dragutin Topic, Yugoslavia	1 Aug 1993	2.38

* Outdoor performances; only the best performance for each athlete is included
Source: IAAF

Top 10 Men's triple jumpers of all time*

	Athlete/country	Date	Distance (metres)
1	Jonathan Edwards, UK	7 Aug 1995	18.29
2	Kenny Harrison, USA	27 July 1996	18.09
3	Willie Banks, USA	16 June 1985	17.97
4 =	James Beckford, Jamaica	20 May 1995	17.92
=	Khristo Markov, Bulgaria	31 Aug 1987	17.92
6	Vladimir Inozemtsev, Ukraine	20 June 1990	17.90
7	João Carlos de Oliveira, Brazil	15 Oct 1975	17.89
8	Mike Conley, USA	27 June 1987	17.87
9	Charles Simpkins, USA	2 Sep 1985	17.86
10	Yoelbi Quesada, Cuba	8 Aug 1997	17.85

* Outdoor performances; only the best performance for each athlete is included
Source: IAAF

When Willie Banks set the triple jump world record at Indianapolis in 1985, he became the first American since Daniel Ahearn 74 years earlier to set the record. Like Ahearn, Banks also never won Olympic gold.

Top 10 Women's long jumpers of all time*

	Athlete/country	Date	Distance (metres)
1	Galina Chistyakova, USSR	11 June 1988	7.52
2	Jackie Joyner-Kersee, USA	22 May 1994, 31 July 1994	7.49
3	Heike Dreschler, East Germany	9 July 1988, 8 July 1992	7.48
4	Anisoara Cusmir-Stanciu, Romania	4 June 1983	7.43
5	Yelena Belevskaya, USSR	18 July 1987	7.39
6	Inesa Kravets, Ukraine	13 June 1992	7.37
7 =	Marion Jones, USA	31 May 1998, 12 Aug 1998	7.31
=	Yelena Kokonova-Khlopotnova, USSR	12 Sep 1985	7.31
9	Maurren Higa Maggi, Brazil	26 June 1999	7.26
10	Larisa Berezhnaya, Russia	25 May 1991	7.24

* Outdoor performances; only the best performance for each athlete is included
Source: IAAF

While she has not managed to break Chistyakova's world-best mark in the long jump, Jackie Joyner-Kersee did set the world heptathlon record during the 1988 Seoul Olympics.

Top 10 Men's long jumpers of all time*

	Athlete/country	Date	Distance (metres)
1	Mike Powell, USA	30 Aug 1991	8.95
2	Bob Beamon, USA	18 Oct 1968	8.90
3	Carl Lewis, USA	30 Aug 1991	8.87
4	Robert Emmiyan, USSR	22 May 1987	8.86
5 =	Larry Myricks, USA	18 July 1988	8.74
=	Erick Walder, USA	2 Apr 1994	8.74
7	Ivan Pedroso, Cuba	18 July 1995	8.71
8	Kareem Streete-Thompson, USA	4 July 1994	8.63
9	James Beckford, Jamaica	5 Apr 1997	8.62
10	Yago Lamela, Spain	24 June 1999	8.56

* Outdoor performances; only the best performance for each athlete is included
Source: IAAF

Going into the 1968 Olympic Games, the men's long jump Olympic record stood at 8.12 metres. Bob Beamon shattered that mark, but it was also broken by runner-up Klaus Beer (East Germany) and the joint world record holder at the time, Ralph Boston (USA).

◀ Jonathan Edwards, triple jump Olympic champion in 2000 and the first male British jumper to win Olympic gold since Lyn Davies in the long jump in 1964.

WORLD CHAMPIONS

- Oldest World Championship records
- Athletes with the most World Championship gold medals
- Athletes with the most IAAF Grand Prix titles
- Medal-winning countries at the World Championships
- First athletes to win three consecutive individual titles at the World Championships

HOW DID IT BEGIN?

The first official IAAF World Championships were held in Helsinki in 1983. They were originally held every four years between Olympic celebrations, but since 1991 have been a biennial event. The venues for all official events have been: Helsinki, Finland (1983); Rome, Italy (1987); Tokyo, Japan (1991); Stuttgart, Germany (1993); Gothenburg, Sweden (1995); Athens, Greece (1997); Seville, Spain (1999); Edmonton, Canada (2001). The 2003 Championships will be held in Paris.

Top 10 Oldest World Championship records

	Event	Athlete/country	Winning time/distance/points	Date
1	Women's 800 metres	Jarmila Kratochvilova, Czechoslovakia	1 min 54.68 sec	9 Aug 1983
2	Women's 400 metres	Jarmila Kratochvilova, Czechoslovakia	47.99 sec	10 Aug 1983
3	Men's marathon	Rob de Castella, Australia	2 hr 10 min 3 sec	14 Aug 1983
4 =	Men's shot put	Werner Günthör, Switzerland	22.23 m	29 Aug 1987
=	Women's marathon	Rosa Mota, Portugal	2 hr 25 min 17 sec	29 Aug 1987
6	Women's high jump	Stefka Kostadinova, Bulgaria	2.09 m	30 Aug 1987
7	Women's discus	Martina Opitz, East Germany	71.62 m	31 Aug 1987
8 =	Heptathlon	Jackie Joyner-Kersee, USA	7,128 pt	1 Sep 1987
=	Men's 800 metres	Billy Konchellah, Kenya	1 min 43.06 sec	1 Sep 1987
10	Women's 200 metres	Silke Gladisch, East Germany	21.74 sec	3 Sep 1987

Source: IAAF

Top 10 Athletes with the most World Championship gold medals*

	Athlete/country	Total
1	Michael Johnson, USA	9
2	Carl Lewis, USA	8
3	Sergey Bubka, USSR/Ukraine	6
4 =	Maurice Greene, USA	5
=	Marion Jones, USA	5
=	Lars Riedel, Germany	5
7 =	Gail Devers, USA	4
=	Haile Gebrselassie, Ethiopia	4
=	Jackie Joyner-Kersee, USA	4
=	Ivan Pedroso, Cuba	4
=	Antonio Pettigrew, USA	4
=	Calvin Smith, USA	4

* Including relays

Despite all his world titles, Michael Johnson had still not broken the world 400 metres record despite 10 years of trying. However, that came to an end when he won his fourth 400-metre consecutive world title in Seville in 1999, and in a new world best.

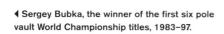

◀ Sergey Bubka, the winner of the first six pole vault World Championship titles, 1983–97.

The 10 Athletes with the most IAAF Grand Prix titles

	Athlete/country	Event(s)/year	Total
1	Merlene Ottey, Jamaica	Overall 1987, 1990 100 metres 1987, 1989, 1991, 1994, 1996 200 metres 1990, 1992	9
2	Sergey Bubka, USSR/Ukraine	Overall 1991, 1993 Pole vault 1985, 1987, 1991, 1993, 1997	7
3 =	Mike Conley, USA	Long jump 1985 Triple jump 1986, 1988, 1990, 1992, 1994	6
=	Ana Fidelia Quirot, Cuba	400 metres 1988, 1990 800 metres 1987, 1989, 1991, 1997	6
5 =	Said Aouita, Morocco	Overall 1986, 1988, 1989 5,000 metres 1986 Mile 1988	5
=	Marion Jones, USA	Overall 1998 100 metres 1998, 2000 200 metres 1997 Long jump 1998	5
=	Noureddine Morceli, Algeria	Overall 1994 Mile 1990 1,500 metres 1991, 1993, 1994	5
=	Maria Mutola, Mozambique	Overall 1995 800 metres 1993, 1995, 1999, 2001	5
=	Sonia O'Sullivan, Ireland	3,000 metres 1993, 1995, 2000 5,000 metres 1992, 1994	5
=	Jan Zelezny, Czechoslovakia	Javelin 1991, 1993, 1995, 1997, 2001	5

Source: IAAF

The IAAF Grand Prix series was launched in 1985 and is a season-long competition at various venues worldwide. Originally points were given for performances in individual events, with an overall champion at the end of the season being declared. Since 1993, the champion in each event has been decided at the end-of-season Grand Prix final.

Top 10 Medal-winning countries at the World Championships

	Country	Gold medals	Silver medals	Bronze medals	Total
1	USA	80	41	47	168
2	USSR/Russia	40	52	53	145
3	Germany/West Germany	21	23	22	66
4	East Germany	21	19	19	59
5	UK	11	22	19	52
6	Kenya	19	16	15	50
7	Jamaica	5	14	23	42
8	Italy	9	13	8	30
9	Cuba	13	10	5	28
10	Spain	6	10	7	23

Source: IAAF

While the United States has won twice as many gold medals as the USSR/Russia, they did not have the first Championship of 1983 all their own way. East Germany dominated the Championship with 10 gold medals, the USA and USSR each collecting eight.

The 10 First athletes to win three consecutive individual titles at the World Championships

	Athlete/country	Event	Years
1 =	Sergey Bubka, USSR/Ukraine	Pole vault	1983, 87, 91
=	Greg Foster, USA	110 metres hurdles	1983, 87, 91
=	Carl Lewis, USA	100 metres	1983, 87, 91
4	Werner Günthör, Switzerland	Shot put	1987, 91, 93
5 =	Moses Kiptanui, Kenya	3,000 metres steeplechase	1991, 93, 95
=	Noureddine Morceli, Algeria	1,500 metres	1991, 93, 95
=	Dan O'Brien, USA	Decathlon	1991, 93, 95
=	Lars Riedel, Germany	Discus	1991, 93, 95
9 =	Haile Gebrselassie, Ethiopia	10,000 metres	1993, 95, 97
=	Michael Johnson, USA	400 metres	1993, 95, 97

The first woman to win three consecutive titles was Astrid Kombernuus (Germany), in the shot put, in 1995, 1997, and 1999.

Carl Lewis went on to win an unprecedented 10 World Championship medals – eight gold, one silver, and one bronze. He twice won a record-equalling three golds at one Championship, in 1983 and 1987, each time in the 100 metres, long jump and sprint relay.

◀ Michael Johnson, winner of the 400-metre title at four consecutive World Championships between 1993 and 1999.

RECORD BREAKERS

- Longest-standing men's world records of all time
- Women's outdoor world records broken most times
- Men's outdoor world records broken most times
- Longest-standing men's outdoor world records
- Longest-standing women's outdoor world records

> It was a lifetime of training for just 10 seconds.
>
> **Jesse Owens,** Olympic 100-metre record holder

Top 10 Longest-standing men's world records of all time*

	Athlete/country#	Event	Date set	Date broken	Duration (y:m:d)		
1	Jesse Owens	Long jump	25 May 1935	12 Aug 1960	25	2	18
2	Patrick Ryan	Hammer	17 Aug 1913	27 Aug 1938	25	0	10
3	Vince Matthews, Ronald Freeman, Larry James, Lee Evans	4 x 400 metres relay	20 Oct 1968	8 Aug 1992	23	9	19
4	Bob Beamon	Long jump	18 Oct 1968	30 Aug 1991	22	10	12
5	Daniel Ahearn	Triple jump	30 May 1911	27 Oct 1931	20	4	28
6	Jesse Owens, Ralph Metcalfe, Foy Draper, Frank Wykoff	4 x 100 metres relay	9 Aug 1936	1 Dec 1956	20	3	23
7	Jesse Owens	100 metres	20 June 1936	3 Aug 1956	20	1	13
8	Ivan Fuqua, Edgar Ablowich, Karl Warner, Bill Carr	4 x 400 metres relay	7 Aug 1932	27 July 1952	19	11	20
9	Peter O'Connor, UK	Long jump	5 Aug 1901	23 July 1921	19	11	13
10	Lee Evans	400 metres	18 Oct 1968	17 Aug 1988	19	9	30

* Outdoor world records

\# All USA unless otherwise stated

Top 10 Women's outdoor world records broken most times*

	Event	Occasions record broken or equalled
1	Javelin	22
2	Pole vault	19
3	Hammer	14
4 =	5,000 metres	11
=	3,000 metres steeplechase	11
6 =	Heptathlon	9
=	High jump	9
8	Long jump	8
9 =	400 metres hurdles	7
=	10,000 metres	7

* Outdoor world records at recognized Olympic events broken or equalled 1 Jan 1981–31 Dec 2001

The first pole vault world record was not established until 1995. Since then, Emma George of Australia has broken the record 11 times.

One of the main reasons that the javelin record has been broken so often is because new specifications were introduced in 1999 – the record has been broken 13 times since the new specifications.

Top 10 Men's outdoor world records broken most times*

	Event	Occasions record broken or equalled
1	Pole vault	20
2	Javelin	11
3 =	5,000 metres	10
=	10,000 metres	10
5 =	Decathlon	9
=	High jump	9
=	100 metres	9
8	4 x 100 metres relay	8
9	1,500 metres	7
10	3,000 metres steeplechase	6

* Outdoor world records at recognized Olympic events broken or equalled 1 Jan 1981–31 Dec 2001

Sergey Bubka (USSR/Ukraine) broke 17 of the 20 pole vault world records.

New marks were set for the javelin in 1986 after a change in specifications. The world record has been broken eight times since the first record was established with the new specifications.

DID YOU KNOW? Jesse Owens set three different world records that each stood for more than 20 years, in the long jump, 100 metres, and 4 x 100 metres relay.

Top 10 Longest-standing men's outdoor world records*

	Athlete/country	Event	Date set
1	Jürgen Schult, East Germany	Discus	6 June 1986
2	Yuriy Syedikh, USSR	Hammer	30 Aug 1986
3	Randy Barnes, USA	Shot	20 May 1990
4	Mike Powell, USA	Long jump	30 Aug 1991
5	Kevin Young, USA	400 metres hurdles	6 Aug 1992
6	Michael Marsh, Leroy Burrell, Dennis Mitchell, Carl Lewis, USA	4 x 100 metres relay	8 Aug 1992
7	Javier Sotomayor, Cuba	High jump	27 July 1993
8	Colin Jackson, UK	110 metres hurdles	20 Aug 1993
9	Jon Drummond, André Cason, Dennis Mitchell, Leroy Burrell, USA	4 x 100 metres relay#	21 Aug 1993
10	Sergey Bubka, Ukraine	Pole vault	3 July 1994

* As at 1 January 2002

\# Equalled world record

Top 10 Longest-standing women's outdoor world records*

	Athlete/country	Event	Date set
1	Jarmila Kratochvilova, Czechoslovakia	800 metres	26 July 1983
2 =	Marita Koch, East Germany	400 metres	6 Oct 1985
=	Silke Möller, Sabine Günther, Ingrid Auerswald, Marlies Göhr, East Germany	4 x 100 metres relay	6 Oct 1985
4	Natalya Lisovskaya, USSR	Shot put	7 June 1987
5	Stefka Kostadinova, Bulgaria	High jump	30 Aug 1987
6	Galina Chistyakova, USSR	Long jump	11 June 1988
7	Gabriele Reinsch, East Germany	Discus	9 July 1988
8	Florence Griffith-Joyner, USA	100 metres	16 July 1988
9	Yordanka Donkova, Bulgaria	100 metres hurdles	20 Aug 1988
10	Jackie Joyner-Kersee, USA	Heptathlon	24 Sep 1988

* As at 1 January 2002

▼ Nazi propaganda had portrayed black people as inferior just before the 1936 Berlin Olympics. Jesse Owens proved them wrong with four gold medals.

THE WORLD MILE RECORD

- Fastest milers of all time
- Fastest miles ever run
- Fastest miles ever run by a woman
- Fastest miles run in Oslo
- First athletes to run the mile in under four minutes
- Youngest men to set the world mile record
- First US runners to run a sub four-minute mile

THE FOUR-MINUTE MILE

Within a little over two years of Roger Bannister's shattering the four-minute-mile bárrier, the number of athletes to do so had risen to 10, although none had succeeded in taking more than two seconds off the record. The time has been progressively reduced in subsequent years, however, by athletes such as Sebastian Coe, Steve Ovett, and Noureddine Morceli. The current world record is held by Hicham El Guerrouj (Morocco), who, in 1999, brought the time down to 3 minutes 43.13 seconds.

Top 10 Fastest milers of all time*

	Athlete/country	Year	Time (min:sec)
1	Hicham El Guerrouj, Morocco	1999	3:43.13
2	Noah Ngeny, Kenya	1999	3:43.40
3	Noureddine Morceli, Algeria	1993	3:44.39
4	Steve Cram, UK	1985	3:46.32
5	Daniel Komen, Kenya	1997	3:46.38
6	Venuste Niyongabo, Burundi	1997	3:46.70
7	Said Aouita, Morocco	1987	3:46.76
8	Bernard Lagat, Kenya	2001	3:47.28
9	Sebastian Coe, UK	1981	3:47.33
10	Laban Rotich, Kenya	1997	3:47.65

* Outdoor records; based on best time of each athlete

Hicham El Guerrouj took the world mile record off Noureddine Morceli in Rome in 1999. A year earlier, also in Rome, he deprived Morceli of the 1,500-metre world record.

Top 10 Fastest miles ever run

	Athlete/country	Year	Time (min:sec)
1	Hicham El Guerrouj, Morocco	1999	3:43.13
2	Noah Ngeny, Kenya	1999	3:43.40
3	Noureddine Morceli, Algeria	1993	3:44.39
4	Hicham El Guerrouj, Morocco	1998	3:44.60
5	Hicham El Guerrouj, Morocco	1997	3:44.90
6	Hicham El Guerrouj, Morocco	2001	3:44.95
7	Noureddine Morceli, Algeria	1995	3:45.19
8	Hicham El Guerrouj, Morocco	1997	3:45.64
9	Hicham El Guerrouj, Morocco	2000	3:45.96
10	Hicham El Guerrouj, Morocco	2000	3:46.24

When Hicham El Guerrouj set the new world mile record in 1999, the old world record was also beaten by the second-place finisher, 20-year-old Noah Ngeny of Kenya.

Top 10 Fastest miles ever run by a woman

	Athlete/country	Year	Time (min:sec)
1	Svetlana Masterkova, Russia	1996	4:12.56
2	Paula Ivan, Romania	1989	4:15.61
3	Natalya Artyomova, USSR	1984	4:15.80
4	Mary Slaney, USA	1985	4:16.71
5	Natalya Artyomova, Russia	1991	4:17.00
6	Sonia O'Sullivan, Ireland	1994	4:17.25
7	Maricica Puica, Romania	1985	4:17.33
8	Maricica Puica, Romania	1982	4:17.44
9	Zola Pieterse (née Budd), UK	1985	4:17.47
10	Mary Slaney, USA	1982	4:18.08

The only two on the above list to have won the Olympic title in the 1,500 metres are Paula Ivan in 1988 and Svetlana Masterkova in 1996.

Top 10 Fastest miles run in Oslo*

	Athlete/country	Date	Time (min:sec)
1	Hicham El Guerrouj, Morroco	4 July 1997	3:44.90
2	Hicham El Guerrouj, Morocco	28 July 2000	3:46.24
3	Steve Cram, UK	27 July 1985	3:46.32
4	Laban Rotich, Kenya	4 July 1997	3:47.65
5	Steve Scott, USA	7 July 1982	3:47.69
6	Noureddine Morceli, Algeria	10 July 1993	3:47.78
7	José Luis González, Spain	27 July 1985	3:47.79
8	John Kibowen, Kenya	4 July 1997	3:47.88
9	William Chirchir, Kenya	28 July 2000	3:47.94
10	Noureddine Morceli, Algeria	5 July 1996	3:48.15

* At the Bislet Stadium, venue for many world records

Many world records have been set at the Bislet Stadium, but only three mile records have been set in Oslo, and all were by Britons: Steve Ovett, Sebastian Coe, and Steve Cram.

▶ Roger Bannister crosses the finishing line at Iffley Road, Oxford on 6 May 1954, unaware that he had become the first man to run the mile in under four minutes.

◀ Roger Bannister (right) with the world mile record holder Hicham El Guerrouj.

The 10 First athletes to run the mile in under four minutes

	Athlete/country	Venue	Time (min:sec)	Date
1	Roger Bannister, England	Oxford, UK	3:59.4	6 May 1954
2	John Landy, Australia	Turku, Finland	3:57.9	21 June 1954
3	Laszlo Tabori, Hungary	London, UK	3:59.0	28 May 1955
4 =	Chris Chataway, England	London, UK	3:59.8	28 May 1955
=	Brian Hewson, England	London, UK	3:59.8	28 May 1955
6	Jim Bailey, Australia	Los Angeles, USA	3:58.6	5 May 1956
7	Gunnar Nielsen, Denmark	Compton, USA	3:59.1	1 June 1956
8	Ron Delany, Ireland	Compton, USA	3:59.4	1 June 1956
9	Derek Ibbotson, England	London, UK	3:59.4	6 Aug 1956
10	István Rózsavölgyi, Hungary	Budapest, Hungary	3:59.0	26 Aug 1956

Chris Chataway, fourth equal in this list, was runner-up to Roger Bannister when he first broke the four-minute barrier. Chataway was also in second place behind John Landy when he became the next man to run the distance in less than four minutes.

The only other occasion on which Bannister ran the mile in under four minutes was at the 1954 Vancouver Commonwealth Games when he beat Landy in what was heralded as the "Race of the Century". It certainly lived up to its billing, with Bannister winning in 3 minutes 58.8 seconds to Landy's 3 minutes 59.6 seconds.

Top 10 Youngest men to set the world mile record*

	Athlete/country	Date record set	Age (y:m:d)		
1	Jim Ryun, USA	17 July 1966	19	2	18
2	Herb Elliott, Australia	6 Aug 1958	20	5	9
3	Filbert Bayi, Tanzania	17 May 1975	21	10	24
4	Sebastian Coe, UK	17 July 1979	22	8	11
5	Peter Snell, New Zealand	27 Jan 1962	23	1	10
6	Noureddine Morceli, Algeria	5 Sep 1993	23	6	5
7	John Walker, New Zealand	12 Aug 1975	23	7	0
8	John Landy, Australia	21 June 1954	24	2	9
9	Steve Ovett, UK	1 July 1980	24	8	23
10	Steve Cram, UK	27 July 1985	24	9	13

* Men's outdoor world records; based on age when they first set the record

The year before he set the world record in Dublin in 1958, Australia's Herb Elliott held the world junior records for the mile, 1,500 metres, two, and three miles. He ran his first mile at the age of 14 and won, in a race against many older boys, with a time of 5 minutes 35 seconds. On 25 January 1958, a month before his 20th birthday, he became the first teenager to run a mile in under four minutes, when he clocked a time of 3 minutes 59.9 at the Olympic Park in Melbourne.

The 10 First US runners to run a sub four-minute mile

	Athlete	Time (min:sec)	Date
1	Don Bowden	3:58.7	1 June 1957
2	Dyrol Burleson	3:58.6	23 April 1960
3	Jim Beatty	3:58.0	28 May 1960
4	Jim Grelle	3:59.9	28 April 1962
5	Keith Forman	3:58.3	26 May 1962
6	Cary Weisiger	3:59.3	26 May 1962
7	Bill Dotson	3:59.0	23 June 1962
8	Bob Seaman	3:58.07	18 August 1962
9	Tom O'Hara	3:59.2	15 February 1963
10	Archie San Romani	3:57.6	5 June 1964

Apart from San Romani, three other United States runners broke the sub four-minute barrier for the first time at the Compton Invitational Mile on 5 June 1964. One of them, in 8th place with a time of 3 minutes 59.0 seconds, was 17-year-old Jim Ryun, who went on to become the greatest US miler of all time – and, at the age of 19 in 1966, the youngest man ever to hold the world mile record. He remains the only American to hold the record. He went into the Olympics as world record holder at 880 yards, 1,500 metres, and the mile, and was unbeaten over the two longer distances in three years, but illness just before the Games, combined with the effects of the high altitude of Mexico City, meant he had to settle for silver medal in the 1,500 metres.

MARATHONS

- Fastest winning times in the London Marathon
- Closest London Marathons
- Fastest winning times in the Boston Marathon
- Fastest winning times in the New York City Marathon

GOING THE DISTANCE

The now-standard distance for the marathon of 26 miles 385 yards was adopted at the 1908 London Olympics. The race was from Windsor to the Olympic Stadium in Shepherd's Bush, London and measured 26 miles, but to make sure the race concluded in front of the Royal Box, where King Edward VII was sitting, the athletes had to run a further 385 yards.

Top 10 Fastest winning times in the London Marathon

	Athlete/country	Year	Time (hr:min:sec)
1	Khalid Khannouchi, USA	2002	2:05:38
2	Antonio Pinto, Portugal	2000	2:06:36
3	Abdelkader El Mouaziz, Morocco	2001	2:07:11
4	Antonio Pinto, Portugal	1997	2:07:55
5 =	Abel Anton, Spain	1998	2:07:57
=	Abdelkader El Mouaziz, Morocco	1999	2:07:57
7	Steve Jones, UK	1985	2:08:16
8	Dionicio Ceron, Mexico	1995	2:08:30
9	Dionicio Ceron, Mexico	1994	2:08:53
10	Douglas Wakiihuri, Kenya	1989	2:09:03

The first London Marathon was run in March 1981. It was the brainchild of former Olympic steeplechaser Chris Brasher, after he had competed in the 1979 New York City Marathon. The women's record was set in 2002 when Britain's Paula Radcliffe won in 2 hours 18 minutes 56 seconds.

Top 10 Closest London Marathons

	Winning athlete/country	Runner-up athlete/country	Year	Winning margin (sec)
1	Dick Beardsley, USA	–		
	Inge Simonsen, Norway	–	1981	dead-heat
2	Joyce Chepchumba, Kenya*	Liz McColgan, UK	1997	1
3	Antonio Pinto, Portugal	Stefano Baldini, Italy	1997	2
4 =	Dionicio Ceron, Mexico	Steve Moneghetti, Australia	1995	3
=	Eamonn Martin, UK	Isidro Rico, Mexico	1993	3
=	Derartu Tulu, Ethiopia	Svetlana Zakharova, Russia	2001*	3
=	Douglas Wakiihuri, Kenya	Steve Moneghetti, Australia	1989	3
8	Antonio Pinto, Portugal	Jan Huruk, Poland	1992	5
9 =	Abel Anton, Spain	Abdelkadar El Mouaziz, Morocco	1998	10
=	Khalid Khannouchi, USA	Paul Tergat, Kenya	2002	10
=	Malgorzata Sobanska, Poland*	Manuela Machado, Portugal	1995	10

* Women's race

The biggest winning margin was in the women's race at the inaugural London Marathon in 1981, when Joyce Smith (UK) won by 7 minutes 15 seconds over Gillian Drake (New Zealand).

▶ Just a few of the thousands of runners in the London Marathon, going past the Tower of London.

> If you want to run a mile, then run a mile. If you want to experience another life, run a marathon.
>
> Emil Zatopek

Top 10 Fastest winning times in the Boston Marathon

	Athlete/country	Year	Time (hr:min:sec)
1	Cosmas Ndeti, Kenya	1994	2:07:15
2	Andres Espinosa, Mexico	1994	2:07:19
3	Moses Tanui, Kenya	1998	2:07:34
4	Joseph Chebet, Kenya	1998	2:07:37
5	Rob de Castella, Australia	1986	2:07:51
6	Gert Thys, South Africa	1998	2:07:52
7	Jackson Kipngok, Kenya	1994	2:08:08
8	Hwang Young-Cho, Korea	1994	2:08:09
9	Ibrahim Hussein, Kenya	1992	2:08:14
10	Gelindo Bordin, Italy	1990	2:08:19

The women's record was set in 1994 when Uta Pippig of Germany won in 2 hours 21 minutes 45 seconds.

Top 10 Fastest winning times in the New York City Marathon

	Athlete/country	Year	Time (hr:min:sec)
1	Tesfaye Jifar, Ethiopia	2001	2:07:43
2	Juma Ikangaa, Tanzania	1989	2:08:01
3	John Kagwe, Kenya	1997	2:08:12
4	Alberto Salazar, USA	1981	2:08:13
5	Steve Jones, UK	1988	2:08:20
6	John Kagwe, Kenya	1998	2:08:45
7	Rod Dixon, New Zealand	1983	2:08:59
8	Joseph Chebet, Kenya	1999	2:09:14
9	Salvador Garcia, Mexico	1991	2:09:28
10 =	Willie Mtolo, South Africa	1992	2:09:29
=	Alberto Salazar, USA	1982	2:09:29

The women's record was also set in 2001 when Margaret Okayo of Kenya won in 2 hours 24 minutes 21 seconds.

At the Start

It is arguable whether golf originated in the Netherlands, Belgium, or Scotland, but the earliest recorded reference dates from the latter in 1457, when King James II banned "gouf", along with "fute-ball". His successors, however, were enthusiasts – Mary, Queen of Scots was the earliest-known female golfer. The first international game took place in Leith in 1682, when the Duke of York and a shoemaker beat two English noblemen. The Edinburgh Golfing Society was founded at Leith in 1735. The "Royal & Ancient" St. Andrews Club in Scotland was founded in 1754, and the Blackheath Club in England in 1766. The first golf match was played in the United States in 1779, and the South Carolina Golf Club was established in 1786. Golf has been played professionally since the 19th century.

GOLF

THE RYDER CUP

THE CUP'S ORIGINS

The Ryder Cup was launched in 1927 by British seed merchant and golf enthusiast Samuel Ryder (1858–1936). It is held every two years (with a break between 1939 and 1945 due to World War II), and the venues alternate between the United States and Europe. The United States originally competed against Great Britain and Ireland, but, since 1979, it has competed against Europe.

Top 10 Most appearances in the Ryder Cup for Europe

	Player/country*#	Years	Apps
1	Nick Faldo	1977–97	11
2	Christy O'Connor Sr.	1955–73	10
3 =	Bernhard Langer, Germany	1981–97	9
=	Dai Rees	1937–61	9
5 =	Peter Alliss	1953–69	8
=	Seve Ballesteros, Spain	1979–85	8
=	Neil Coles	1961–77	8
=	Bernard Gallacher	1969–83	8
=	Bernard Hunt	1953–69	8
=	Sam Torrance	1981–95	8
=	Ian Woosnam	1983–97	8

* Great Britain & Ireland up to 1977

\# All UK unless otherwise stated

Alf Padgham (1933, 1935, 1937), John Panton (1951, 1953, 1961), and Alf Perry (1933, 1935, 1937) uniquely all played in three Ryder Cups without winning a match, a feat no USA golfer has equalled.

Top 10 Most appearances in the Ryder Cup for the USA

	Player	Years	Apps
1 =	Billy Casper	1961–75	8
=	Ray Floyd	1969–93	8
=	Lanny Wadkins	1977–93	8
4 =	Gene Littler	1961–75	7
=	Sam Snead	1937–59	7
6 =	Tom Kite	1979–93	6
=	Jack Nicklaus	1969–81	6
=	Arnold Palmer	1961–73	6
=	Gene Sarazen	1927–37	6
=	Lee Trevino	1969–81	6

Two of Sam Snead's seven appearances were as captain: in 1951 in Pinehurst, North Carolina, and in 1959 at Eldorado Country Club, Palm Springs, California. On both occasions, he led the United States to victory, winning both his matches in 1951 and winning one and halving the other in 1959. He was also the non-playing captain in 1969.

Top 10 European players with the most wins in the Ryder Cup

	Player/country*#	Wins
1	Nick Faldo	23
2	Seve Ballesteros, Spain	20
3	Bernhard Langer	18
4	José Maria Olázabal, Spain	15
5 =	Peter Oosterhuis	14
=	Ian Woosnam	14
7 =	Bernard Gallacher	13
=	Tony Jacklin	13
9 =	Neil Coles	12
=	Colin Montgomerie	12

* Great Britain & Ireland up to 1977

\# All UK unless otherwise stated

Nick Faldo and Peter Oosterhuis have each won a record six singles matches in the Ryder Cup. Peter Oosterhuis beat Arnold Palmer in the singles in each of his first two Ryder Cup matches. Nick Faldo's first singles win was over Tom Watson in 1977, and both Faldo and Oosterhuis have beaten Johnny Miller in singles matches.

Top 10 American players with the most wins in the Ryder Cup

	Player	Wins
1	Arnold Palmer	22
2 =	Billy Casper	20
=	Lanny Wadkins	20
4 =	Jack Nicklaus	17
=	Lee Trevino	17
6	Tom Kite	15
7	Gene Littler	14
8	Hale Irwin	13
9	Ray Floyd	12
10 =	Sam Snead	10
=	Tom Watson	10

Arnold Palmer, Billy Casper, Sam Snead, and Lee Trevino have each won a record six singles matches for the USA. Arnold Palmer's first Ryder Cup match was in the foursomes with Billy Casper in 1961. They beat Dai Rees and Ken Bousfield 2 & 1. Palmer's first singles was the same year when he halved with Peter Alliss. He bowed out by losing 4 & 2 to Peter Oosterhuis in 1973 at Muirfield Golf Course in Scotland.

> I look into their eyes, shake their hand, pat their back, and wish them luck, but I am thinking, 'I am going to bury you.'
>
> **Seve Ballesteros**

Top 10 Biggest winning matches in the Ryder Cup

	Match	Year	Margin
1	George Duncan beat Walter Hagen (USA)	1929	10 & 8
2 =	Walter Hagen/Denny Shute (USA) beat George Duncan/Arthur Havers	1931	10 & 9
=	Ed Oliver/Lew Worsham (USA) beat Henry Cotton/Arthur Lees	1947	10 & 9
4	Fred Daly beat Ted Kroll (USA)	1953	9 & 7
5 =	Leo Diegel (USA) beat Abe Mitchell	1929	9 & 8
=	Abe Mitchell beat Olin Dutra (USA)	1933	9 & 8
=	Paul Runyan/Horton Smith (USA) beat Bill Cox/Edward Jarman	1935	9 & 8
8 =	Johnny Farrell/Jim Turnesa (USA) beat George Duncan/Archie Compston	1927	8 & 6
=	Denny Shute (USA) beat Bert Hodson	1931	8 & 6
=	Charles Whitcombe beat Johnny Farrell (USA)	1929	8 & 6

The biggest winning margins since 1953 occurred in 1987 when Tom Kite (USA) beat Howard Clark 8 & 7, and in 1997 when Fred Couples (USA) beat Ian Woosnam 8 & 7. The 1929 Ryder Cup – the first on British soil, at Moortown, Leeds – was not only notable for the first UK win, but also produced some high-scoring matches. The United States led by one point going into the singles and it was the "Battle of the Captains", George Duncan versus Walter Hagen, that saw the UK skipper win 10 & 8 and set his side on the way to victory. Charles Whitcombe beat Johnny Farrell 10 & 8, Archie Compston beat Gene Sarazen 6 & 4, and victory was secured for the home team when 22-year-old newcomer Henry Cotton beat Al Watrous 4 & 3.

Top 10 Biggest winning margins in the Ryder Cup

	Winners	Score	Year	Winning captain	Margin
1	USA	23½–8½	1967	Ben Hogan	15
2	USA	23–9	1963	Arnold Palmer	14
3 =	USA	11–1	1947	Ben Hogan	10
=	USA	21–11	1975	Arnold Palmer	10
5	USA	18½–9½	1981	Dave Marr	9
6 =	USA	9½–2½	1951	Sam Snead	7
=	USA	19½–12½	1965	Byron Nelson	7
8 =	USA	9–3	1931	Walter Hagen	6
=	USA	9–3	1935	Walter Hagen	6
=	USA	19–13	1973	Jack Burke	6
=	USA	17–11	1979	Billy Casper	6

The biggest winning margin by either the British or the European team was in 1985 when Europe, captained by Tony Jacklin, won 16½–11½. Five men played in the United States' two biggest wins of 1963 and 1967. They were: Arnold Palmer, Johnny Pott, Billy Casper, Julius Boros, and Gene Littler.

▼ European team captain Seve Ballesteros proudly holds the trophy after victory over the USA in the Ryder Cup at the Valderrama Golf Cub in Sotogrande, Spain, in 1997.

TOURNAMENT & MONEY WINNERS

- Players with the most wins on the US Tour in a career
- Most wins on the US Tour in a calendar year
- Career money-winners on the US Seniors Tour
- Career money-winners on the European PGA Tour
- Career money-winners of all time
- Career earnings by women

> It's nice to have the opportunity to play for so much money, but it's nicer to win.
> **Patty Sheenan**

Top 10 Players with the most wins on the US Tour in a career

	Player*	Tour wins
1	Sam Snead	81
2	Jack Nicklaus	70
3	Ben Hogan	63
4	Arnold Palmer	60
5	Byron Nelson	52
6	Billy Casper	51
7 =	Walter Hagen	40
=	Cary Middlecoff	40
9	Gene Sarazen	38
10	Lloyd Mangrum	36

* All USA

For many years, Sam Snead's total number of career wins was put at 84. However, the PGA Tour amended this figure in 1990 after discrepancies were found in their previous lists. They deducted 11 wins from his total, but added eight others that should have been included, giving a revised total of 81.

The most successful woman on the US Women's Tour is Kathy Whitworth, with 88 tour wins. The highest-placed overseas player is Gary Player (South Africa) with 22 wins.

Top 10 Most wins on the US Tour in a calendar year

	Player*	Year	Wins
1	Byron Nelson	1945	18
2	Ben Hogan	1946	13
3	Sam Snead	1950	11
4	Ben Hogan	1948	10
5 =	Paul Runyan	1933	9
=	Tiger Woods	2000	9
7 =	Harry Cooper	1937	8
=	Johnny Miller	1974	8
=	Byron Nelson	1944	8
=	Arnold Palmer	1960	8
=	Henry Picard	1939	8
=	Gene Sarazen	1930	8
=	Horton Smith	1929	8
=	Sam Snead	1938	8
=	Tiger Woods	1999	8

* All USA

Having won eight Tour events in 1944, Byron Nelson shattered the US record the following year with a stunning 18 wins. His remarkable year included a run of 11 consecutive tournament wins, also a US record.

Top 10 Career money-winners on the US Seniors Tour

	Player/country*	Career winnings ($)#
1	Hale Irwin	13,921,874
2	Jim Colbert	10,553,940
3	Gil Morgan	9,749,317
4	Lee Trevino	9,426,642
5	Dave Stockton	9,140,870
6	Bob Charles, New Zealand	8,564,577
7	Ray Floyd	8,229,505
8	Larry Nelson	8,086,397
9	George Archer	8,000,911
10	Jim Dent	7,832,042

* All USA unless otherwise stated
\# As at the end of the 2001 season

Hale Irwin joined the Seniors Tour in 1995 after 20 victories on the regular Tour stretching from 1971 to 1994. After joining the Seniors, he won an additional 32 tournaments to the end of the 2001 season.

Top 10 Career money-winners on the European PGA Tour

	Player/country*	Career winnings (£)#
1	Colin Montgomerie, Scotland	8,569,356
2	Bernhard Langer, Germany	6,353,160
3	Darren Clarke, Northern Ireland	5,823,837
4	Ian Woosnam, Wales	5,052,725
5	Lee Westwood, England	4,866,873
6	José Maria Olázabal, Spain	4,526,266
7	Ernie Els, South Africa	4,186,122
8	Retief Goosen, South Africa	4,073,606
9	Nick Faldo, England	3,988,090
10	Miguel Angel Jiménez, Spain	3,735,393

* As at the end of the 2001 season

Colin Montgomerie, who turned professional in 1987, first topped the European money list in 1993, and was number one for the following six seasons.

◀ Prior to the arrival of Tiger Woods, the last man to show anything like domination of world golf was Jack Nicklaus.

Top 10 Career money-winners of all time

	Player/country*	Career winnings ($)#
1	Tiger Woods	26,191,227
2	Davis Love III	17,994,690
3	Phil Mickelson	17,837,998
4	David Duval	15,312,553
5	Scott Hoch	14,553,202
6	Vijay Singh, Fiji	14,524,452
7	Nick Price, Zimbabwe	14,477,425
8	Hal Sutton	13,885,946
9	Mark Calcavecchia	13,409,349
10	Greg Norman, Australia	13,344,142

* All USA unless otherwise stated

\# As at the end of the 2001 season

Tiger Woods turned professional in August 1996 and won nearly $800,000 in just eight tournaments in his rookie year. The following year he was top money winner with over $2,000,000, and in 2000 won a record $9,188,320.

▶ Not only a top money-winner but also a low scorer – in the 2001 Standard Register Ping tournament at Moon Valley, Phoenix, Annika Sorenstam shot a record 13 under par 59.

Top 10 Career earnings by women

	Player/country*	Career winnings (£)#
1	Annika Sorenstam, Sweden	8,306,464
2	Karrie Webb, Australia	7,698,299
3	Betsy King	7,187,444
4	Dottie Pepper	6,658,613
5	Juli Inkster	6,512,487
6	Beth Daniel	6,433,001
7	Meg Mallon	5,954,573
8	Pat Bradley	5,743,605
9	Laura Davies, UK	5,695,525
10	Rosie Jones	5,683,934

* All USA unless otherwise stated

\# As at the end of the 2001 season

Annika Sorenstam won more tournaments on the US LPGA Tour in the 1990s than anyone else – 18. She is also one of only two women to win $1,000,000 in a season on three occasions; Karrie Webb is the other.

THE MAJOR RECORDS

Top 10 Biggest winning margins in the Majors

	Player/country	Year	Tournament	Venue	Winning margin
1	Tiger Woods, USA	2000	US Open	Pebble Beach	15
2	Tom Morris Sr., UK	1862	British Open	Prestwick	13
3 =	Tom Morris Jr., UK	1870	British Open	Prestwick	12
=	Tiger Woods, USA	1997	US Masters	Augusta	12
5	Willie Smith, USA	1899	US Open	Baltimore	11
6 =	Jim Barnes, USA	1921	US Open	Columbia	9
=	Jack Nicklaus, USA	1965	US Masters	Augusta	9
8 =	James Braid, UK	1908	British Open	Prestwick	8
=	Ray Floyd, USA	1976	US Masters	Augusta	8
=	J. H. Taylor, UK	1900	British Open	St. Andrews	8
=	J. H. Taylor, UK	1913	British Open	Hoylake	8
=	Tiger Woods, USA	2000	British Open	St. Andrews	8

The biggest winning margin in the other Major, the US PGA Championship, was in 1980, when Jack Nicklaus won by seven strokes over Andy Bean at Oak Hill.

THE FOUR MAJORS

The four Majors are the British Open, the US Open, the US Masters, and the US PGA. The oldest is the British Open, first played at Prestwick in 1860 and won by Willie Park. The youngest of the four Majors is the US Masters, played over the beautiful Augusta National course in Georgia. Entry is by invitation only, and the first winner was Horton Smith in 1934.

◀ One of golf's first greats, Tom Morris Sr. He and his son, "Young Tom", together won eight British Open titles.

Top 10 Most frequent runners-up in the Majors

	Player/country*	British Open	US Open	US PGA	US Masters	Total
1	Jack Nicklaus	7	4	4	4	19
2	Arnold Palmer	1	4	3	2	10
3 =	Greg Norman, Australia	1	2	2	3	8
=	Sam Snead	0	4	2	2	8
5 =	J. H. Taylor, UK	6	1	0	0	7
=	Tom Watson	1	2	1	3	7
7 =	Ben Hogan	0	2	0	4	6
=	Byron Nelson	0	1	3	2	6
=	Gary Player, South Africa	0	2	2	2	6
=	Harry Vardon, UK	4	2	0	0	6

* All USA unless otherwise stated

In addition to the four players above, the only other player to finish as runner-up in all four Majors was Craig Wood (USA).

Top 10 Players to win the most Majors in a career

	Player/country*	British Open	US Open	US PGA	US Masters	Total
1	Jack Nicklaus	3	4	5	6	18
2	Walter Hagen	4	2	5	0	11
3 =	Ben Hogan	1	4	2	2	9
=	Gary Player, South Africa	3	1	2	3	9
5	Tom Watson	5	1	0	2	8
6 =	Bobby Jones	3	4	0	0	7
=	Arnold Palmer	2	1	0	4	7
=	Gene Sarazen	1	2	3	1	7
=	Sam Snead	1	0	3	3	7
=	Harry Vardon, UK	6	1	0	0	7
=	Tiger Woods	1	1	2	3	7

* All USA unless otherwise stated

No man has won all four Majors in one year. Ben Hogan, in 1953, won three of the four, but did not compete in the PGA Championship. Bobby Jones achieved a unique Grand Slam in 1930 by winning the British Open and US Open, as well as winning the amateur titles in both countries.

Top 10 Lowest four-round totals in the Majors

	Player/country	Venue	Year	Total
1	David Toms, USA	Atlanta	2001*	265
2	Phil Mickelson, USA	Atlanta	2001*	266
3 =	Steve Elkington, Australia	Riviera	1995*	267
=	Colin Montgomerie, UK	Riviera	1995*	267
=	Greg Norman, Australia	Royal St. George's, Sandwich	1993#	267
6 =	Steve Lowery, USA	Atlanta	2001*	268
=	Nick Price, Zimbabwe	Turnberry	1994#	268
=	Tom Watson, USA	Turnberry	1977#	268
9 =	Nick Faldo, UK	Royal St. George's, Sandwich	1993#	269
=	Davis Love III, USA	Winged Foot	1997*	269
=	Jack Nicklaus, USA	Turnberry	1977#	269
=	Jesper Parnevik, Sweden	Turnberry	1994#	269
=	Nick Price, Zimbabwe	Southern Hills	1994*	269
=	Tiger Woods, USA	St. Andrews	1999#	269

* US PGA Championship
# British Open Championship

In the US Masters, the lowest four-round total is 270 by Tiger Woods, USA, in Augusta, Georgia, 1997. In the US Open, the lowest four-round total is 272 by Jack Nicklaus, USA, at Baltusrol Golf Club, Springfield, New Jersey, 1980, Lee Janzen, USA, at Baltusrol, 1993, and Tiger Woods, USA, in Pebble Beach, California, 2000.

◀ Jose-Maria Olázabal of Spain at the 18th green, Augusta, 1995. It was not to be back-to-back Masters victories for the Spaniard as he lost his title to American Ben Crenshaw.

GOLF

- Biggest winning margins in the US Masters
- First players to hole in one at the US Masters
- Lowest winning totals in the US Masters
- Finishers in the first US Masters, 1934
- Players with the most US Masters titles

THE AUGUSTA COURSE

The US Masters, the brainchild of American amateur golfer Robert Tyre "Bobby" Jones, is the only Major played on the same course each year, in Augusta, Georgia. The course was built on the site of an old nursery, and the abundance of flowers, shrubs, and plants is a reminder of its former days, with each of the 18 holes named after the plants growing adjacent to it.

Top 10 Biggest winning margins in the US Masters

	Player/country*	Year	Score	Runner(s)-up*	Score	Margin
1	Tiger Woods	1997	270	Tom Kite	282	12
2	Jack Nicklaus	1965	271	Arnold Palmer, Gary Player, South Africa	280	9
3	Ray Floyd	1976	271	Ben Crenshaw	279	8
4	Arnold Palmer	1964	276	Dave Marr, Jack Nicklaus	282	6
5 =	Nick Faldo, UK	1996	276	Greg Norman, Australia	281	5
=	Claude Harmon	1948	279	Cary Middlecoff	284	5
=	Ben Hogan	1953	274	Porky Oliver	279	5
8 =	Seve Ballesteros, Spain	1980	275	Gibby Gilbert, Jack Newton, Australia	279	4
=	Seve Ballesteros, Spain	1983	280	Ben Crenshaw, Tom Kite	284	4
=	Jimmy Demaret	1940	280	Lloyd Mangrum	284	4
=	Bernhard Langer, Germany	1993	277	Chip Beck	281	4
=	Sam Snead	1952	286	Jack Burke Jr.	290	4

* All USA unless otherwise stated

Top 10 First players to hole in one at the US Masters

	Player/country*	Hole	Year
1	Ross Somerville#	16	1934
2	Willie Goggin	16	1935
3	Ray Billows#	16	1940
4	Claude Harmon	12	1947
5	John Dawson#	16	1949
6	Leland Gibson	6	1954
7	Billy Joe Patton#	6	1954
8	William Hyndman III#	12	1959
9	Clive Clark, UK	16	1968
10	Charles Coody	6	1972

* All USA unless otherwise stated
\# Amateur

The only other occasion, apart from 1954 above, when two men holed in one at the same US Masters tournament was in 1992 when Jeff Sluman (USA) aced the 4th and Corey Pavin (USA) aced the 16th.

Top 10 Lowest winning totals in the US Masters

	Player/country*	Year	Score
1	Tiger Woods	1997	270
2 =	Ray Floyd	1976	271
=	Jack Nicklaus	1965	271
4	Tiger Woods	2001	272
5 =	Ben Crenshaw	1995	274
=	Ben Hogan	1953	274
7 =	Seve Ballesteros, Spain	1980	275
=	Fred Couples	1992	275
9 =	Nick Faldo, UK	1996	276
=	Jack Nicklaus	1975	276
=	Arnold Palmer	1964	276
=	Tom Watson	1977	276
=	Tiger Woods	2002	276

* All USA unless otherwise stated

> There isn't a flaw in his golf or his make-up. He will win more majors than Arnold Palmer and me combined.
>
> **Jack Nicklaus** on Tiger Woods

Top 10 Finishers in the first US Masters, 1934

	Player*	Round 1	Round 2	Round 3	Round 4	Total
1	Horton Smith	70	72	70	72	284
2	Craig Wood	71	74	69	71	285
3 =	Billy Burke	72	71	70	73	286
=	Paul Runyan	74	71	70	71	286
5	Ed Dudley	74	69	71	74	288
6	Willie MacFarlane	74	73	70	74	291
7 =	Al Espinosa	75	70	75	72	292
=	Jimmy Hines	70	74	74	74	292
=	Harold McSpaden	77	74	72	69	292
=	Macdonald Smith	74	70	74	74	292

* All USA

Horton Smith sank a 20-foot birdie putt at the 17th and then parred the 18th to snatch victory by one stroke.

Top 10 Players with the most US Masters titles

	Player/country*	Years	Wins
1	Jack Nicklaus	1963, 1965–66, 1972, 1975, 1986	6
2	Arnold Palmer	1958, 1960, 1962, 1964	4
3 =	Jimmy Demaret	1940, 1947, 1950	3
=	Nick Faldo, UK	1989–90, 1996	3
=	Gary Player, South Africa	1961, 1974, 1978	3
=	Sam Snead	1949, 1952, 1954	3
=	Tiger Woods	1997, 2001–02	3
8 =	Seve Ballesteros, Spain	1980, 1983	2
=	Ben Crenshaw	1984, 1995	2
=	Ben Hogan	1951, 1953	2
=	Bernhard Langer, Germany	1985, 1993	2
=	Byron Nelson	1937, 1942	2
=	José-Maria Olázabal, Spain	1994, 1999	2
=	Horton Smith	1934, 1936	2
=	Tom Watson	1977, 1981	2

* All USA unless otherwise stated

◄ Not only did Tiger Woods win the 1997 US Masters with a record winning margin, he was also the youngest-ever winner of the event at 22 years 3 months.

THE BRITISH OPEN

- Biggest winning margins in the British Open

- Most British Open titles

- All-time lowest four-round totals in the British Open

- Youngest winners of the British Open

> "Any golfer worth his salt has to cross the sea and try to win the British Open.
> **Jack Nicklaus**"

Top 10 Biggest winning margins in the British Open

	Player/country*	Year	Score	Runner(s)-up*	Score	Margin
1	Tom Morris Sr.	1862	163	Willie Park	176	13
2	Tom Morris Jr.	1870	149	Bob Kirk, David Strath	161	12
3 =	James Braid	1908	291	Tom Ball	299	8
=	J. H. Taylor	1900	309	Harry Vardon	317	8
=	J. H. Taylor	1913	304	Ted Ray	312	8
=	Tiger Woods, USA	2000	269	Thomas Bjorn, Denmark Ernie Els, South Africa	277	8
7 =	Walter Hagen, USA	1929	292	Johnny Farrell, USA	298	6
=	Bobby Jones, USA	1927	285	Aubrey Boomer Fred Robson	291	6
=	Johnny Miller, USA	1976	279	Seve Ballesteros, Spain Jack Nicklaus, USA	285	6
=	Arnold Palmer, USA	1962	276	Kel Nagle, Australia	282	6
=	Harry Vardon	1903	300	Tom Vardon	306	6

* All UK unless otherwise stated

J. H. Taylor (left), James Braid (centre), and Harry Vardon. In the 21 years between 1894 and 1914, they won 16 British Open titles.

Top 10 Most British Open titles

	Player/country	Years	Titles
1	Harry Vardon, UK	1896, 1898–99, 1903, 1911, 1914	6
2 =	James Braid, UK	1901, 1905–06, 1908, 1910	5
=	J. H. Taylor, UK	1894–95, 1900, 1909, 1913	5
=	Peter Thomson, Australia	1954–56, 1958, 1965	5
=	Tom Watson, USA	1975, 1977, 1980, 1982–83	5
6 =	Walter Hagen, USA	1922, 1924, 1928–29	4
=	Bobby Locke, South Africa	1949–50, 1952, 1957	4
=	Tom Morris Sr., UK	1861–62, 1864, 1867	4
=	Tom Morris Jr., UK.	1868–70, 1872	4
=	Willie Park Sr., UK	1860, 1863, 1866, 1875	4

The best total by a current tour player is three wins each by Seve Ballesteros (Spain) and Nick Faldo (UK).

▼ Tiger Woods on his way to winning his first British Open at St. Andrews. It was the second of three Majors for Woods in 2000.

Top 10 All-time lowest four-round totals in the British Open

	Player/country	Venue	Year	Total
1	Greg Norman, Australia	Royal St. George's	1993	267
2 =	Nick Price, Zimbabwe	Turnberry	1994	268
=	Tom Watson, USA	Turnberry	1977	268
4 =	Nick Faldo, UK	Royal St. George's	1993	269
=	Jack Nicklaus, USA	Turnberry	1977	269
=	Jesper Parnevik, Sweden	Turnberry	1994	269
=	Tiger Woods, USA	St. Andrews	2000	269
8 =	Nick Faldo, UK	St. Andrews	1990	270
=	Bernhard Langer, Germany	Royal St. George's	1993	270
10 =	Tom Lehman, USA	Lytham	1996	271
=	Tom Watson, USA	Muirfield	1980	271
=	Fuzzy Zoeller, USA	Turnberry	1994	271

The first time the Open Championship was played over four rounds of 18 holes was at Muirfield in 1892, when the amateur Harold H. Hilton won with a total of 305. The record has kept falling since then and, at Turnberry in 1977, Tom Watson destroyed the British Open records, winning with a record 268. This remained unbeaten until 1993, when Australia's Greg Norman became the first champion to shoot four rounds under 70 when he won with 267 at Sandwich. The lowest individual round is 63, which has been achieved by seven golfers: Mark Hayes (USA), Turnberry 1977; Isao Aoki (Japan), Muirfield 1980; Greg Norman (Australia), Turnberry 1986; Paul Broadhurst (UK), St. Andrews 1990; Jodie Mudd (USA), Royal Birkdale 1991; Nick Faldo (UK), Sandwich 1993; and Payne Stewart (USA), Sandwich 1993.

Top 10 Youngest winners of the British Open

	Player/country	Age (y:m)
1	Tom Morris Jr., UK	17y 5m
2	Willie Auchterlonie, UK	21y 1m
3	Seve Ballesteros, Spain	22y 3m
4	John H. Taylor, UK	23y 3m
5	Gary Player, South Africa	23y 8m
6	Bobby Jones, USA	24y 3m
7	Tiger Woods, USA	24y 6m
8	Peter Thomson, Australia	24y 11m
9 =	Arthur Havers, UK	25y 0m
=	Tony Jacklin, UK	25y 0m

The ages of Arthur Havers and Tony Jacklin were an identical 25 years and 5 days when they won the Open in 1923 and 1969, respectively. The dates of birth for Tom Kidd and Jack Simpson, the 1873 and 1884 winners, have never been established. Hugh Kirkaldy, the 1891 winner, was born in 1865 and could have been either 25 or 26 when he won the title but, again, his exact date of birth has never been confirmed.

THE US OPEN & THE US PGA

- Lowest winning totals in the US PGA Championship

- Biggest winning margins in the US Open

- Lowest rounds in the US Open

- Most wins in the US PGA Championship

- Best finishes by Sam Snead in the US Open

Top 10 Lowest winning totals in the US PGA Championship*

	Player/country#	Year	Venue	Score
1	David Toms	2001	Atlanta	265
2	Steve Elkington, Australia	1995	Riviera	267
3 =	Davis Love III	1997	Winged Foot	269
=	Nick Price, Zimbabwe	1994	Southern Hills	269
5	Tiger Woods	2000	Valhalla	270
6 =	Bobby Nichols	1964	Columbus	271
=	Vijay Singh, Fiji	1998	Sahalee	271
8 =	Paul Azinger	1993	Inverness Club, Toledo	272
=	Ray Floyd	1982	Southern Hills	272
=	David Graham, Australia	1979	Oakland Hills	272
=	Jeff Sluman	1988	Oak Tree	272

* Since 1958, when it became a stroke-play tournament

\# All USA unless otherwise stated

◄ When he won the 1965 Greater Greensboro Open, Sam Snead became, at the age of 52, the oldest winner of a US Tour event.

Any player can win a US Open, but it takes a helluva player to win two.
Walter Hagen

Top 10 Biggest winning margins in the US Open

	Player/country*	Year	Score	Runner(s)-up*	Score	Margin
1	Tiger Woods	2000	272	Miguel Angel Jimenez, Spain		
				Ernie Els, South Africa	287	15
2	Willie Smith	1899	315	George Low, W. H. Way, Val Fitzjohn	326	11
3	Jim Barnes	1921	289	Walter Hagen, Fred McLeod	298	9
4 =	Fred Herd	1898	328	Alex Smith	335	7
=	Tony Jacklin, UK	1970	281	Dave Hill	288	7
=	Alex Smith	1906	295	Willie Smith	302	7
7 =	Laurie Auchterlonie	1902	307	Stewart Gardner, Walter J. Travis	313	6
=	Ralph Guldhal	1938	284	Dick Metz	290	6
=	Ben Hogan	1953	283	Sam Snead	289	6
10	Willie Anderson	1904	303	Gil Nicholls	308	5

* All USA unless otherwise stated

In his record-breaking win, Woods opened with a first round 65 and led by one from Jimenez. One of only three men to break par in round two, Woods went six shots clear of Jimenez and Thomas Bjorn with a 69. He stretched his lead to 10 shots in round three, ahead of Ernie Els, and completed his 15-stroke winning margin with a final round 67.

Top 10 Most wins in the US PGA Championship

	Player/country*	Years	Wins
1 =	Walter Hagen	1921, 1924–27	5
=	Jack Nicklaus	1962, 1971, 1973, 1975, 1980	5
3 =	Gene Sarazen	1922–23, 1933	3
=	Sam Snead	1942, 1949, 1951	3
5 =	Jim Barnes	1916, 1919	2
=	Leo Diegel	1928–29	2
=	Ray Floyd	1969, 1982	2
=	Ben Hogan	1946, 1948	2
=	Byron Nelson	1940, 1945	2
=	Larry Nelson	1981, 1987	2
=	Gary Player, South Africa	1962, 1972	2
=	Nick Price, Zimbabwe	1992, 1994	2
=	Paul Runyan	1934, 1938	2
=	Denny Shute	1936–37	2
=	Dave Stockton	1970, 1976	2
=	Lee Trevino	1974, 1984	2
=	Tiger Woods	1999–2000	2

* All USA unless otherwise stated

Top 10 Lowest rounds in the US Open*

	Player#	Years	Score
1 =	Johnny Miller	1973	63
=	Jack Nicklaus	1980	63
=	Tom Weiskopf	1980	63
4 =	Mark Brooks	2001	64
=	Keith Clearwater	1967	64
=	Ben Crenshaw	1981	64
=	Tommy Jacobs	1964	64
=	Peter Jacobsen	1988	64
=	Tom Kite	2001	64
=	Lee Mackey Jr.	1950	64
=	Rives McBee	1966	64
=	Loren Roberts	1994	64
=	Vijay Singh, Fiji	2001	64
=	Curtis Strange	1989	64

* Over 18 holes, unless otherwise stated

\# All USA unless otherwise stated

When Lee Mackey Jr. became the first man to shoot a 64, he beat the three-year-old record of 65 set by James McHale Jr. at St. Louis Country Club in 1947.

Top 10 Best finishes by Sam Snead in the US Open

	Venue	Year	Position
1 =	Oakland Hills	1937	2nd
=	Medinah	1949	Tied 2nd
=	St. Louis	1947	2nd
=	Oakmont	1953	2nd
5	The Olympic Club	1955	Tied 3rd
6 =	Philadelphia	1939	5th
=	Riviera	1948	5th
8 =	Inverness	1957	Tied 8th
=	Winged Foot	1959	Tied 8th
10	Oak Hill	1968	Tied 9th

Snead never won the US Open, despite winning all of the other three Majors. The closest he came to winning the title was in 1947, when he lost in a play-off to Lew Worsham by one shot. Snead had holed an 18-foot putt to earn the right to play-off, but he missed from less than three feet on the last hole, costing him his one and only chance at the Open.

- Longest holes at St. Andrews
- Winners of the women's Majors
- Winners of the World Cup
- Winners of the Vardon Trophy
- Winners of the US Women's Open

> Don't play too much golf. Two rounds a day are plenty.
>
> Harry Vardon

MISCELLANEOUS RECORDS

Top 10 Longest holes at St. Andrews*

	Hole name	Hole no.	Par	Yards
1	Long Hole	14	5	523
2	Hole o'Cross (out)	5	5	514
3	Road Hole	17	4	461
4	Ginger Beer	4	4	419
5	Dyke	2	4	411
6	Cartgate (in)	15	4	401
7	Hole o'Cross (in)	13	4	398
8	Heathery (out)	6	4	374
9	Burn	1	4	370
10	High Hole (out)	7	4	359

* Old (Championship) course

St. Andrews is unquestionably the "home" of golf, and the game was first recorded as being played there in 1552. The Society of St. Andrews Golfers was formed in 1754 and the original course was laid out alongside St. Andrews Bay. It consisted of 22 holes, but with only 12 huge greens. It is now a par-72 course measuring 6,566 yards. There are five 18-hole courses at St. Andrews: the Old Course, New Course, Jubilee, Eden, and Strathtyrum courses. There is also the 9-hole Balgove course. St. Andrews has hosted the Open Championship a record 26 times.

Top 10 Winners of the women's Majors

	Player*	Titles
1	Patty Berg	16
2 =	Louise Suggs	13
=	Mickey Wright	13
4	Babe Zaharias	12
5 =	Juli Inkster#	9
=	Betsy Rawls	8
7	JoAnne Carner#	7
8 =	Pat Bradley#	6
=	Betsy King#	6
=	Patty Sheehan#	6
=	Glenna C. Vare	6
=	Kathy Whitworth	6

* All USA

\# Current player

The present-day Majors are the US Open, LPGA Championship, Nabisco Championship, British Open, and the amateur championships of both the United States and Great Britain. Also taken into account in this Top 10 list are wins in the former Majors: the Western Open (1937–67), Titleholders Championship (1930–72), and the Du Maurier Classic (1977–2000).

▶ Australia's Karrie Webb during the 2001 US Women's Open at Pine Needles Lodge and Golf Club. Webb went on to win by eight strokes over Se Ri Pak.

Top 10 Winners of the World Cup

	Country	Years	Wins
1	United States	1955-56, 1960-64, 1966-67, 1969, 1971, 1973, 1975, 1978-79, 1983, 1988, 1992-95, 1999-2000	23
2 =	Australia	1954, 1959, 1970, 1989	4
=	South Africa	1965, 1974, 1996, 2001	4
=	Spain	1976-77, 1982, 1984	4
5	Canada	1968, 1980, 1985	3
6	Ireland	1958, 1997	2
7 =	Argentina	1953	1
=	England	1998	1
=	Germany	1990	1
=	Japan	1957	1
=	Sweden	1991	1
=	Taiwan	1972	1
=	Wales	1987	1

The first World Cup, then known as the Canada Cup, was contested in 1953 at Beaconfield Golf Club, Montreal, and was won by Argentina. The trophy was the brainchild of Canadian industrialist John Jay Hopkins, who donated the trophy to be contested by two-man teams of professional golfers who represented their country. Its name was changed to the World Cup in 1967, and in 2000 it became the EMC World Cup. There were no tournaments in 1981 and 1986.

Top 10 Winners of the Vardon Trophy

	Player/country*	Years	Wins
1 =	Billy Casper	1960, 1963, 1965-66, 1968	5
=	Lee Trevino	1970-72, 1974, 1980	5
3 =	Arnold Palmer	1961-62, 1964, 1967	4
=	Sam Snead	1938, 1949-50, 1955	4
5 =	Ben Hogan	1940-41, 1948	3
=	Greg Norman, Australia	1989-90, 1994	3
=	Tom Watson	1977-79	3
=	Tiger Woods	1999, 2000-01	3
9 =	Fred Couples	1991-92	2
=	Bruce Crampton, Australia	1973, 1975	2
=	Tom Kite	1981-82	2
=	Lloyd Mangrum	1951, 1953	2
=	Nick Price, Zimbabwe	1993, 1997	2

* All USA unless otherwise stated

Inaugurated in 1937, the Vardon Trophy was awarded until 1941 on a point system, but since then has been awarded by the US PGA to the player on the regular tour with the lowest scoring average. The first winner was Harry Cooper. The trophy is named after six-time British Open winner Harry Vardon, who also won the US Open in 1900. The first man to win with an average under 70 was Jimmy Demaret in 1947 (69.90). Greg Norman, in 1994, was the first player to win with less than 69 (68.81), while Tiger Woods won it in 2000 with the first average under 68 (67.79).

Top 10 Winners of the US Women's Open

	Player*	Years	Titles
1 =	Betsy Rawls	1951, 1953, 1957, 1960	4
=	Mickey Wright	1958-59, 1961, 1964	4
3 =	Susie Berning	1968, 1972-73	3
=	Hollis Stacy	1977-78, 1984	3
=	Babe Zaharias	1948, 1950, 1954	3
6 =	Donna Caponi	1969-70	2
=	JoAnne Carner#	1971, 1976	2
=	Betsy King#	1989-90	2
=	Patty Sheehan#	1992, 1994	2
=	Annika Sorenstam, Sweden#	1995-96	2
=	Louise Suggs	1949, 1952	2
=	Karrie Webb#	2000-01	2

* All USA unless otherwise stated

\# Current player

BOXING

At the Start

One of man's most primitive means of attack and defence, fist fighting developed as a sport some 6,000 years ago. It was added to the Olympic Games in 688 BC, when a fighter called Onomastus of Smyrna emerged as the first champion. As spikes and studs were attached to the hands, the sport became ever more akin to gladiatorial contests and was banned in medieval Europe. Bare-knuckle fighting was revived in England in the 17th century, and the first recorded match in the United Kingdom took place in 1681, when the Duke of Albemarle organized a bout between his butler and his butcher. In 1719, fight expert James Figg set up a boxing academy in London. The transition to gloved fighting and the introduction from 1867 of the Queensberry Rules mark the transition to the modern sport.

- First boxers to regain the World Heavyweight title

- Heaviest combined weight of boxers at a Championship fight

- Heaviest boxers to contest a World Heavyweight title fight

- Oldest World Heavyweight champions

- World Heavyweight champions with the best undefeated professional records

GOING THE DISTANCE

The last World Heavyweight title fight to go 15 rounds was when Michael Spinks beat Larry Holmes to retain his IBF title in Las Vegas on 19 April 1986. The last time a heavyweight contest went beyond 15 rounds was on 5 April 1915 when Jess Willard deprived Jack Johnson of his title amidst controversy in Havana, Cuba, over 26 rounds.

HEAVYWEIGHT BOXING

The 10 First boxers to regain the World Heavyweight title

	Boxer/country*	Lost to	Year	Won back from	Year
1	Floyd Patterson	Ingemar Johansson, Sweden	1959	Ingemar Johansson	1960
2	Muhammad Ali	Joe Frazier	1971	George Foreman	1974
3	Muhammad Ali	Leon Spinks	1978	Leon Spinks	1978
4	Tim Witherspoon	Pinklon Thomas	1984	Tony Tubbs	1986
5	Evander Holyfield	Riddick Bowe	1992	Riddick Bowe	1993
6	George Foreman	Muhammad Ali	1974	Michael Moorer	1994
7	Michael Moorer	George Foreman	1994	Axel Schulz, Germany	1996
8	Mike Tyson	James "Buster" Douglas	1990	Frank Bruno, UK	1996
9	Evander Holyfield	Michael Moorer	1994	Mike Tyson	1996
10	Lennox Lewis, UK	Oliver McCall	1994	Oliver McCall	1997

* All USA unless otherwise stated

Floyd Patterson had an interesting career as the World Heavyweight champion. He became the youngest-ever champion when he beat Archie Moore for the vacant title in 1956. His opponent in his second defence of the title was Pete Rademacher, who was making his professional debut in the fight. In June 1960, Patterson became the first man to regain the title by beating Sweden's Ingemar Johansson, the man who had taken his title from him a year earlier. He lost his title with a first-round knockout by Sonny Liston in 1962.

Top 10 Heaviest combined weight of boxers at a Championship fight

	Boxers*/weight (lb)	Date	Combined weight (lb)
1	Lennox Lewis (247) v Michael Grant (250)	29 Apr 2000	497
2	Primo Carnera (259½) v Paulino Uzcudun (229¼)	22 Oct 1933	488¾
3 =	Lennox Lewis (251) v Oliver McCall (237)	2 July 1997	488
=	Lennox Lewis (244) v Andrew Golota (244)	14 Oct 1997	488
5	Riddick Bowe (243) v Michael Dokes (244)	6 Feb 1993	487
6	Lennox Lewis (242) v Henry Akinwande (237½)	12 July 1997	479½
7	George Foreman (256) v Axel Schulz (221)	22 Apr 1995	477
8	Max Baer (209½) v Primo Carnera (263¼)	14 June 1934	472¾
9	George Foreman (250) v Michael Moorer (222)	5 Nov 1994	472
10 =	Tim Witherspoon (227) v Tony Tubbs (244)	17 Jan 1986	471
=	Lennox Lewis (243) v Shannon Briggs (228)	28 Mar 1998	471

* Winner first; all USA except: Lennox Lewis (UK), Primo Carnera (Italy), Paulino Uzcudun (Spain), Henry Akinwande (UK), and Axel Schulz (Germany)

Lennox Lewis, who appears in the list on five occasions, never fought at less than 233 lb, his weight during his first defence of his WBC title in 1993 against Frank Bruno. The heaviest man to have boxed professionally was Jimmy Black (USA) who weighed in at around 360 lb in the early 1970s. When he fought Claude McBride on 1 June 1971, the combined weight of the two men was 700 lb.

Top 10 Heaviest boxers to contest a World Heavyweight title fight*

	Boxer/country#	Opponent#	Year	Weight (lb)
1	Primo Carnera†, Italy	Tommy Loughran	1934	270
2	George Foreman	Evander Holyfield†	1991	257
3	Abe Simon	Joe Louis†	1942	255½
4	Leroy Jones	Larry Holmes†	1980	254½
5	Lennox Lewis, UK	Hasim Rahman†	2001	253
6 =	Buddy Baer	Joe Louis†	1942	250
=	Michael Grant	Lennox Lewis†, UK	2000	250
8	Frank Bruno†, UK	Oliver McCall	1995	248
9	Lennox Lewis†, UK	Hasim Rahman	2001	246½
10 =	Riddick Bowe	Evander Holyfield†	1993	246
=	James "Buster" Douglas	Evander Holyfield†	1990	246

* Based on their heaviest weight at which they fought
\# All USA unless otherwise stated
† Winner

Top 10 Oldest World Heavyweight champions*

	Boxer/country#	Date of win	Age (y:m:d)
1	George Foreman†	5 Nov 1994	46:9:14
2	Evander Holyfield†	12 Aug 2000	37:9:13
3	Jersey Joe Walcott	18 July 1951	37:6:5
4	Muhammad Ali†	15 Sep 1978	36:7:29
5	Lennox Lewis†, UK	17 Nov 2001	36:2:15
6	Evander Holyfield†	9 Nov 1996	34:0:21
7	Bob Fitzsimmons, UK	17 Mar 1897	33:9:24
8	Frank Bruno, UK	2 Sep 1995	33:9:16
9	Trevor Berbick, Jamaica	22 Mar 1986	33:7:21
10	Jess Willard	5 Apr 1915	33:3:7

* Based on age when they first won or regained world title
\# All USA unless otherwise stated
† Age at time of regaining title

Jersey Joe Walcott is the oldest man to have won the title for the first time.

Top 10 World Heavyweight champions with the best undefeated professional records*

	Boxer/country#	Year of first title	Record W–L–D
1	Rocky Marciano	1952	43–0–0
2	George Foreman	1973	37–0–0
3	Frans Botha†, South Africa	1995	36–0–0
4	Michael Moorer	1994	35–0–0
5	Riddick Bowe	1992	32–0–0
6 =	Larry Holmes	1978	28–0–0
=	Michael Spinks	1985	28–0–0
=	Mike Tyson	1986	28–0–0
9	Michael Dokes	1982	26–0–1
10 =	Joe Frazier§	1970	25–0–0
=	Evander Holyfield	1990	25–0–0

* When they won their first heavyweight title
\# All USA unless otherwise stated
† Botha was stripped of the IBF title shortly after winning it from Axel Schulz of Germany in December 1995 because of illegal use of steroids
§ When Frazier won the New York version of the title in 1968, his record was 21–0–0

▶ Rocky Marciano, "The Brockton Blockbuster", retired as undefeated World Heavyweight champion in 1955 with a record of 49 wins from 49 fights.

HEAVYWEIGHT CHAMPIONS

> Honey, I forgot to duck.
>
> **Jack Dempsey** to his wife, after his 1926 defeat by Gene Tunney

Top 10 Attendances at World Heavyweight title fights

	Fight	Venue	Date	Attendance
1	Jack Dempsey v Gene Tunney	Philadelphia	23 Sep 1926	120,757
2	Jack Dempsey v Gene Tunney	Chicago	22 Sep 1927	104,943
3	Jack Dempsey v Luis Angel Firpo	New York	14 Sep 1923	82,000
4	Georges Carpentier v Jack Dempsey	Jersey City	2 July 1921	80,183
5	Max Schmeling v Jack Sharkey	New York	12 June 1930	79,222
6	Joe Louis v Max Schmeling	New York	22 June 1938	70,043
7	Muhammad Ali v George Foreman	Kinshasa, Zaïre	30 Oct 1974	65,000
8	Muhammad Ali v Leon Spinks	New Orleans	15 Sep 1978	63,350
9	Primo Carnera v Joe Louis	New York	25 June 1935	62,000
10	Max Schmeling v Jack Sharkey	Long Island	21 June 1932	61,863

The Jack Dempsey-Gene Tunney contest at Soldier Field, Chicago in 1927 was notable for the famous "Battle of the Long Count" in which Tunney was floored in the seventh round. Dempsey stood over him while the time keeper commenced the count, but the referee would not start until Dempsey had moved to a neutral corner. When he did so, the referee started counting. Tunney got up on the count of nine – a full 14 seconds after the timekeeper had started the count.

The 10 Last fights of Muhammad Ali

	Opponent	Venue	Decision	Title(s)	Date
1	Trevor Berbick	Nassau, Bahamas	Lost points 10	None	11 Dec 1981
2	Larry Holmes	Las Vegas	Lost TKO 11	WBC	2 Oct 1980
3	Leon Spinks	New Orleans	Won points 15	WBA	15 Sep 1978
4	Leon Spinks	Las Vegas	Lost points 15	WBA/WBC	15 Feb 1978
5	Earnie Shavers	New York	Won points 15	WBA/WBC	29 Sep 1977
6	Alfredo Evangelista	Landover, Maryland	Won points 15	WBA/WBC	16 May 1977
7	Ken Norton	New York	Won points 15	WBA/WBC	28 Sep 1976
8	Richard Dunn	Munich, Germany	Won TKO 5	WBA/WBC	24 May 1976
9	Jimmy Young	Landover, Maryland	Won points 15	WBA/WBC	30 Apr 1976
10	Jean-Pierre Coopman	San Juan, Puerto Rico	Won KO 5	WBA/WBC	20 Feb 1976

Ali's fight with Earnie Shavers at Madison Square Garden in 1977 made history as the first championship bout to have a female judge, Eva Shain.

Ali's last opponent, Jamaican-born Trevor Berbick, had a brief spell as World Heavyweight champion. Having lost to Larry Holmes on points in Las Vegas in 1981, he captured the WBC version of the title five years later by beating Pinklon Thomas on points over 12 rounds. He held the title for just eight months before losing it to Mike Tyson in just two rounds.

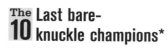

◀ Lennox Lewis, Britain's first World Heavyweight champion of the 20th century and the first since Bob Fitzsimmons in 1899.

The 10 Shortest World Heavyweight title fights

	Winner/country*	Loser/country*	Date	Duration (sec)
1	Mike Dokes	Mike Weaver	10 Dec 1982	63
2	Tommy Burns, Canada	Jem Roche, Ireland	17 Mar 1908	88
3	Mike Tyson	Michael Spinks	27 June 1988	91
4	Mike Tyson	Carl Williams	21 July 1989	93
5	Lennox Lewis, UK	Andrew Golota	4 Oct 1997	95
6	Joe Frazier	Dave Zyglewicz	22 Apr 1969	96
7	Mike Tyson	Bruce Seldon	9 Nov 1996	109
8	Muhammad Ali	Sonny Liston	25 May 1965	112
9	George Foreman	Joe Roman, Puerto Rico	1 Sep 1973	120
10	Riddick Bowe	Michael Dokes	6 Feb 1993	139

* All USA unless otherwise stated

▼ He claimed he was "The Greatest" and the rest of the world never argued with him. Muhammad Ali, formerly Cassius Clay.

The 10 Last bare-knuckle champions*

	Boxer/country	Nickname	Reign begins	Reign ends
1	John L. Sullivan, USA	Boston Strong Boy	1882	1889
2	Paddy Ryan, USA	–	1880	1882
3	Joe Goss, UK	–	1876	1880
4	Tom Allen, UK	–	1873	1876
5	Jem Mace, UK	The Gypsy	1870	1873
6	Mike McCoole, Ireland	The Deck Hand Champion	1869	1870
7	Tom King*, UK	–	1863	1869
8	Joe Coburn, Ireland	–	1863	1865
9	John Camel Heenan, USA	The Benica Boy	1860	1863
10	John Morrissey, Ireland	Old Smoke	1853	1859

* To 1863 as Champions of America, since then as Champions of the World

Tom King beat John Heenan for the first world title at Wadhurst, England, on 10 December 1863, while Joe Coburn remained as the American champion. The last bare-knuckle contest for the world title was between John L. Sullivan and Jake Kilrain in Richburg, Mississippi, on 8 July 1889.

Top 10 Most wins in World Heavyweight title fights

	Boxer/country*	Bouts	Wins
1	Joe Louis	27	26
2	Muhammad Ali/Cassius Clay	25	22
3	Larry Holmes	25	21
4	Lennox Lewis, UK	15	14
5 =	Tommy Burns, Canada	13	12
=	Mike Tyson	15	12
7 =	Joe Frazier	11	10
=	Evander Holyfield	15	10
=	Jack Johnson	11	10
10	Ezzard Charles	13	9

* All USA unless otherwise stated

This list also represents the Top 10 most World Heavyweight title bouts, with the exception of Floyd Patterson (USA) who would be in at 9th with 12 fights. James J. Jeffries, with eight wins from eight fights, represents the best record of boxers undefeated in World Heavyweight Championship fights.

- Boxing World Champions with the most consecutive successful defences
- Most winners of the International Boxing Hall of Fame's Fighter of the Year award
- First Olympic champions to win professional world titles
- World Champions with the longest professional careers

"THE RING"

Boxing's "Bible", *The Ring*, was founded by Nat Fleischer in 1922. From 1928, the magazine presented its annual Fighter of the Year Award. The first winner was Gene Tunney. Since 1945, there has also been an award for the Fight of the Year, in which Muhammad Ali featured a record six times.

BOXING GREATS

Top 10 Boxing World Champions with the most consecutive successful defences*

	Boxer/country	Weight division	Years	Defences
1	Joe Louis, USA	Heavyweight#	1937–49	25
2	Ricardo Lopez, Mexico	WBC/WBA Strawweight	1990–98	22
3 =	Henry Armstrong, USA	Welterweight#	1938–40	19
=	Khaosai Galaxy, Thailand	WBA Junior-bantamweight	1984–91	19
=	Eusebio Pedroza, Panama	WBA Featherweight	1978–85	19
6 =	Wilfredo Gomez, Puerto Rico	WBC Junior-featherweight	1977–83	17
=	Myung Woo Yuh, South Korea	WBA Junior-flyweight	1985–91	17
8	Orlando Canizares, USA	IBF Bantamweight	1988–94	16
9	Bernard Hopkins, USA	IBF/WBC/WBA Middleweight	1995–2002	15
10 =	Miguel Canto, Mexico	WBC Flyweight	1975–79	14
=	Bob Foster, USA	Light-heavyweight#	1968–74	14

* One champion per division listed

\# Undisputed champion

Top 10 Most winners of the International Boxing Hall of Fame's Fighter of the Year award*

	Boxer/country#	Years	Wins
1	Muhammad Ali	1963†, 1972§, 1974–75, 1978	5
2	Joe Louis	1936, 1938–39, 1941	4
3 =	Joe Frazier	1967, 1970–71	3
=	Evander Holyfield	1987, 1996–97	3
=	Rocky Marciano	1952, 1954–55	3
6 =	Ezzard Charles	1949–50	2
=	George Foreman	1973, 1976	2
=	Marvin Hagler	1983, 1985§	2
=	Thomas Hearns	1980, 1984	2
=	Ingemar Johansson, Sweden	1958–59	2
=	Sugar Ray Leonard	1979, 1981§	2
=	Tommy Loughran	1929, 1931	2
=	Floyd Patterson	1956, 1960	2
=	Barney Ross	1934§–35	2
=	Dick Tiger, Nigeria	1962, 1965	2
=	Mike Tyson	1986, 1988	2

* Formerly The Ring Fighter of the Year award

All USA unless otherwise stated

† As Cassius Clay

§ Shared award

Top 10 First Olympic champions to win professional world titles

	Boxer/country	Olympic title/year	First pro. title/year
1	Fidel la Barba, USA	Flyweight 1924	Flyweight 1925
2	Frankie Genaro, USA	Flyweight 1920	Flyweight 1927
3	Jackie Fields, USA	Featherweight 1924	Welterweight 1929
4	Pascual Perez, Argentina	Flyweight 1948	Flyweight 1954
5	Floyd Patterson, USA	Middleweight 1952	Heavyweight 1956
6	Cassius Clay, USA	Light-heavyweight 1960	Heavyweight 1964
7	Nino Benvenuti, Italy	Light-middleweight 1960	Junior-middleweight 1965
8	Joe Frazier, USA	Heavyweight 1964	Heavyweight 1968
9	George Foreman, USA	Heavyweight 1968	Heavyweight 1973
10	Mate Parlov, Yugoslavia	Light-heavyweight 1972	Light-heavyweight 1978

Willie Smith (USA) took the Olympic Bantamweight title in 1924 and three years later won the British version of the world title. However, he is not universally acknowledged as the World Champion. Joe Frazier, 1964, George Foreman, 1968, and Lennox Lewis, 1988, are the only Olympic Heavyweight/super-heavyweight Champions to go on to win the professional World Heavyweight title. Ray Mercer won the Heavyweight title in 1988 and later went on to win the WBO version of the title.

◀ Two of the best-known fighters in the 1980s, Sugar Ray Leonard (left) and Marvin Hagler. Their World title fight at Caesar's Palace in 1987 was staged before a full house.

Top 10 World Champions with the longest professional careers

	Boxer/country	Fought professionally	Years
1 =	Bob Fitzsimmons, UK	1883–1914	31
=	Jack Johnson, USA	1897–1928	31
3 =	George Foreman, USA	1969–97	28
=	Archie Moore, USA	1935–63	28*
5	Joe Brown, USA	1943–70	27
6 =	Billy Murphy, New Zealand	1881–1907	26
=	Willie Pep, USA	1940–66	26
8 =	Jack Britton, USA	1905–30	25
=	Young Griffo, Australia	1886–1911	25
=	Harold Johnson, USA	1946–71	25
=	Charles "Kid" McCoy, USA	1891–1916	25
=	Sugar Ray Robinson, USA	1940–65	25

* Archie Moore engaged in an exhibition bout in 1965, which, if counted, increases his career span to 30 years

Dates of many fights in the last century are not recorded, so it is impossible to establish the exact length of some careers. The longest career of any professional boxer is believed to be that of Bobby Dobbs, who fought for 39 years between 1875 and 1914. His last fight is alleged to have been when he was 56.

BOXING

- First countries to produce World Champions
- First World Champions under Queensberry Rules
- First men to regain world titles
- First American-born World Champions
- First men to win world titles at three different weights

QUEENSBERRY RULES

The original Queensberry Rules, as drawn up in 1867 by John Sholto Douglas, the 8th Marquess of Queensberry, contained 12 rules. The three most significant, which are still adhered to today, were: (a) boxers should wear gloves, (b) all rounds should last three minutes (previously a round ended when a fighter was knocked down), and (c) wrestling (as permitted under the London Rules) was outlawed.

BOXING FIRSTS

The 10 First countries to produce World Champions*

Country#	Boxer	Weight	Year
1 Ireland	Jack "Nonpareil" Dempsey	Middleweight	1884
2 USA	Paddy Duffy	Welterweight	1888
3 UK	Ike Weir	Featherweight	1889
4 Canada	George LaBlanche	Middleweight	1889
5 New Zealand	Billy Murphy	Featherweight	1890
6 Australia	Young Griffo	Featherweight	1890
7 Switzerland	Frank Erne	Lightweight	1899
8 Barbados	Joe Walcott	Welterweight	1901
9 Austria	Jack Root	Light-heavyweight	1903
10 Denmark	Battling Nelson	Lightweight	1908

* Under Queensberry Rules

\# Of birth

Despite producing many of the early World Champions, Ireland did not stage its first world title fight until 1908 when Canada's Tommy Burns made the seventh defence of his World Heavyweight title against local hero Jem Roche from Wexford, in Dublin. He did not remain a hero for long – Burns knocked him out in the first round.

The 10 First World Champions under Queensberry Rules*

Boxer/country	Weight	Year
1 Jack Dempsey, Ireland	Middleweight	1884
2 Jack McAuliffe, Ireland	Lightweight	1887
3 Paddy Duffy, USA	Welterweight	1888
4 Ike Weir, UK	Featherweight	1889
5 George Dixon, Canada	Bantamweight	1890
6 James J. Corbett, USA	Heavyweight	1892
7 Jack Root, Austria	Light-heavyweight	1903
8 Jimmy Wilde, UK	Flyweight	1916
9 Johnny Dundee, Italy	Junior-lightweight	1921
10 Mushy Callahan, USA	Junior-welterweight	1926

* First champion per division listed

Jack "Nonpareil" Dempsey, not to be confused with the heavyweight champion of the same name, was the sport's first World Champion with gloves. Born in County Kildare, Ireland, in 1862, Dempsey won the World Middleweight title at the age of 21. He lost it to Bob Fitzsimmons in 1891. Four years later, he attempted to win the welterweight title but was thwarted by Tommy Ryan.

The 10 First men to regain world titles

Boxer/country*	Weight	Year
1 Mysterious Billy Smith	Welterweight	1898
2 George Dixon, Canada	Featherweight	1898
3 Rube Ferns	Welterweight	1901
4 Stanley Ketchel	Middleweight	1908
5 Billy Papke	Middleweight	1910
6 Ted "Kid" Lewis, UK	Welterweight	1917
7 Jack Britton	Welterweight	1919
8 Peter Herman	Bantamweight	1921
9 Joe Lynch	Bantamweight	1922
10 Johnny Dundee, Italy	Junior-lightweight	1923

* All USA-born unless otherwise stated

Billy Papke was the first man to regain a world title on two occasions. Having lost the middleweight crown to Stanley Ketchel in 1909, he regained it with a third-round knockout of Willie Lewis eight months later. He lost it again to Johnny Thompson in February 1911, but beat Jim Sullivan four months later to regain it.

▶ Thomas Hearns on his way to beating Nate Miller in April 1999 and capturing the vacant IBO Cruiserweight title.

◀ Ghanaian World Champion Azumah Nelson won the WBC Super-featherweight title in 1995 at the age of 37.

The 10 First American-born World Champions*

	Boxer	Birth place	Weight	Date of first title
1	Paddy Duffy	Boston, Massachusetts	Welterweight	30 Oct 1888
2	James J. Corbett	San Francisco	Heavyweight	7 Sep 1892
3	Tommy Ryan	Redwood, New York	Welterweight	26 July 1894
4	Charles "Kid" McCoy	Rush County, Indiana	Welterweight	2 Mar 1896
5	George "Kid" Lavigne	Bay City, Michigan	Lightweight	1 June 1896
6	Solly Smith	Los Angeles	Featherweight	4 Oct 1897
7	Jimmy Barry	Chicago	Bantamweight	6 Dec 1897
8	James J. Jeffries	Carroll, Ohio	Heavyweight	9 June 1899
9	Terry McGovern	Johnstown, Pennsylvania	Bantamweight	12 Sep 1899
10	Rube Ferns	Pittsburgh, Kansas	Welterweight	15 Jan 1900

* Under Queensberry Rules

The first recognized world champion under Queensberry Rules was middleweight Jack "Nonpareil" Dempsey, who captured the title in 1884. However, although he represented the USA, Dempsey was in fact born in County Kildare in the Republic of Ireland.

The 10 First men to win world titles at three different weights

	Boxer/country	Weights/years of first titles
1	Bob Fitzsimmons, UK	Middle 1891, Heavy 1897, Light-heavy 1903
2	Tony Canzoneri, USA	Feather* 1927, Light 1930, Junior-welter 1931
3	Barney Ross, USA	Light 1933, Junior-welter 1933, Welter 1934
4	Henry Armstrong, USA	Feather 1937, Welter 1938, Light 1938
5	Wilfred Benitez, USA	Junior-welter 1976, Welter 1979, Junior-middle 1981
6	Alexis Arguello, Nicaragua	Feather 1974, Junior-light 1978, Light 1981
7	Roberto Duran, Panama	Light 1972, Welter 1980, Junior-middle 1983
8	Wilfredo Gomez, Puerto Rico	Junior-feather 1977, Feather 1984, Junior-light 1985
9	Thomas Hearns, USA	Welter 1980, Junior-middle 1982, Light-heavy 1987
10	Sugar Ray Leonard, USA	Welter 1979, Junior-middle 1981, Middle 1987

* New York version of the title

At the Start

Tennis has its roots in a game played in France in an indoor court. As "real", or royal, tennis, it was played in England from the medieval period, and as "field tennis" during the late 18th and early 19th centuries. In 1874, Major Walter Clopton Wingfield patented *sphairistiké* (Greek for "ball games"), or lawn tennis, as a more vigorous version of badminton (which developed from the ancient children's game of battledore and shuttlecock). The Marylebone Cricket Club revised Wingfield's original rules and, in 1877, the game came under the aegis of the Wimbledon-based All England Croquet Club, which added the name Lawn Tennis to its own, holding the first championships in 1877. The world's first national governing body for tennis was the United States Lawn Tennis Association, which was formed at the Fifth Avenue Hotel, New York on 21 May 1881.

GRAND SLAM CHAMPIONS

- Most Grand Slam men's singles titles
- Most Grand Slam women's singles titles
- Most Grand Slam men's titles
- First players to perform the Grand Slam
- Most Grand Slam women's titles

LOSING STREAK

Despite reaching four US Open finals, Bjorn Borg was a runner-up on each occasion, something that happened to him only once in a Wimbledon final and not at all in six French Open finals.

Top 10 Most Grand Slam men's singles titles

	Player/country	A	F	W	US	Total
1	Pete Sampras, USA	2	0	7	4	13
2	Roy Emerson, Australia	6	2	2	2	12
3 =	Bjorn Borg, Sweden	0	6	5	0	11
=	Rod Laver, Australia	3	2	4	2	11
5	Bill Tilden, USA	0	0	3	7	10
6 =	Jimmy Connors, USA	1	0	2	5	8
=	Ivan Lendl, Czechoslovakia	2	3	0	3	8
=	Fred Perry, UK	1	1	3	3	8
=	Ken Rosewall, Australia	4	2	0	2	8
10 =	Andre Agassi, USA	3	1	1	2	7
=	Henri Cochet, France	0	4	2	1	7
=	René Lacoste, France	0	3	2	2	7
=	William Larned, USA	0	0	0	7	7
=	John McEnroe, USA	0	0	3	4	7
=	John Newcombe, Australia	2	0	3	2	7
=	Bill Renshaw, UK	0	0	7	0	7
=	Richard Sears, USA	0	0	0	7	7
=	Mats Wilander, Sweden	3	3	0	1	7

A – Australian Open; F – French Open; W – Wimbledon; US – US Open

Top 10 Most Grand Slam women's singles titles

	Player/country	A	F	W	US	Total
1	Margaret Court* (née Smith), Australia	11	5	3	7	26
2	Steffi Graf, West Germany/Germany	4	6	7	5	22
3	Helen Wills-Moody, USA	0	4	8	7	19
4 =	Chris Evert-Lloyd, USA	2	7	3	6	18
=	Martina Navratilova, Czechoslovakia/USA	3	2	9	4	18
6	Billie Jean King (née Moffitt), USA	1	1	6	4	12
7 =	Maureen Connolly, USA	1	2	3	3	9
=	Monica Seles, Yugoslavia/USA	4	3	0	2	9
9 =	Suzanne Lenglen#, France	0	2	6	0	8
=	Molla Mallory (née Bjurstedt), USA	0	0	0	8	8

A – Australian Open; F – French Open; W – Wimbledon; US – US Open

* Includes two wins in Amateur Championships in 1968 and 1969, which were held alongside the Open Championship

\# Lenglen also won four French singles titles pre-1925 when the tournament was a "closed" event

◀ Billie Jean King, winner of more Wimbledon titles than any other player.

Top 10 Most Grand Slam men's titles

	Player/country	Singles	Doubles	Mixed	Total
1	Roy Emerson, Australia	12	16	0	28
2	John Newcombe, Australia	7	17	1	25
3	Frank Sedgman, Australia	5	9	8	22
4	Bill Tilden, USA	10	6	5	21
5	Rod Laver, Australia	11	6	3	20
6 =	John Browmwich, Australia	2	13	4	19
=	Neale Fraser, Australia	3	11	5	19
8 =	Jean Borotra, France	4	9	5	18
=	Ken Rosewall, Australia	8	9	1	18
=	Fred Stolle, Australia	2	10	6	18
=	Todd Woodbridge, Australia	0	12	6	18

Top 10 First players to perform the Grand Slam*

	Player/country	Event	Year
1	Donald Budge, USA	Singles	1938
2 =	Ken McGregor, Australia	Doubles	1951
=	Frank Sedgman, Australia	Doubles	1951
4	Maureen Connolly, USA	Singles	1953
5	Maria Bueno#, Brazil	Doubles	1960
6	Rod Laver, Australia	Singles	1962
7 =	Ken Fletcher, Australia	Mixed	1963
=	Margaret Smith, Australia	Mixed	1963
9	Owen Davidson†, Australia	Mixed	1967
10	Rod Laver, Australia	Singles	1969

* Winning singles, doubles, or mixed doubles at all four Grand Slam events in one year

\# Bueno completed the doubles Grand Slam in 1960 with two different partners: Christine Truman (UK) and Darlene Hard (USA)

† Davidson completed the mixed doubles Grand Slam in 1967 with two different partners: Lesley Turner (Australia) and Billie Jean King (USA)

Apart from Budge, Connolly, and Laver, the only other players to have performed the singles Grand Slam are: Margaret Court (Australia) in 1970 and Steffi Graf (West Germany) in 1988. Graf also won the Olympic title in the same year. The last player to perform the Grand Slam was Martina Hingis (Switzerland), who won the Ladies' Doubles at all four events in 1998.

◀ "Pistol Pete" – Pete Sampras of the USA, one of the world's greatest tennis players, and a dominant force in the men's game in the 1990s.

Top 10 Most Grand Slam women's titles

	Player/country	Singles	Doubles	Mixed	Total
1	Margaret Court (née Smith), Australia	24	19	19	62
2	Martina Navratilova, Czechoslovakia/USA	18	31	7	56
3	Bille Jean King (née Moffitt), USA	12	16	11	39
4	Margaret Du Pont, USA	6	21	10	37
5 =	Louise Brough, USA	6	21	8	35
=	Doris Hart, USA	6	14	15	35
7	Helen Wills-Moody, USA	19	9	3	31
8	Elizabeth Ryan, USA	0	17	9	26
9	Suzanne Lenglen, France	12	8	5	25
10	Steffi Graf, West Germany/Germany	22	1	0	23

Steffi Graf's only doubles title was at Wimbledon in 1988 when she partnered Gabriela Sabatini (Argentina) to victory.

TENNIS

- Most US Open men's titles
- Most US Open women's titles
- Most US Open women's singles titles
- Most US Open men's singles titles
- Most singles matches won in a US Open career

DID YOU KNOW?

Organized lawn tennis started in the United States following the formation of the US Lawn Tennis Association on 21 May 1881, and on 31 August that year the first national championships got underway on the courts of the Newport [Rhode Island] Casino. The men's singles and doubles were the only events contested, with competitors playing in a wide variety of attire, including coloured blazers and cravats. The first winner of the singles title was Richard Sears, who dominated the event in its early years, winning the first seven titles, until deposed by Henry Slocum in 1888.

US OPEN RECORDS

Top 10 Most US Open men's titles

	Player/country*	Years	Singles	Doubles	Mixed	Total titles
1	Bill Tilden	1913–29	7	5	4	16
2	Richard Sears	1881–87	7	6	0	13
3 =	Neale Fraser, Australia	1957–60	2	3	3	8
=	George M. Lott Jr.	1928–34	0	5	3	8
=	John McEnroe	1979–89	4	4	0	8
=	Billy Talbert	1942–48	0	4	4	8
7 =	Jack Kramer	1940–47	2	4	1	7
=	Bill Larned	1901–11	7	0	0	7
=	Vincent Richards	1918–26	0	5	2	7
=	Holcombe Ward	1899–1906	1	6	0	7

* All USA unless otherwise stated

Jack Kramer turned professional shortly after winning the US Open and Wimbledon in 1947. He made his professional debut on 26 December 1947 against Bobby Riggs at Madison Square Garden. Despite a heavy snowfall and the cancellation of most public transport, over 15,000 fans turned out – some arriving on skis.

Top 10 Most US Open women's titles

	Player/country*	Years	Singles	Doubles	Mixed	Total titles
1	Margaret Du Pont (née Osborne)	1941–60	3	13	9	25
2	Margaret Court# (née Smith), Australia	1961–75	7	5	8	20
3	Louise Brough	1942–57	1	12	4	17
4	Hazel Wightman (née Hotchkiss)	1909–28	4	6	6	16
5 =	Sarah Cooke (née Palfrey)	1930–45	2	9	4	15
=	Martina Navratilova, Czechoslovakia/USA	1977–90	4	9	2	15
7 =	Juliette Atkinson	1894–1902	3	7	3	13
=	Billie Jean King (née Moffitt)	1964–80	4	5	4	13
=	Molla Mallory (née Bjurstedt)	1915–26	8	2	3	13
=	Helen Wills-Moody	1922–31	7	4	2	13

* All USA unless otherwise stated

Includes two wins in Amateur Championships of 1968 and 1969, which were held alongside the Open Championship

Margaret Du Pont was one of the leading exponents of the doubles game, winning 21 doubles titles at Grand Slam events. She enjoyed a long career, first entering the US Top 10 rankings in 1938. Twenty years later she was still ranked number five.

▶ Chris Evert-Lloyd, the only player to win 100 matches in the US Open.

Top 10 Most US Open women's singles titles

	Player/country*	Years	Titles
1	Molla Mallory (née Bjurstedt)	1915–26	8
2 =	Margaret Court (née Smith)#, Australia	1962–70	7
=	Helen Wills-Moody	1923–31	7
4	Chris Evert-Lloyd	1975–82	6
5	Steffi Graf, West Germany/Germany	1988–96	5
6 =	Pauline Betz	1942–46	4
=	Maria Bueno, Brazil	1959–66	4
=	Helen Jacobs	1932–35	4
=	Billie Jean King (née Moffitt)	1967–74	4
=	Alice Marble	1936–40	4
=	Elizabeth Moore	1896–1905	4
=	Martina Navratilova	1983–87	4
=	Hazel Wightman (née Hotchkiss)	1909–19	4

* All USA unless otherwise stated

Includes two wins in Amateur Championships of 1968 and 1969, which were held alongside the Open Championship

Top 10 Most US Open men's singles titles

	Player/country*	Years	Titles
1 =	William Larned	1901–11	7
=	Richard Sears	1881–87	7
=	Bill Tilden	1920–29	7
4	Jimmy Connors	1974–83	5
5 =	John McEnroe	1979–84	4
=	Pete Sampras	1990–96	4
=	Robert Wrenn	1893–97	4
8 =	Oliver Campbell	1890–92	3
=	Ivan Lendl, Czechoslovakia	1985–87	3
=	Fred Perry, UK	1933–36	3
=	Malcolm Whitman	1898–1900	3

* All USA unless otherwise stated

Top 10 Most singles matches won in a US Open career

	Player/country*	Years	Total wins
1	Chris Evert-Lloyd	1971–89	101
2	Jimmy Connors	1970–92	98
3	Martina Navratilova, Czechoslovakia/USA	1973–93	89
4	Vic Seixas	1940–69	75
5 =	Steffi Graf, West Germany/Germany	1984–2000	73
=	Ivan Lendl, Czechoslovakia	1979–94	73
7	Bill Tilden	1916–30	71
8	R. Norris Williams	1912–35	69
9 =	John McEnroe	1977–92	65
=	Molla Mallory (née Bjurstedt)	1915–29	65

* All USA unless otherwise stated

WIMBLEDON RECORDS

- Most Wimbledon men's titles
- First players to win three Wimbledon titles in one year
- Lowest-seeded Wimbledon men's champions
- Most Wimbledon women's titles
- Most Wimbledon men's singles titles
- Most Wimbledon women's singles titles

THE LADIES' PLATE
The Wimbledon women's singles plate is known as the Venus Rosewater Dish and is a copy of a pewter original exhibited in the Louvre, Paris.

Top 10 Most Wimbledon men's titles

	Player/country	Years	Singles	Doubles	Mixed	Total titles
1	William Renshaw, UK	1880–89	7	7	0	14
2	Lawrence Doherty, UK	1897–1905	5	8	0	13
3	Reginald Doherty, UK	1897–1905	4	8	0	12
4	John Newcombe, Australia	1965–74	3	6	0	9
5 =	Ernest Renshaw, UK	1880–89	1	7	0	8
=	Tony Wilding, New Zealand	1907–14	4	4	0	8
7 =	Wilfred Baddeley, UK	1891–96	3	4	0	7
=	Bob Hewitt, Australia/South Africa	1962–79	0	5	2	7
=	Rod Laver, Australia	1959–69	4	1	2	7
=	John McEnroe, USA	1979–84	3	4	0	7
=	Pete Sampras, USA	1993–2000	7	0	0	7
=	Todd Woodbridge, Australia	1993–2000	0	6	1	7
=	Mark Woodforde, Australia	1993–2000	0	6	1	7

Top 10 First players to win three Wimbledon titles in one year*

	Player/country	Year
1	Suzanne Lenglen, France	1920
2	Suzanne Lenglen, France	1922
3	Suzanne Lenglen, France	1925
4	Donald Budge, USA	1937
5	Donald Budge, USA	1938
6 =	Alice Marble, USA	1939
=	Bobby Riggs, USA	1939
8	Louise Brough, USA	1948
9	Louise Brough, USA	1950
10	Doris Hart, USA	1951

* Singles, doubles, and mixed doubles

The last person to win all three titles in one year was Billie Jean King (USA) in 1973. The last man to perform the feat was Frank Sedgman (Australia) in 1952.

Top 10 Lowest-seeded Wimbledon men's champions

	Player/country	Year	Seed
1 =	Boris Becker, Germany	1985	U*
=	Goran Ivanisevic, Croatia	2001	U*
=	Richard Krajicek, Netherlands	1996	U*
4	Andre Agassi, USA	1992	12
5 =	Pat Cash, Australia	1987	11
=	Jaroslav Drobny, Egypt	1954	11
7 =	Bob Falkenburg, USA	1948	7
=	Sidney Wood, UK	1931	7
9 =	Arthur Ashe, USA	1975	6
=	Dick Savitt, USA	1951	6
=	Michael Stich, Germany	1991	6

* Unseeded

The 1927 Championship was the first with seeding, and that year's final was between the fourth seed, Henry Cochet (France), and his fellow countryman and number one seed Jean Borotra. The first time the number one seed won the men's title was in 1929 when Cochet beat Borotra. The 1996 final between Krajicek (Netherlands) and MalVai Washington (USA) is the only singles final, men's or women's, to be contested by two unseeded players.

◀ An aerial view of Wimbledon's centre and outside courts.

Top 10 Most Wimbledon women's titles

	Player/country	Years	Singles	Doubles	Mixed	Total titles
1	Billie Jean King (née Moffitt), USA	1961–79	6	10	4	20
2 =	Martina Navratilova, Czechoslovakia/USA	1976–95	9	7	3	19
=	Elizabeth Ryan, USA	1914–34	0	12	7	19
4	Suzanne Lenglen, France	1919–25	6	6	3	15
5	Louise Brough, USA	1946–55	4	5	4	13
6	Helen Wills-Moody, USA	1927–38	8	3	1	12
7 =	Margaret Court (née Smith), Australia	1953–75	3	2	5	10
=	Doris Hart, USA	1947–55	1	4	5	10
9 =	Maria Bueno, Brazil	1958–66	3	5	0	8
=	Steffi Graf, West Germany/Germany	1988–98	7	1	0	8

Top 10 Most Wimbledon men's singles titles

	Player/country	Years	Titles
1 =	William Renshaw, UK	1881–89	7
=	Pete Sampras, USA	1993–2000	7
3 =	Bjorn Borg, Sweden	1976–80	5
=	Laurence Doherty, UK	1902–06	5
5 =	Reginald Doherty, UK	1897–1900	4
=	Rod Laver, Australia	1961–69	4
=	Tony Wilding, New Zealand	1910–13	4
8 =	Wilfred Baddeley, UK	1891–95	3
=	Boris Becker, West Germany	1985–89	3
=	Arthur Gore, UK	1901–09	3
=	John McEnroe, USA	1981–84	3
=	John Newcombe, Australia	1967–71	3
=	Fred Perry, UK	1934–36	3
=	Bill Tilden, USA	1920–30	3

Top 10 Most Wimbledon women's singles titles

	Player/country	Years	Titles
1	Martina Navratilova, Czechoslovakia/USA	1978–90	9
2	Helen Wills-Moody, USA	1927–38	8
3 =	Dorothea Chambers (née Douglass), UK	1903–14	7
=	Steffi Graf, West Germany/Germany	1988–1996	7
5 =	Blanche Hillyward, (née Bingley), UK	1886–1900	6
=	Billie Jean King, USA	1966–75	6
=	Suzanne Lenglen, France	1919–25	6
8 =	Lottie Dodd, UK	1887–93	5
=	Charlotte Sterry (née Cooper), UK	1895–1908	5
10	Louise Brough, USA	1948–55	4

◀ Martina Navratilova holding up the Wimbledon Ladies' Championship plate, which she won a record nine times.

AUSTRALIAN & FRENCH OPEN RECORDS

- Most French Open men's singles titles
- Most French Open women's singles titles
- Most French Open titles
- Most Australian Open singles titles
- Most Australian Open titles

FIRST AND LAST

Bjorn Borg's sixth and last French Open win was in 1981, when he beat Ivan Lendl in the final. It was Lendl's first Grand Slam final appearance.

Top 10 Most French Open men's singles titles

	Player/country	Years	Titles
1	Bjorn Borg, Sweden	1974–81	6
2	Henri Cochet, France	1926–32	4
3 =	Gustavo Kuerten, Brazil	1997–2001	3
=	René Lacoste, France	1925–29	3
=	Ivan Lendl, Czechoslovakia	1986–87	3
=	Mats Wilander, Sweden	1985–88	3
7 =	Sergi Bruguera, Spain	1993–94	2
=	Jim Courier, USA	1991–92	2
=	Jaroslav Drobny, Egypt	1951–52	2
=	Roy Emerson, Australia	1963–67	2
=	Jan Kodes, Czechoslovakia	1970–71	2
=	Rod Laver, Australia	1962–69	2
=	Frank Parker, USA	1948–49	2
=	Nicola Pietrangeli, Italy	1959–60	2
=	Ken Rosewall, Australia	1953–68	2
=	Manuel Santana, Spain	1961–64	2
=	Tony Trabert, USA	1954–55	2
=	Gottfried von Cramm, Germany	1934–36	2

Max Decugis (France) won a record eight titles in the pre-1925 championships.

Top 10 Most French Open women's singles titles

	Player/country	Years	Titles
1	Chris Evert-Lloyd, USA	1974–86	7
2	Steffi Graf, West Germany/ Germany	1987–99	6
3	Margaret Court (née Smith), Australia	1962–73	5
4	Helen Wills-Moody, USA	1928–32	4
5 =	Arantxa Sanchez Vicario, Spain	1989–98	3
=	Monica Seles, Yugoslavia	1990–93	3
=	Hilde Sperling, Germany	1935–37	3
8 =	Maureen Connolly, USA	1953–54	2
=	Margaret Du Pont (née Osborne), USA	1946–49	2
=	Doris Hart, USA	1950–52	2
=	Ann Jones (née Haydon), UK	1961–66	2
=	Suzanne Lenglen*, France	1925–26	2
=	Simone Mathieu, France	1938–39	2
=	Martina Navratilova, USA	1982–84	2
=	Margaret Scriven, UK	1933–34	2
=	Lesley Turner, Australia	1963–65	2

* Lenglen also won four French titles pre-1925 when the tournament was a "closed" event

Top 10 Most French Open titles*

	Player/country	Singles	Doubles	Mixed	Total titles
1	Margaret Court (née Smith), Australia	5	4	4	13
2 =	Doris Hart, USA	2	5	4	11
=	Martina Navratilova, Czechoslovakia/USA	2	7	2	11
4	Simone Mathieu, France	2	6	2	10
5 =	Françoise Durr, France	1	5	3	9
=	Chris Evert-Lloyd, USA	7	2	0	9
7 =	Jean Borotra, France	1	5	2	8
=	Henri Cochet, France	4	3	1	8
=	Roy Emerson, Australia	2	6	0	8
10 =	Bjorn Borg, Sweden	6	0	0	6
=	Gigi Fernandez, USA	0	6	0	6
=	Steffi Graf, West Germany/Germany	6	0	0	6
=	Helen Wills-Moody, USA	4	2	0	6
=	Natasha Zvereva, Belarus	0	6	0	6

* Men and women

◀ Margaret Court, winner of 36 French and Australian titles.

Top 10 Most Australian Open singles titles*

	Player/country#	Years	Titles
1	Margaret Court (née Smith)	1960–73	11
2 =	Nancye Bolton (née Wynne)	1937–51	6
=	Roy Emerson	1961–67	6
4	Daphne Akhurst	1925–30	5
5 =	Evonne Cawley (née Goolagong)	1974–77	4
=	Jack Crawford	1931–35	4
=	Steffi Graf, West Germany/ Germany	1988–94	4
=	Ken Rosewall	1953–72	4
=	Monica Seles, Yugoslavia/USA	1991–96	4
10 =	Andre Agassi, USA	1995–2001	3
=	James Anderson	1922–25	3
=	Joan Hartigan	1933–36	3
=	Martina Hingis, Switzerland	1997–99	3
=	Rod Laver	1960–69	3
=	Martina Navratilova, Czechoslovakia/USA	1981–85	3
=	Adrian Quist	1936–48	3
=	Mats Wilander, Sweden	1983–88	3

* Men and women
\# All Australia unless otherwise stated

Top 10 Most Australian Open titles*

	Player/country#	Years	Singles	Doubles	Mixed	Total titles
1	Margaret Court (née Smith)	1960–73	11	8	4	23
2	Nancye Bolton (née Wynne)	1926–51	6	10	4	20
3	Thelma Long	1936–58	2	12	4	18
4 =	Daphne Akhurst	1924–30	5	4	4	13
=	Adrian Quist	1936–50	3	10	0	13
6 =	John Bromwich	1938–50	2	8	1	11
=	Jack Crawford	1929–35	4	4	3	11
=	Martina Navratilova, Czechoslovakia/USA	1975–89	3	8	0	11
9 =	Evonne Cawley (née Goolagong)	1971–83	4	5	0	9
=	Roy Emerson	1961–69	6	3	0	9

* Men and women
\# All Australia unless otherwise stated

▼ Although he won six French singles titles, Sweden's Bjorn Borg never played in the Australian Open.

THE DAVIS CUP

- Davis Cup teams
- Most appearances in Davis Cup finals
- Davis Cup-winning countries
- Davis Cup-winning captains
- Highest-scoring sets in Davis Cup finals

> I guess I was the first Englishman to bring the American attitude to the game of lawn tennis.
>
> Fred Perry

Top 10 Davis Cup teams

	Country	Points*
1	Sweden	69
2	USA	62
3	Australia	59
4	France	47
5	Germany/West Germany	46
6	Czechoslovakia/Czech Republic	40
7	Italy	36
8	Spain	29
9	USSR/Russia	24
10 =	Argentina	18
=	India	18
=	Switzerland	18

* Based on five points for winning the tournament, four for runner-up, three for losing semi-finalist, and so on

This is for matches played since 1981, when the World Group, featuring the top 16 nations, was introduced. They play a straight knockout tournament during the course of the year, with the final played each December.

With 11 points, the UK teams would enter the list at number 19.

Top 10 Most appearances in Davis Cup finals

	Country	Finals
1	USA	59
2	Australasia/Australia	46
3	British Isles/UK	17
4	France	14
5	Sweden	12
6	Italy	7
7	West Germany/Germany	5
8 =	Romania	3
=	Spain	3
9 =	Czechoslovakia	2
=	India*	2
=	Russia	2

* India also qualified for the 1974 final against South Africa but refused to play because of the South African government's apartheid policies

Top 10 Davis Cup-winning countries

	Country	Years	Wins
1	USA	1900–95	31
2	Australasia/Australia	1907–99	27
3 =	British Isles/UK	1903–36	9
=	France	1927–2001	9
5	Sweden	1975–98	7
6	West Germany/Germany	1988–93	3
7 =	Czechoslovakia	1980	1
=	Italy	1976	1
=	South Africa	1974	1
=	Spain	2000	1

DID YOU KNOW? Italy's Nicola Pietrangeli played in a record 66 Davis Cup ties from 1954–72 and also a record 164 rubbers, winning 120 of them.

Top 10 Davis Cup-winning captains

	Captain	Country	Years	Wins
1	Harry Hopman	Australia	1939–67	16
2 =	Norman Brookes	Australasia/Australia	1907–19	6
=	Norris Williams	USA	1921–26	6
4 =	William Collins	Britain	1903–06	4
=	Neale Fraser	Australia	1973–86	4
=	Pierre Gillou	France	1927–30	4
=	Herbert Roper-Barrett	Great Britain	1933–36	4
8 =	Walter Pate	USA	1937–46	3
=	Niki Pilic	Germany	1988–93	3
=	Hans Olsson	Sweden	1984–87	3

(Richard) Norris Williams II has the unique distinction of being the only Davis Cup captain to survive the *Titanic* sinking of 1912. He was in a first-class cabin, with ticket number PC 17597, which cost £61 7s 7d (£61.38p). He dived off the ship and clung to a half-submerged lifeboat for six hours before being rescued. Sadly, his father went down with the ship.

Top 10 Highest-scoring sets in Davis Cup finals

	Match	Year	Score
1 =	Maurice McLoughlin, USA v Norman Brookes, Australia	1914	17–15
=	Bill Tilden/Richard Williams, USA v James Anderson/John Hawkes, Australia	1923	17–15
3	Alex Olmedo/Ham Richardson, USA v Mal Anderson/Neale Fraser, Australia	1958	16–14
4 =	Fred Perry, UK v Francis Shields, USA	1934	15–13
=	Donald Budge, USA v Charles Hare, UK	1937	15–13
=	Manuel Santana, Spain v Roy Emerson, Australia	1965	15–13
=	Arthur Ashe, USA v Ilie Nastase, Romania	1969	15–13
8 =	Vic Seixas/Tony Trabert, USA v Rex Hartwig/Lew Hoad, Australia	1955	14–12
9 =	Arthur Gore/Herbert Roper-Barrett, UK v Norman Brookes/Anthony Wilding, Australia	1907	13–11
=	James Anderson/John Hawkes, Australia v Bill Tilden/Richard Williams, USA	1923	13–11
=	Jacques Brugnon/Henri Cochet, France v Wilmer Allison/John Van Ryn, USA	1932	13–11
=	Ken McGregor, Australia v Ted Schroeder, USA	1950	13–11
=	Ted Schroeder, USA v Mervyn Rose, Australia	1951	13–11
=	Lew Hoad, Australia v Tony Trabert, Australia	1953	13–11
=	Vic Seixas, USA v Mal Anderson, Australia	1957	13–11
=	Mal Anderson, Australia v Barry MacKay, USA	1958	13–11
=	Arthur Ashe, USA v Christian Kuhnke, West Germany	1970	13–11
=	Henrik Sundstrom, Sweden v John McEnroe, USA	1984	13–11
=	Pat Cash, Australia v Stefan Edberg, Sweden	1986	13–11*
=	Pat Cash, Australia v Stefan Edberg, Sweden	1986	13–11#

* First set

\# Second set

The fifth and final game of the 1977 final between Tony Roche (Australia) and Corrado Barazzutti (Italy) was unfinished at 12–12 in the first set.

◀ Jim Courier, Andre Agassi, USA team coach Tom Gullikson, and Pete Sampras of the USA team pose with the Davis Cup Trophy after beating Russia 3–2 to win the title in 1995.

TENNIS

- Men with most tournament wins
- Women with most tournament wins
- Women with most career wins
- Women spending most weeks at top of ATP world rankings
- Men spending most weeks at top of ATP world rankings
- Career earnings by men
- Career earnings by women

> Nobody reminds me of me, I'm an original.
> **Jimmy Connors**

ATP & WTA RECORD BREAKERS

Top 10 Men with most tournament wins*

	Player/country	Wins
1	Jimmy Connors, USA	109
2	Ivan Lendl, Czechoslovakia/USA	94
3	John McEnroe, USA	77
4	Pete Sampras, USA	63
5 =	Bjorn Borg, Sweden	62
=	Guillermo Vilas, Argentina	62
7	Ilie Nastase, Romania	57
8 =	Andre Agassi, USA	49
=	Boris Becker, Germany	49
10	Rod Laver, Australia	47

* In singles events in the Open era, 1968–1 January 2002

Top 10 Women with most tournament wins*

	Player/country	Wins
1	Martina Navratilova, Czechoslovakia/USA	167
2	Chris Evert-Lloyd, USA	157
3	Steffi Graff, West Germany/Germany	107
4	Evonne Cawley (née Goolagong), Australia	88
5	Margaret Court (née Smith), Australia	79
6	Billie Jean King (née Moffitt), USA	67
7	Virginia Wade, UK	55
8	Monica Seles, Yugoslavia/USA	51
9 =	Lindsay Davenport, USA	38
=	Martina Hingis, Switzerland	38

* In singles events in the Open era, 1968–1 January 2002

Top 10 Women with most career wins*

	Player/country	Wins
1	Chris Evert-Lloyd, USA	1,304
2	Steffi Graf, West Germany/Germany	900
3	Martina Navratilova, Czechoslovakia/USA	773
4	Arantxa Sanchez Vicario, Spain	734
5	Conchita Martinez, Spain	635
6	Gabriela Sabatini, Argentina	632
7	Pam Shriver, USA	625
8	Helena Sukova, Czechoslovakia	614
9	Zina Jackson (née Garrison), USA	587
10	Wendy Turnbull, Australia	577

* Singles only in the Open era, 1968–11 February 2002
Source: WTA

Chris Evert-Lloyd also has the best ratio of wins with 1,304 wins and just 144 losses from 75 tournaments, representing a win ratio of .901.

Top 10 Women spending most weeks at top of WTA world rankings*

	Player/country	Weeks
1	Steffi Graf, West Germany/Germany	377
2	Martina Navratilova, Czechoslovakia/USA	331
3	Chris Evert-Lloyd, USA	262
4	Martina Hingis, Switzerland	209
5	Monica Seles, Yugoslavia/USA	178
6	Lindsay Davenport, USA	38
7	Tracy Austin, USA	22
8	Arantxa Sanchez Vicario, Spain	11
9	Jennifer Capriati, USA	6
10	Venus Williams, USA	1

* As at 1 March 2002
Source: WTA

The Sanex WTA Rankings are computer rankings based on a player's performance over the year and take into account their best 17 results at singles and best 11 at doubles. Points are awarded based on performance at each event played.

◀ Jimmy Connors was ranked world number one five years in a row, from 1974 to 1978.

Top 10 Men spending most weeks at top of ATP world rankings*

Player/country	Weeks
1 Pete Sampras, USA	286
2 Ivan Lendl, Czechoslovakia/USA	270
3 Jimmy Connors, USA	268
4 John McEnroe, USA	170
5 Bjorn Borg, Sweden	109
6 Andre Agassi, USA	87
7 Stefan Edberg, Sweden	72
8 Jim Courier, USA	58
9 Gustavo Kuerten, Brazil	43
10 Ilie Nastase, Romania	40

* As at 1 January 2002
Source: ATP

Top 10 Career earnings by men*

Player/country	Winnings ($)
1 Pete Sampras, USA	42,357,490
2 Boris Becker, West Germany/Germany	25,079,186
3 Andre Agassi, USA	23,482,490
4 Yevgeny Kafelnikov, Russia	21,423,535
5 Ivan Lendl, Czechoslovakia/USA	21,262,417
6 Stefan Edberg, Sweden	20,630,941
7 Goran Ivanisevic, Croatia	19,682,620
8 Michael Chang, USA	18,904,768
9 Jim Courier, USA	13,978,963
10 Gustavo Kuerten, Brazil	13,014,235

* As at 1 January 2002

Top 10 Career earnings by women*

Player/country	Winnings ($)*
1 Steffi Graff, West Germany/Germany	21,895,277
2 Martina Navratilova, Czechoslovakia/USA	20,344,061
3 Martina Hingis, Switzerland	16,845,441
4 Arantxa Sanchez Vicario, Spain	16,472,594
5 Lindsay Davenport, USA	14,036,870
6 Monica Seles, Yugoslavia/USA	13,518,919
7 Jana Novotna, Czechoslovakia	11,249,134
8 Conchita Martinez, Spain	9,779,780
9 Venus Williams, USA	9,319,337
10 Chris Evert-Lloyd, USA	8,896,195

* As at 1 January 2002

◀ Steffi Graf ended Martina Navratilova's five-year reign as number one by deposing her in 1986.

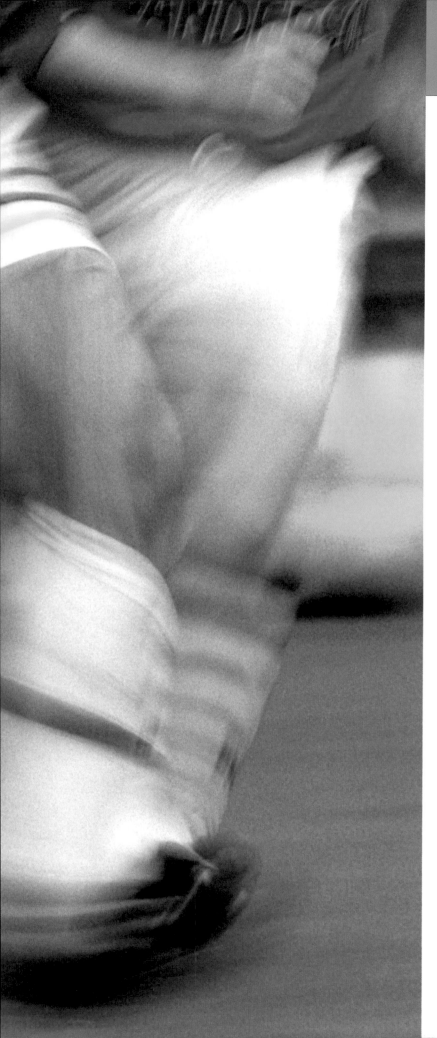

FOOTBALL

At the Start

Football-like games were played in China over 2,500 years ago, and were also popular pastimes in ancient Greece and Rome. Throughout Europe in the Middle Ages, local customs – especially on Shrove Tuesday – often centred around sometimes violent football matches between rival villages. Shakespeare was aware of football, referring to it in two of his plays. The first rules, the Cambridge Rules, were drawn up in 1848 and clubs were set up in the 1850s – Sheffield FC, dating from 1855, is the oldest still in existence. The Football Association (the letters "s-o-c" in "association" are the origin of the name "soccer") was founded in 1863. Inter-team games, facilitated by the growth of the railway system and work-free Saturday afternoons, led to the formation of the Football League in the 1888–89 season.

FOOTBALL

WORLD CUP RECORDS

- ● World Cup countries
- ● Highest World Cup scores
- ● Goalscorers in the final stages of the World Cup
- ● Goals in one World Cup tournament

WORLD CUP RECORDS

The World Cup was launched in Uruguay in 1930 after many years of discussion, and it was largely thanks to the FIFA president Jules Rimet that the trophy eventually got under way, the first World Cup trophy being named after him. Thirteen teams took part in the first tournament and Uruguay, the hosts, won the first competition when they beat neighbours Argentina 4–2 in the final in front of 93,000 partisan fans in Montevideo.

Top 10 World Cup countries*

	Country	Tournaments won	Played	Won	Drawn	Lost	For	Against	Points
1	Brazil	4	80	53	14	13	173	78	120
2	Germany#	3	78	45	17	16	162	103	107
3	Italy	3	66	38	16	12	105	62	92
4	Argentina	2	57	29	10	18	100	69	68
5	England	1	45	20	13	12	62	42	53
6	France	1	41	21	6	14	86	58	48
7	Spain	0	40	16	10	14	61	48	42
8	Yugoslavia	0	37	16	8	13	60	46	40
9	Uruguay	2	37	15	8	14	61	52	38
10 =	Netherlands	0	32	14	9	9	56	36	37
=	Sweden	0	38	14	9	15	66	60	37

* Based on two points for a win and one point for a draw; matches resolved on penalties are classed as a draw

Including West Germany

Brazil is the only country to have played in the final stages of every World Cup since its introduction in 1930. They appeared in their first final in 1950 but lost to Uruguay on home soil. Their first triumph was in Sweden in 1958 when the world witnessed the emergence of the great Pelé.

Top 10 Highest World Cup scores*

	Winners/losers	Date	Score
1	Australia v American Samoa	11 April 2001	31–0
2	Australia# v Tonga†	9 April 2001	22–0
3	Iran v Guam	24 November 2000	19–0
4	Iran# v Maldives	2 June 1997	17–0
5	Tajikistan v Guam	26 November 2000	16–0
6 =	Australia v Solomon Islands	11 June 1997	13–0
=	Fiji v American Samoa	7 April 2001	13–0
=	New Zealand v Fiji	16 August 1981	13–0
9 =	Oman v Laos	30 April 2001	12–0
=	Syria# v Maldives	4 June 1997	12–0
=	Syria v Philippines	30 April 2001	12–0
=	United Arab Emirates# v Brunei	14 April 2001	12–0
=	West Germany v Cyprus	21 May 1969	12–0

* All in qualifying matches

Away team

† "Away" fixture, but played on Australian soil

Australia beat American Samoa again on 16 April 2001, but on this occasion by only 11–0, so that in three matches within just seven days they scored a staggering 64 goals without conceding any. The highest score in the final stages of the World Cup occurred in 1982 when Hungary beat El Salvador 10–1.

Top 10 Goalscorers in the final stages of the World Cup

	Player/country	Years	Goals
1	Gerd Müller, West Germany	1970–74	14
2	Just Fontaine, France	1958	13
3	Pelé, Brazil	1958–70	12
4 =	Jürgen Klinsman, West Germany/Germany	1990–98	11
=	Sandor Kocsis, Hungary	1954	11
6 =	Teófilio Cubillas, Peru	1970–78	10
=	Grzegorz Lato, Poland	1974–82	10
=	Gary Lineker, England	1986–90	10
=	Helmut Rahn, West Germany	1954–58	10
10 =	Roberto Baggio, Italy	1990–98	9
=	Gabriel Batistuta, Argentina	1994–98	9
=	Eusébio, Portugal	1966	9
=	Jairzinho, Brazil	1970–74	9
=	Ademir, Brazil	1950	9
=	Paolo Rossi, Italy	1978–82	9
=	Karl–Heinz Rummenigge, West Germany	1978–86	9
=	Uwe Seeler, West Germany	1958–70	9
=	Leonidas da Silva, Brazil	1934–38	9
=	Vavà, Brazil	1958–62	9

▼ Pelé played in four tournaments between 1958 and 1970, scoring the first of his 12 World Cup goals against Wales in 1958.

Top 10 Goals in one World Cup tournament

	Player	Country	Year	Goals
1	Just Fontaine	France	1958	13
2	Sandor Kocsis	Hungary	1954	11
3	Gerd Müller	West Germany	1970	10
4 =	Ademir	Brazil	1950	9
=	Eusébio	Portugal	1966	9
6 =	Leonidas da Silva	Brazil	1938	8
=	Guillermo Stábile	Argentina	1930	8
8 =	Jairzinho	Brazil	1970	7
=	Grzegorz Lato	Poland	1974	7
=	Gyula Zsengeller	Hungary	1938	7

FOOTBALL

- Most capped international players

- Biggest wins in major international tournaments

- Goalscorers in international football

- World Cup coaches

- Countries in the European Championship

INTERNATIONAL FOOTBALL

Top 10 Most capped international players

	Player	Country	Years	Caps*
1	Claudio Suárez	Mexico	1992–2002	170
2 =	Mohamed Al-Deayea	Saudi Arabia	1990–2002	162
3 =	Hossam Hassan	Egypt	1985–2002	160
4 =	Cobi Jones	USA	1992–2002	153
5 =	Lothar Matthäus	West Germany/Germany	1980–2000	150
6 =	Mohammed Al-Khilaiwi	Saudi Arabia	1992–2001	143
=	Thomas Ravelli	Sweden	1981–97	143
8	Majed Abdullah	Saudi Arabia	1978–94	140
9	Peter Schmeichel	Denmark	1987–2001	129
10	Marcelo Balboa	USA	1988–2000	128

* As at 1 May 2002

The most capped British Isles footballer is Peter Shilton (England) with 125 caps, who is ranked joint 13th.

THE FIRST MATCHES

The first unofficial match between two countries was on 5 March 1870 when England played Scotland at Kennington Oval, London. They drew 1–1. The first official match was the same fixture, but at the West of Scotland Cricket Club on 30 November 1872. This time the sides drew 0–0. The first International match outside the UK was at Uccle, near Brussels, on 1 May 1904, when Belgium and France drew 3–3.

> We enjoy the expectations people have of us. The higher they are, the more pressure, the better we like it.
>
> **Jürgen Klinsmann,** German captain, during the 1998 World Cup finals

Top 10 Biggest wins in major international tournaments

	Winners/losers	Tournament	Score
1	Australia v American Samoa	2002 World Cup Qualifier	31–0
2	Australia v Tonga	2002 World Cup Qualifier	22–0
3	Kuwait v Bhutan	2000 Asian Championship Qualifier	20–0
4 =	China v Guam	2000 Asian Championship Qualifier	19–0
=	Iran v Guam	2002 World Cup Qualifier	19–0
6	Tahiti v American Samoa	2000 Oceania Championship Qualifier	18–0
7 =	Australia v Cook Islands	2000 Oceania Championship	17–0
=	China v Maldives	1992 Olympic Games Qualifier	17–0
=	Iran v Maldives	1998 World Cup Qualifier	17–0
10 =	Denmark v France	1908 Olympic Games	17–1
=	Tajikistan v Guam	2002 World Cup Qualifier	16–0

The record wins for other major tournaments are: Copa America: Argentina v Ecuador, 1942, 12–0; European Championship: Spain v Malta, 1984, 12–1; British Championship: England v Ireland, 1899, 13–2.

Top 10 Goalscorers in international football

	Player	Country	Years	Matches	Goals*
1	Ferenc Puskás	Hungary/Spain	1945–56	84	83
2	Pelé	Brazil	1957–71	91	77
3 =	Ali Daei	Iran	1993–2001	103	76
=	Sandor Kocsis	Hungary	1948–56	68	75
5	Gerd Müller	West Germany	1966–74	62	68
6	Majed Abdullah	Saudi Arabia	1978–94	140	67
7	Imre Schlosser	Hungary	1906–27	68	60
8	Hossam Hassan	Egypt	1985–2002	160	59
9	Jassem Al-Houwaidi	Kuwait	1992–2001	69	58
10 =	Gabriel Batistuta	Argentina	1991–2001	75	55
=	Kazuyoshi Miura	Japan	1990–2000	91	55

* As at 1 May 2002

The most goals by a British Isles player is 49 by Bobby Charlton, England. He is ranked joint 16th.

Top 10 World Cup coaches*

	Coach/home country	Country	Years	Matches
1	Helmut Schön, Germany	West Germany	1966–78	25
2	Mario Zagalo, Brazil	Brazil	1970–98	20
3 =	Vicenzo Bearzot, Italy	Italy	1978–86	18
=	Josef Herberger, Germany	Germany/West Germany	1934–62	18
5	Velibor Milutinovic, Yugoslavia	Mexico, Costa Rica, USA, Nigeria	1986–98	17
6	Guy Thys, Belgium	Belgium	1982–90	16
7 =	Lajos Baróti, Hungary	Hungary	1958–78	15
=	Carlos Alberto Parreira, Brazil	Kuwait, UAE, Brazil, Saudi Arabia	1982–98	15
9 =	Franz Beckenbauer, Germany	West Germany	1986–90	14
=	Carlos Bilardo, Argentina	Argentina	1986–90	14
=	Walter Winterbottom, England	England	1950–62	14

* Based on number of matches played in the final stages of the World Cup

In the four World Cups that Helmut Schön took Germany to, he led his side to two finals: in 1966 when they lost to England and in 1974 when they beat the Netherlands 2–1. His last World Cup game was a 3–2 defeat by Austria in 1978.

Top 10 Countries in the European Championship*

	Country	Tournaments won	P	W	D	L	F	A	Pts
1	Germany	3	33	17	10	6	49	31	44
2	Netherlands	1	25	15	6	4	45	23	36
3	France	2	23	12	6	5	40	29	30
4	Italy	1	24	10	9	5	26	17	29
5	Soviet Union/Russia	1	25	9	7	9	30	30	25
6	Spain	1	25	7	8	10	26	32	22
7	England	0	23	7	7	9	25	26	21
8	Czechoslovakia/Czech Rep	1	19	7	6	6	26	23	20
9	Portugal	0	13	7	3	3	19	10	17
10	Yugoslavia	0	20	5	5	10	31	45	15

* Two points for a win and one for a draw in all matches played in the final stages

The only other country to have won the tournament is Denmark in 1992, who are in 11th place, although technically they should not have taken part in the final stages of the tournament as they finished second to Yugoslavia in the qualifying tournament. However, the Yugoslavs were excluded from the tournament due to domestic troubles, and the Danes took their place.

◀ The Australian Socceroos' 31–0 demolition of American Samoa took place at the Coffs Harbour International Sports Stadium, Australia, in April 2001.

PREMIER LEAGUE RECORDS

- Most Premiership goals scored
- Most matches won in the Premiership
- Goalscorers in the Premiership
- Most Premiership goals in a season
- Most Premiership own goals scored
- Most drawn matches in the Premiership

THE PREMIERSHIP

The FA Barclaycard Premiership was launched in the 1992–93 season when 22 clubs broke away from the Football League. Manchester United, runners–up to Leeds United in the last old Division One campaign the previous season, were the inaugural Premiership champions, winning their first League title since 1966–67.

Top 10 Most Premiership goals scored

	Club	Goals
1	Manchester United	722
2	Liverpool	581
3	Arsenal	558
4	Newcastle United	551
5	Chelsea	518
6	Leeds United	486
7	Tottenham Hotspur	457
8	Aston Villa	434
9	Everton	426
10	West Ham United	420

All clubs have played 350 Premiership matches.

Manchester United's first goal in the new Premiership was against Sheffield United, at Bramall Lane, on 15 August 1992 and was scored by Mark Hughes. United lost 2–1. They lost 3–0 to Everton in their first home game but then scored their first Premiership goal at Old Trafford against Ipswich Town.

Top 10 Most matches won in the Premiership

	Club	Wins
1	Manchester United	220
2	Arsenal	180
3	Liverpool	173
4	Newcastle United	157
5	Leeds United	155
6	Chelsea	146
7	Aston Villa	133
8	West Ham United	122
9	Tottenham Hotspur	120
10	Blackburn Rovers	114

All clubs, except Blackburn Rovers (274), have played 350 Premiership matches.

Manchester United had to wait until their fourth match in the Premiership before registering their first victory, a 1–0 win at Southampton thanks to a Dion Dublin goal. Their first win at Old Trafford was on 2 September 1992 when Mark Hughes scored the only goal in a 1–0 win.

Top 10 Goalscorers in the Premiership*

	Player	Club(s)	Goals
1	Alan Shearer	Blackburn Rovers/Newcastle United	204
2	Andy Cole	Newcastle United/Manchester United/Blackburn Rovers	145
3 =	Les Ferdinand	Queen's Park Rangers/Newcastle United/Tottenham Hotspur	132
=	Robbie Fowler	Liverpool/Leeds United	132
5	Ian Wright	Arsenal	113
6 =	Teddy Sheringham	Nottingham Forest/Tottenham Hotspur/Manchester United	117
=	Dwight Yorke	Aston Villa/Manchester United	108
8	Matt Le Tissier	Southampton	101
9	Dion Dublin	Manchester United/Coventry City/Aston Villa	97
10	Michael Owen	Liverpool	83

* To end of 2001–02 season

Although he started his career at Southampton, Alan Shearer never played for them in the Premiership as he left the club the season before the start of the new League. Shearer's first Premiership goal was on the opening day of the 1992–93 season, when he scored two against Crystal Palace. He scored 16 goals that season despite missing half of it through injury.

▶ Alan Shearer became the youngest player to score a hat-trick in the old First Division when he netted three times for Southampton against Arsenal in April 1988.

> I wasn't born with the skills of a Best or a Pelé. My game is commitment. I'm committed. I have been all my life.
>
> **Alan Shearer**

Top 10 Most Premiership goals in a season

	Player	Club	Season	Goals
1 =	Andy Cole	Newcastle United	1993–94	34
=	Alan Shearer	Blackburn Rovers	1994–95	34
3 =	Alan Shearer	Blackburn Rovers	1993–94	31
=	Alan Shearer	Blackburn Rovers	1995–96	31
5	Kevin Phillips	Sunderland	1999–2000	30
6	Robbie Fowler	Liverpool	1995–96	28
7 =	Les Ferdinand	Newcastle United	1995–96	25
=	Robbie Fowler	Liverpool	1994–95	25
=	Matt Le Tissier	Southampton	1993–94	25
=	Alan Shearer	Newcastle United	1996–97	25
=	Chris Sutton	Norwich City	1993–94	25

Top 10 Most Premiership own goals scored

	Club	Own goals
1	Manchester United	22
2	Leeds United	16
3 =	Chelsea	15
=	Liverpool	15
=	Tottenham Hotspur	15
6 =	Coventry City	13
=	Middlesbrough	13
=	Southampton	13
9 =	Aston Villa	12
=	Newcastle United	12

The first own goal in the Premiership was scored on 5 September 1992 when Nottingham Forest goalkeeper Mark Crossley put the ball into his own net against Blackburn Rovers at Ewood Park. The most own goals scored in a season is six by Manchester United in the 1996–97 season.

Top 10 Most drawn matches in the Premiership

	Club	Draws
1 =	Aston Villa	104
=	Chelsea	104
3	Everton	103
4 =	Arsenal	99
=	Coventry City	99
6	Tottenham Hotspur	98
7	Leeds United	96
8	West Ham United	92
9	Liverpool	89
10	Wimbledon	82

All clubs, except Wimbledon (274) and Coventry (312) have played 350 Premiership matches.

Coventry were very much the draw specialists of the Premiership. In each of their first six seasons in the new League, they drew at least 13 matches per season, and in 1997–98 drew 16 matches. The most matches drawn in a single season is 18, shared jointly by Manchester City (1993–94), Sheffield United (1993–94), and Southampton (1994–95).

TEAM RECORDS

- Longest current spells in the "Top Flight"
- Clubs with the most Football League titles
- Clubs with the most British titles
- Clubs to score the most goals in a Football League season
- Clubs with the most FA Cup wins

BOB PAISLEY

The man behind many of Liverpool's triumphs was Bob Paisley who guided the club to a record six First Division titles, three European Champions' Cup wins, three Milk Cup (League Cup) wins, one UEFA Cup win, and a European Super Cup triumph. He spent nearly 50 years with the club as player, coach, and manager. Hardly surprising, given his record, he was Manager of the Year six times.

Top 10 Longest current spells in the "Top Flight"

	Club	Years
1	Arsenal	83
2	Everton	48
3	Liverpool	40
4	Manchester United	27
5 =	Southampton	24
=	Tottenham Hotspur	24
7	Aston Villa	14
8	Chelsea	13
9	Leeds United	12
10 =	Newcastle United	9
=	West Ham United	9

"Top flight" refers to either the old First Division or, since 1992–93, the Premiership. Coventry City ended 34 years in the top flight in 2001 when they were relegated from the Premier League.

Top 10 Clubs with the most Football League titles*

	Club	Years	Titles
1	Liverpool	1894–1990	22
2	Manchester United	1908–2001	16
3	Arsenal	1931–2002	12
4 =	Aston Villa	1894–1981	10
=	Everton	1891–1987	10
=	Sunderland	1892–1999	10
7 =	Manchester City	1899–2002	9
=	Sheffield Wednesday	1900–1959	9
9 =	Preston North End	1889–2000	8
=	Wolverhampton Wanderers	1889–1989	8

* Includes all divisions of the Football League and, since 1992–93, the Premiership

The first of Liverpool's 22 League titles was the old Second Division title in 1893–94. Their first Division One (now the Premiership) title was in the 1900–01 season.

> I only drink when we win a trophy. Maybe people think I'm an alcoholic.
>
> **Ian Ferguson**, Glasgow Rangers player

Top 10 Clubs with the most British titles

	Team	League titles	FA Cup	League Cup	Total
1	Glasgow Rangers	49	30	21	101
2	Glasgow Celtic	38	31	12	81
3	Liverpool	18	6	6	30
4	Manchester United	14	10	1	25
5	Arsenal	12	8	2	22
6	Aston Villa	7	7	5	19
7	Aberdeen	4	7	5	16
8 =	Everton	9	5	0	14
=	Heart of Midlothian	4	6	4	14
10	Tottenham Hotspur	2	8	3	13

The rivalry between Celtic and Rangers has been going on for over 110 years since Rangers won the first Scottish title (shared with Dumbarton), with Celtic in third place. Celtic won a record nine titles in a row between 1966 and 1973. Rangers eventually equalled that record in 1997 and it was, perhaps inevitably, Celtic who prevented them from winning their tenth title the following season.

Top 10 Clubs to score the most goals in a Football League season

	Club	Season	Division	Goals
1	Peterborough United	1960–61	4	134
2 =	Aston Villa	1930–31	1	128
=	Bradford City	1928–29	3 (North)	128
4 =	Arsenal	1930–31	1	127
=	Millwall	1927–28	3 (South)	127
6	Doncaster Rovers	1946–47	3 (North)	123
7	Middlesbrough	1926–27	2	122
8 =	Everton	1927–28	1	121
=	Lincoln City	1951–52	3 (North)	121
10	Chester	1964–65	4	119

In 1931–32, Coventry City scored 108 goals in Division Three (South), yet finished in 12th place. In 1957–58, Manchester City scored 104 First Division goals – and conceded 100. The last team to score 100 goals was Manchester City (108) in the First Division in 2001–02. The record for the Premiership is 97 goals by Manchester United in the 1999–2000 season.

Top 10 Clubs with the most FA Cup wins

	Team	First win	Last win	Total
1	Manchester United	1909	1999	10
2 =	Arsenal	1930	2002	8
=	Tottenham Hotspur	1901	1991	8
4	Aston Villa	1887	1957	7
5 =	Blackburn Rovers	1884	1928	6
=	Liverpool	1965	2001	6
=	Newcastle United	1910	1955	6
8 =	Everton	1906	1995	5
=	The Wanderers	1872	1878	5
=	West Bromwich Albion	1888	1968	5

The first ever FA Cup final was played in 1872 at the Kennington Oval cricket ground. A crowd of about 2,000 saw Wanderers beat Royal Engineers 1–0. Matches were played at Wembley (except for the 1970 replay, which took place at Old Trafford) from 1923, when Bolton Wanderers met West Ham United in front of a record crowd of 126,047, until the ground's closure in 2001. The Millennium Stadium in Cardiff is now the home of English football. Tottenham Hotspur have won eight out of the nine FA Cup finals they have appeared in. Their only blemish was in their eighth appearance in 1987 when they lost to Coventry City 3–2. Spurs' cup-winning pattern is remarkably consistent: they won in 1901, 1921, 1961, 1981, and 1991.

◄ Manchester United skipper Roy Keane holding aloft the FA Cup trophy after Manchester United beat Newcastle United 2–0 in the 1989 final. It was Keane's third winner's medal.

- Goalscorers for England
- Goalscorers for Northern Ireland
- Goalscorers for Scotland
- Goalscorers for Wales
- Goalscorers in a Football League season
- Goalscorers at Wembley
- Goalscorers in a Football League career

> I have always had a tremendous desire to be top scorer in the League or whatever competition or whatever game. If I have scored two in the first half and don't get one in the second I will be disappointed.
>
> **Gary Lineker,**
> England international
> footballer, 1991

TOP GOALSCORERS

Top 10 Goalscorers for England*

	Player	Years	Goals
1	Bobby Charlton	1958–70	49
2	Gary Lineker	1984–92	48
3	Jimmy Greaves	1959–67	44
4 =	Tom Finney	1946–58	30
=	Nat Lofthouse	1950–58	30
=	Alan Shearer	1991–2000	30
7	Vivian Woodward	1903–11	29
8	Steve Bloomer	1895–1907	28
9	David Platt	1989–96	27
10	Bryan Robson	1980–91	26

* In full internationals

Bobby Charlton's 49 goals came from a one-time record 106 internationals. He made his international debut against Scotland at Hampden Park, Glasgow, in April 1958 and scored a goal in England's 4–0 victory over the Scots.

Top 10 Goalscorers for Northern Ireland*

	Player	Years	Goals
1	Colin Clarke	1986–93	13
2 =	Gerry Armstrong	1977–86	12
=	Joe Bambrick	1929–38	12
=	Iain Dowie	1990–2000	12
=	Billy Gillespie	1913–31	12
=	Jimmy Quinn	1985–96	12
7	Olphie Stanfield	1887–97	11
8 =	Billy Bingham	1951–64	10
=	Johnny Crossan	1960–68	10
=	Jimmy McIlroy	1952–66	10
=	Peter McParland	1954–62	10

* In full internationals

Remarkably, six of Joe Bambrick's 12 goals came in one game, against Wales on 1 February, 1930, a British international record for one game.

Top 10 Goalscorers for Scotland*

	Player	Years	Goals
1 =	Kenny Dalglish	1972–87	30
=	Denis Law	1959–74	30
3	Hugh Gallacher	1924–35	23
4	Lawrie Reilly	1949–57	22
5	Ally McCoist	1986–98	19
6 =	Bob Hamilton	1899–1911	14
=	Mo Johnston	1984–92	14
8 =	Bob McColl	1896–1908	13
=	John Smith	1877–84	13
=	Andrew Wilson	1920–23	13

* In full internationals

If "own goals" scored by Scotland's opponents were included as an entry, it would rank sixth, with 15.

Kenny Dalglish's tally came from 102 matches (he is the only man to play for Scotland 100 times), while Denis Law's came from just 55.

Top 10 Goalscorers for Wales*

	Player	Years	Goals
1	Ian Rush	1980–96	28
2 =	Ivor Allchurch	1951–66	23
=	Trevor Ford	1947–57	23
4	Dean Saunders	1986–2001	22
5 =	Mark Hughes	1984–99	16
=	Cliff Jones	1954–69	16
7	John Charles	1950–65	15
8 =	D. J. Astley	1931–39	12
=	Billy Lewis	1885–98	12
=	John Toshack	1969–80	12

* In full internationals

If "own goals" scored by Wales' opponents were included as an entry, it would rank eighth, with 13.

Ivor Allchurch's brother Len also played for Wales but never scored a goal, and John Charles' brother Mel also played for his county, scoring on six occasions.

◀ Seven goals in the last two games of the 1927–28 season secured a new League record of 60 goals for Dixie Dean.

Top 10 Goalscorers in a Football League season

	Player/club	Division	Season	Goals
1	Dixie Dean (Everton)	1	1927-28	60
2	George Camsell (Middlesbrough)	2	1926-27	59
3 =	Ted Harston (Mansfield Town)	3 North	1936-37	55
=	Joe Payne (Luton Town)	3 South	1936-37	55
5	Terry Bly (Peterborough United)	4	1960-61	52
6 =	Clarrie Bourton (Coventry City)	3 South	1931-32	49
=	"Pongo" Waring (Aston Villa)	1	1930-31	49
8	Harry Morris (Swindon Town)	3 South	1926-27	47
9 =	Derek Dooley (Sheffield Wednesday)	2	1951-52	46
=	Alf Lythgoe (Stockport County)	3 North	1933-34	46
=	Peter Simpson (Crystal Palace)	3 South	1930-31	46

In the same season that Dixie Dean established the English record, Jimmy Smith of Ayr United established the Scottish League record of 66 goals in a season, which, as Dean's record, still stands. The post-war First Division record is 41, by Jimmy Greaves (Chelsea) in 1960–61.

Top 10 Goalscorers at Wembley*

	Player#	Goals
1	Bobby Charlton	27
2	Gary Lineker	25
3	Jimmy Greaves	20
4	Alan Shearer	18
5	Geoff Hurst	17
6 =	David Platt	16
=	Bryan Robson	16
8	Kevin Keegan	12
9 =	Nat Lofthouse	11
=	Ian Rush	11

* As at the closure of the original stadium in October 2000
# All England internationals, except Ian Rush who played for Wales

England's first international at Wembley was the 1–1 draw with Scotland on 12 April 1924. England's first ever goal on the hallowed turf was scored by Billy Walker, later famed as the manager of FA Cup-winning teams Sheffield Wednesday (1935) and Nottingham Forest (1959).

Top 10 Goalscorers in a Football League career

	Player	Seasons	Goals
1	Arthur Rowley	1946–65	434
2	Dixie Dean	1923–37	379
3	Jimmy Greaves	1957–71	357
4	Steve Bloomer	1892–1914	352
5	George Camsell	1923–39	346
6	John Aldridge	1978–98	329
7	Vic Watson	1920–36	317
8	John Atyeo	1951–66	315
9	Joe Smith	1908–29	314
10 =	Henry Bedford	1919–34	309
=	Harry Johnson	1919–36	309

Dixie Dean scored 349 goals for Everton, a record for a single club. All of John Atyeo's 315 goals were for Bristol City, his only League club. Jimmy Greaves' goals were uniquely all in the First Division.

▶ Probably two of the most important and finest goals Bobby Charlton scored for England were in the 2–1 win over Portugal in the semi-final of the 1966 World Cup at Wembley.

FOOTBALL

AROUND EUROPE

- Most successful clubs in Europe
- Most appearances in European campaigns
- Most Domestic League titles
- Most Spanish titles
- Most German titles
- Most Italian titles
- Most French titles

> " When people think of Italy, after the Mafia and pizza, they think of AC Milan.
> **Silvio Berlusconi,**
> President of AC Milan and Italy, 1997 "

Top 10 Most succesful clubs in Europe*

	Club/country	Champions' League	UEFA Cup	Cup-winners Cup	Total
1	Real Madrid, Spain	9	2	0	11
2	Barcelona, Spain	1	3	4	8
3 =	AC Milan, Italy	5	0	2	7
=	Liverpool, England	4	3	0	7
5 =	Ajax, Netherlands	4	1	1	6
=	Bayern Munich, Germany	4	1	1	6
=	Juventus, Italy	2	3	1	6
8	Inter Milan, Italy	2	3	0	5
9 =	Anderlecht, Belgium	0	1	2	3
=	Feyenoord, Netherlands	1	2	0	3
=	Manchester United, England	2	0	1	3
=	Parma, Italy	0	2	1	3
=	Tottenham Hotspur, England	0	2	1	3
=	Valencia, Spain	0	2	1	3

* Based on wins in the Champions' League/Cup, UEFA Cup/Fairs Cup, and Cup-winners Cup

◀ The European Cup's most successful team, Real Madrid. They were the winners of the first five tournaments between 1956 and 1960.

Top 10 Most appearances in European campaigns

	Club/country	Titles	Campaigns
1	Barcelona, Spain	8	47
2	Real Madrid, Spain	11	45
3	Rangers, Scotland	1	44
4 =	Anderlecht, Belgium	3	43
5 =	Benfica, Portugal	2	42
=	Sporting Lisbon, Portugal	1	42
7 =	FC Porto, Portugal	1	41
=	Juventus, Italy	6	41
=	Rapid Vienna, Austria	0	41
10 =	CSKA Sofia, Bulgaria	0	40
=	Olympiakos, Greece	0	40

The most campaigns by an English club is 29 by Liverpool, who have won seven European trophies.

Top 10 Most Domestic League titles*

	Club	Country	Titles
1	Rangers	Scotland	49
2	Linfield	Northern Ireland	44
3	Celtic	Scotland	38
4 =	Olympiakos	Greece	31
=	Rapid Vienna#	Austria	31
6	Benfica	Portugal	30
7 =	Ajax	Holland	28
=	CSKA Sofia	Bulgaria	28
=	Real Madrid	Spain	28
10	Anderlecht	Belgium	26
=	Ferencvaros	Hungary	26
=	Jeunesse Esch	Luxembourg	26
=	Juventus	Italy	26

* Amongst UEFA-affiliated countries, as at end of 2001-02 season, except Hungarian League, which was not completed at time of going to press

Includes one wartime German League title

Top 10 Most Spanish titles*

	Club	League titles	Cup wins	Total
1	Real Madrid	28	17	45
2	Athletic Bilbao	8	23	41
3	Barcelona	16	24	40
4	Atletico Madrid	9	9	18
5	Valencia	5	6	11
6	Real Zaragoza	0	5	5
7	Seville	1	3	4
8	Deportivo la Coruña	1	2	3
=	Español	0	3	3
=	Real Sociedad	2	1	3
=	Real Union de Irun	0	3	3

* League and Domestic Cup

Football was played on a regional basis in Spain until the formation of the first national league in 1928–29. Barcelona pipped Real Madrid to the first title by two points.

Top 10 Most German titles*

	Club	League titles	Cup wins	Total
1	Bayern Munich	17	10	27
2	1FC Nuremberg	9	3	12
3	Schalke 04	7	4	11
4	SV Hamburg	6	3	9
5 =	Borussia Dortmund	6	2	8
=	Borussia Moenchengladbach	5	3	8
7 =	1FC Cologne	3	4	7
=	VfB Stuttgart	4	3	7
=	Werder Bremen	3	4	7
10	1FC Kaiserslautern	4	2	6

* League and Domestic Cup

The first organized soccer in Germany was in 1902–03 with a series of Regional Leagues and the champions meeting in an end-of-season play-off. The first winners were Leipzig. However, the present-day Bundesliga was not formed until 1963 and the first winners were Cologne. The first German Cup winners were Nuremberg in 1935.

◀ In 12 seasons with Bayern Munich, Lothar Matthaus won six Bundesliga titles and five German Cup Winners' medals.

Top 10 Most Italian titles*

	Club	League titles	Cup wins	Total
1	Juventus	26	9	35
2	AC Milan	16	4	20
3	Inter Milan	13	3	16
4	Torino	8	4	12
5	AS Roma	3	8	11
6	Genoa	9	1	10
7	Bologna	7	2	9
8	Fiorentina	2	6	8
9	Pro Verceilli	7	0	7
10 =	Lazio	2	3	5
=	Napoli	2	3	5
=	Sampdoria	1	4	5

* League and Domestic Cup

The first Italian champions were Genoa in 1898. They also won the title for the next two years. Juventus won their first title in 1926. The first fully national Serie A started in 1929–30 and was won by Inter Milan.

Top 10 Most French titles

	Club	League titles	Cup wins	Total
1	Marseille	8	10	18
2	Saint-Etienne	10	6	16
3	Monaco	7	6	13
4	Nantes	8	3	11
5 =	Bordeaux	5	3	8
=	Lille	3	5	8
=	Stade de Reims	6	2	8
8	Nice	4	3	7
9 =	Paris St. Germain	2	4	6
=	Racing Club Paris	1	5	6

* League and Domestic Cup

Lille were the first French champions in 1933 and it was not until 1957 that Saint-Etienne won the first of their record 10 League titles. Olympique Pantin won the first French Cup Final in 1918. The country's top team, Marseille, won their first League title in 1937 and were Cup winners for the first time in 1926.

TRANSFERS & AWARDS

- ● Transfer fees in world football
- ● Transfer fees between English clubs
- ● World Footballer of the Year awards
- ● European Footballer of the Year awards

BENDING THE RULES

Over the years, football authorities have, on occasions, attempted to limit the ceiling on transfer fees, but with little success. After Alf Common's first £1,000 move in 1905, a limit of £350 per player was put on transfers, but clubs got round the rules by selling two players for £700, with one being worth virtually nothing and the sought-after player commanding the full transfer fee!

Top 10 Transfers fees in world football

	Player/country	From	To	Year	Fee (£)
1	Zinedine Zidane, France	Juventus, Italy	Real Madrid, Spain	2001	47,700,000
2	Luis Figo, Portugal	Barcelona, Spain	Real Madrid, Spain	2000	37,400,000
3	Hernan Crespo, Italy	Parma, Italy	Lazio, Italy	2000	35,700,000
4	Gianluigi Buffon, Italy	Parma, Italy	Juventus, Italy	2001	32,600,000
5	Gaizka Mendieta, Spain	Valencia, Spain	Lazio, Italy	2001	28,900,000
6	Juan Sebastian Veron, Argentina	Lazio, Italy	Manchester United, England	2001	28,100,000
7	Rui Costa, Portugal	Fiorentina, Italy	AC Milan, Italy	2001	28,000,000
8	Pavel Nedved, Czech Republic	Lazio, Italy	Juventus, Italy	2001	25,500,000
9	Christian Vieri, Italy	Lazio, Italy	Inter Milan, Italy	1999	24,000,000*
10	Nicolas Anelka, France	Arsenal, England	Real Madrid, Spain	1999	23,500,000

* Vieri's transfer was part of a package deal with Nicola Ventola, who was valued at £7 million, with Vieri at £24 million

The world's first £100,000 player was Omar Sivori when he moved to Juventus (Italy) from River Plate (Argentina) in 1957; the world's first million-pound player was Giuseppe Savoldi when he was transferred from Bologna (Italy) to Napoli (Italy) in 1975; the world's first £10 million-pound player was Gianluigi Lentini when he went from Torino (Italy) to AC Milan (Italy) in June 1992, and the first to be transferred for £20 million was the Brazilian Denilson, when he moved from São Paolo (Brazil) to Real Betis (Spain) in 1998. Born in Marseille in 1972, Zinedine Zidane started his career at Cannes before moving to Bordeaux and then to Juventus in 1996. He spent five seasons with the Italian club, scoring 25 goals in 130 matches before his record move to Real Madrid.

Top 10 Transfer fees between English clubs

	Player	From	To	Year	Fee (£)
1	Rio Ferdinand	West Ham United	Leeds United	2000	18,000,000
2	Alan Shearer	Blackburn Rovers	Newcastle United	1996	15,000,000
3	Dwight Yorke	Aston Villa	Manchester United	1998	12,600,000
4 =	Robbie Fowler	Liverpool	Leeds United	2001	11,000,000
=	Emile Heskey	Leicester City	Liverpool	2000	11,000,000
=	Frank Lampard	West Ham United	Chelsea	2001	11,000,000
7	Chris Sutton	Blackburn Rovers	Chelsea	1999	10,000,000
8 =	Stan Collymore	Nottingham Forest	Liverpool	1995	8,500,000
9	Dean Richards	Southampton	Tottenham Hotspur	2001	8,100,000
10 =	Dietar Hammann	Newcastle United	Liverpool	1999	8,000,000
=	Francis Jeffers	Everton	Arsenal	2001	8,000,000

Transfer fees appear to have spiralled in recent years, but it was a similar story in 1979 when Trevor Francis became Britain's first million-pound footballer. In 1962, Manchester United made Denis Law Britain's first £100,000 player when they bought him from the Italian club Torino. The first four-figure transfer fee came in 1905, when Middlesbrough paid Sunderland £1,000 for Alf Common, and the first £100 deal was clinched way back in 1892 when Aston Villa bought Willie Groves from West Bromwich.

When Bill Nicholson signed Jimmy Greaves for Spurs from Milan in 1961 he paid £99,999, but would not pay the other £1 because he did not want Greaves to have to carry the burden of being "Britain's first £100,000 footballer".

Top 10 World Footballer of the Year awards*

	Player/country	1st	2nd	3rd	4th	5th	Pts
1	Zinedine Zidane, France	2	0	1	2	0	17
2	Ronaldo, Brazil	2	1	0	0	0	14
3	Romario, Brazil	1	1	0	1	0	11
4 =	Roberto Baggio, Italy	1	0	1	0	1	9
=	Luis Figo, Portugal	1	1	0	0	0	9
=	Rivaldo, Brazil	1	0	1	0	1	9
=	Hristo Stoitchkov, Bulgaria	0	2	0	0	1	9
=	George Weah, Liberia	1	1	0	0	0	9
9	David Beckham, England	0	2	0	0	0	8
10 =	Marco van Basten, Netherlands	1	0	0	0	1	6
=	Gabriel Batistuta, Argentina	0	0	1	1	1	6
=	Dennis Bergkamp, Netherlands	0	0	2	0	0	6
=	Jean-Pierre Papin, France	0	1	0	1	0	6

* Based on top five finishes in the annual poll: five points for a win, four points for a second placing, etc

Awarded since 1991 under the auspices of FIFA, the World Footballer of the Year award is made to the player who is voted the top player by the coaches of national teams. Each coach votes for three players who obtain, respectively, five, three, and one points.

Top 10 European Footballer of the Year awards*

	Player/country	Gold	Silver	Bronze	Total
1 =	Franz Beckenbauer, West Germany	2	2	1	5
=	Michel Platini, France	3	0	2	5
3 =	Johann Cruyff, Netherlands	3	0	1	4
=	Raymond Kopa, France	1	1	2	4
=	Gerd Müller, West Germany	1	1	2	4
=	Luis Suárez, Spain	1	2	1	4
7 =	Marco van Basten, Netherlands	3	0	0	3
=	Bobby Charlton, England	1	2	0	3
=	Eusébio, Portugal	1	2	0	3
=	Kevin Keegan, England	2	1	0	3
=	Ronaldo, Brazil	1	1	1	3
=	Karl-Heinz Rummenigge, West Germany	2	1	0	3
=	Alfredo di Stéfano, Spain	2	1	0	3
=	Zinedine Zidane, France	1	1	1	3

Ths list is based on the gold, silver, and bronze medals won in the annual awards.

▶ **Zinedine Zidane,** the man behind France's 1998 World Cup triumph, went on to help his country to capture the European Championship two years later.

CROWDS & GROUNDS

- ● Highest record attendances in the Football League
- ● Smallest English football grounds
- ● Largest English football grounds
- ● Largest Scottish football grounds
- ● Venues for the FA Cup Final
- ● Highest average football league attendances since World War II

MAINE ROAD

Manchester City moved to their Maine Road ground in 1922 after the 4,000-seater stand at their old Hyde Road ground was damaged by fire. They acquired a new site at Moss Side for £5,500. Nearly 57,000 supporters attended the first match at the new Maine Road ground against Sheffield United on 23 August 1923. When seating was installed in the Platt Lane End stand in 1950, City had more seated accommodation than any other ground in Britain.

Top 10 Highest record attendances in the Football League

	Club	Year	Attendance
1	Manchester City	1934	84,569
2	Chelsea	1935	82,905
3	Everton	1948	78,299
4	Aston Villa	1946	76,588
5	Sunderland	1933	75,118
6	Tottenham Hotspur	1938	75,038
7	Charlton Athletic	1938	75,031
8	Arsenal	1935	73,295
9	Sheffield Wednesday	1934	72,841
10	Manchester United	1939	70,504

These records are likely to stand for all time due to drastic reductions in ground capacities over the last 20 years or so as a result of safety precautions.

Top 10 Largest English football grounds*

	Club	Ground	Capacity
1	Manchester United	Old Trafford	68,174
2	Newcastle United	St. James' Park	52,218
3	Sunderland	Stadium of Light	48,300
4	Liverpool	Anfield	45,362
5	Aston Villa	Villa Park	42,584
6	Chelsea	Stamford Bridge	42,420
7	Leeds United	Elland Road	40,204
8	Everton	Goodison Park	40,170
9	Sheffield Wednesday	Hillsborough	39,859
10	Arsenal	Highbury	38,500

* Based on capacity at the start of the 2001–02 season

Sheffield Wednesday is the only club from outside the Premiership.

Top 10 Smallest English football grounds*

	Club	Ground	Capacity
1	Barnet	Underhill	5,560
2	Macclesfield Town	Moss Rose Ground	6,028
3	Blackpool	Bloomfield Road	6,100
4	Cheltenham Town	Whaddon Road	6,114
5	Torquay United	Plainmoor	6,283
6	Kidderminster Harriers	Aggborough Stadium	6,293
7	Rushden & Diamonds	Nene Park	6,553
8	Brighton & Hove Albion	Withdean Stadium	6,960
9	Hartlepool United	Victoria Park	7,229
10	Colchester United	Layer Road	7,556

* Based on capacity at the start of the 2001–02 season

▶ Ole Gunnar Solskjaer equalizes Nottingham Forest's fourth-minute goal at Old Trafford in September 1996. Manchester United went on to win 4–1 in front of nearly 55,000 Old Trafford fans.

◀ Probably one of the best-known sporting venues in the world – Wembley Stadium, home of English soccer for nearly 80 years.

Top 10 Largest Scottish football grounds*

	Club	Ground	Capacity
1	Celtic	Celtic Park	60,506
2	Queen's Park	Hampden Park	52,000
3	Rangers	Ibrox	50,444
4	Aberdeen	Pittodrie	22,199
5	Kilmarnock	Rugby Park	18,128
6	Hearts	Tynecastle	18,000
7	Hibernian	Easter Road	17,500
8	Morton/Clydebank	Cappielow Park	14,891
9	Partick Thistle	Firhill	14,538
10	Dundee United	Tannadice Park	14,223

* Based on capacity figures at the start of the 2001-02 season

Morton and Clydebank share the Cappielow Park ground in Greenock. Despite being a Third Division side, Queen's Park play at Hampden Park, which explains their high capacity.

Top 10 Venues for the FA Cup Final*

	Venue	Year first used	No of times used
1	Wembley Stadium, London	1923	77
2	Kennington Oval, London	1872	22
3	Crystal Palace, London	1895	21
4 =	Old Trafford, Manchester	1911	3
=	Stamford Bridge, London	1920	3
6 =	Goodison Park, Liverpool	1894	2
=	Millennium Stadium, Cardiff	2001	2
8 =	Baseball Ground, Derby	1886	1
=	Bramall Lane, Sheffield	1912	1
=	Burnden Park, Bolton	1901	1
=	Fallowfield, Manchester	1893	1
=	Lillie Bridge, London	1873	1

* Including replays

Since the first FA Cup Final at Kennington Oval in 1872, a total of 12 grounds have been used to stage the most famous cup competition in the world. Bramall Lane, home of Sheffield United, stands alone as the only present-day League ground to have played host to both the FA Cup Final and a cricket Test match.

Top 10 Highest average Football League attendances since World War II

	Club	Season	Average attendance
1	Manchester United	2001–02	67,558
2	Manchester United	2000–01	67,544
3	Manchester United	1999–2000	58,017
4	Manchester United	1967–68	57,552
5	Newcastle United	1947–48	56,283
6	Tottenham Hotspur	1950–51	55,509
7	Manchester United	1998–99	55,188
8	Manchester United	1997–98	55,168
9	Manchester United	1996–97	55,081
10	Arsenal	1947–48	54,982

Manchester United have topped the 50,000 average a record 15 times.

FOOTBALL

FOOTBALLING MISCELLANY

- Most Football League appearances
- Oldest Football League clubs
- Longest-serving Football League managers
- Countries with most registered football clubs
- Most common scores in the English & Premier League
- Richest football clubs in the world
- Olympic football countries

FASHION SETTERS

Notts County have left their mark on Italian fashion; Italian giants Juventus played in old Notts County colours in their early days and still play in the same black and white striped shirts as County. Juventus originally played in pink shirts, but when one of its English players, John Savage, was sent to find replacements, he returned with replicas of County's shirts.

Top 10 Most Football League appearances*

	Player	Years	Appearances
1	Peter Shilton	1966–97	1,005
2	Tony Ford	1975–2002	931
3	Tommy Hutchison	1965–91	795
4	Terry Paine	1957–77	824
5	Robbie James	1973–94	782
6	Alan Oakes	1959–84	777
7	John Trollope	1960–80	770
8	Jimmy Dickinson	1946–65	764
9	Roy Sproson	1950–72	761
10	Mick Tait	1975–97	760

* To end of 2000–01 season

Trollope's total of 770 is a record for one club. He spent his entire career with Swindon Town. Shilton's career was spent with Leicester City (286 appearances), Stoke City (110), Nottingham Forest (202), Southampton (188), Derby County (175), Plymouth Argyle (34), Bolton Wanderers (1), and Leyton Orient (9). In total, Shilton played in a record 1,390 senior matches. The record for the Scottish League is held by Graeme Armstrong, with 879 appearances between 1975 and 1999.

Top 10 Oldest Football League clubs

	Club	Year formed
1	Notts County	1862
2	Stoke City	1863
3	Nottingham Forest	1865
4	Chesterfield	1866
5	Sheffield Wednesday	1867
6	Reading	1871
7	Wrexham	1873
8	Aston Villa	1874 (Mar)
9	Bolton Wanderers	1874 (July)
10	Birmingham City	1875

Birmingham City dates its origin to September 1875, slightly pre-dating Blackburn Rovers, which started in November the same year. Scotland's oldest club is Queen's Park, formed in 1867. Queen's Park remains the only amateur team in League football in either Scotland or England.

Top 10 Longest-serving Football League managers*

	Manager	Club	Appointed
1	Dario Gradi	Crewe Alexandra	June 1983
2	Sir Alex Ferguson	Manchester United	November 1986
3	Stan Ternent	Burnley	June 1988
4	George Burley	Ipswich Town	December 1994
5	Peter Reid	Sunderland	March 1995
6	Alan Curbishley	Charlton Athletic	June 1995
7	Barry Fry	Peterborough United	May 1996
8	Arsene Wenger	Arsenal	September 1996
9	Brian Laws	Scunthorpe United	February 1997
10	Ronnie Moore	Rotherham United	May 1997

* As at 1 May 2002

▶ In addition to making over 1,000 Football League appearances, Peter Shilton played for England a record 125 times between 1970 and 1990.

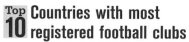

> There are 91 managers in England who think they'd love my job –
> until they got it.
>
> **Alex (later Sir Alex) Ferguson, 1996**

Top 10 Countries with most registered football clubs

	Country	No of registered clubs
1	South Africa	51,944
2	Russia	43,700
3	England	42,000
4	Germany	26,760
5	France	21,629
6	Italy	20,961
7	Uzbekistan	15,000
8	Japan	13,047
9	Brazil	12,987
10	Spain	10,240

Top 10 Most common scores in the English and Premier League*

	Scoreline	Occurrences
1	1–1	18,366
2	1–0	15,644
3	2–1	14,297
4	2–0	13,184
5	0–0	11,386
6	0–1	9,572
7	1–2	8,712
8	3–1	8,695
9	2–2	8,242
10	3–0	8,027

* From 1888–89 to 2000–01; includes the old First Division

Several scorelines have been registered just once, the highest-scoring game being Tranmere Rovers' 13–4 win over Oldham Athletic in a Third Division (North) match on Boxing Day 1935.

Top 10 Richest football clubs in the world

	Club/country	Turnover 1999–2000 (£)
1	Manchester United, England	117,000,000
2	Real Madrid, Spain	103,700,000
3	Bayern Munich, Germany	91,600,000
4	AC Milan, Italy	89,700,000
5	Juventus, Italy	88,400,000
6	Lazio, Italy	79,400,000
7	Chelsea, England	76,700,000
8	Barcelona, Spain	75,200,000
9	Inter Milan, Italy	68,900,000
10	Roma, Italy	64,100,000

Source: Deloitte & Touche

Whilst clubs like Manchester United and Real Madrid have an annual turnover of more than £100,000,000, they also have extremely high wage bills, such as the £80,000 per week each to Raul and Zidane (Real Madrid) and Roy Keane (Manchester United).

Top 10 Olympic football countries

	Country	Gold medal	Silver medal	Bronze medal	Total
1 =	Denmark	1	3	1	5
=	Hungary	3	1	1	5
=	USSR	1	3	1	5
=	Yugoslavia	1	3	1	5
5	East Germany	1	1	2	4
6 =	Brazil	0	2	1	3
=	Great Britain/England	3	0	0	3
=	Netherlands	0	0	3	3
=	Poland	1	2	0	3
=	Spain	1	2	0	3
=	Sweden	1	0	2	3

Football was seen at the first Modern Olympics in 1896 when a visiting Danish team played Smyrna (now the Turkish town of Izmir) 15–0. No medals were awarded. It was not until the 1908 London Olympics that soccer gained official recognition and medals were first awarded. Since then, with the exception of the 1932 Los Angeles Games, soccer has been played at every Olympics.

At the Start

Cricket almost certainly evolved from the medieval bat and ball games that gave rise to such variations as stool ball, which is still played in Sussex, and baseball. It was played in the mid-16th century and by British settlers in the United States as early as 1709. The first inter-county match, between Kent and London, took place 10 years later. By the mid-18th century, cricket was firmly established – especially in Kent, Sussex, and Hampshire. The game's first rules were drawn up in 1744. The Marylebone Cricket Club (MCC) was established in 1787, and still governs the laws of the game. The first Test match was played in Australia in 1877.

CRICKET

- Highest individual Test innings
- Highest innings in a Test match
- Most wickets taken in a Test career
- Most Test dismissals by a wicketkeeper
- Most runs in a Test career

THE FIRST TEST MATCH

The first Test match was played at Melbourne on 15–19 March 1877 when James Lillywhite's touring side took on the Australians and lost by 45 runs. Amazingly, when the centenary Test was played in 1977, Australia won by an identical score. The first Test on English soil took place at The Oval on 6–8 September 1880.

TEST RECORDS

Top 10 Highest individual Test innings

	Batsman	Match	Venue	Year	Score
1	Brian Lara	West Indies v England	St. John's	1993–94	375
2	Gary Sobers	West Indies v Pakistan	Kingston	1957–58	365*
3	Len Hutton	England v Australia	The Oval	1938	364
4	Sanath Jayasuriya	Sri Lanka v India	Colombo	1997–98	340
5	Hanif Mohammad	Pakistan v West Indies	Bridgetown	1957–58	337
6	Walter Hammond	England v New Zealand	Auckland	1932–33	336*
7 =	Don Bradman	Australia v England	Leeds	1930	334
=	Mark Taylor	Australia v Pakistan	Peshawar	1998–99	334*
9	Graham Gooch	England v India	Lord's	1990	333
10	Andrew Sandham	England v West Indies	Kingston	1929–30	325

* Not out

▶ Not only was Allan Border a prolific runmaker in Test cricket, he was also an outstanding captain, leading his side to 32 wins in 93 Tests.

◀ Lord's, the most-used Test cricket ground,
with 102 matches played on it.

Top 10 Highest innings in a Test match

	Match	Venue	Year	Score
1	Sri Lanka v India	Colombo	1997–98	952-6
2	England v Australia	The Oval	1938	903-7d
3	England v West Indies	Kingston	1929–30	849
4	West Indies v Pakistan	Kingston	1957–58	790-3d
5	Australia v West Indies	Kingston	1954–55	759-8d
6	Australia v England	Lord's	1930	729-6d
7	Pakistan v England	The Oval	1987	708
8	Australia v England	The Oval	1934	701
9	Pakistan v India	Lahore	1989–90	699-5
10	Australia v England	The Oval	1930	695

Top 10 Most Test dismissals by a wicketkeeper

	Wicketkeeper	Country	Tests	Catches	Stumped	Total
1	Ian Healy	Australia	119	366	29	395
2	Rodney Marsh	Australia	96	343	12	355
3	Jeff Dujon	West Indies	81	267	5	272
4	Alan Knott	England	95	250	19	269
5	Alex Stewart	England	115	220	11	231
6	Wasim Bari	Pakistan	81	201	27	228
7	Godfrey Evans	England	91	173	46	219
8	Syed Kirmani	India	88	160	38	198
9	Adam Parore	New Zealand	75	187	7	194
10	Deryck Murray	West Indies	62	181	8	189

Top 10 Most wickets taken in a Test career

	Player	Country	Matches	Wickets
1	Courtney Walsh	West Indies	132	519
2	Kapil Dev	India	131	434
3	Richard Hadlee	New Zealand	86	431
4	Shane Warne	Australia	98	430
5	Wasim Akram	Pakistan	104	414
6	Curtly Ambrose	West Indies	98	405
7	Muttiah Muralitharan	Sri Lanka	72	404
8	Ian Botham	England	102	383
9	Glenn McGrath	Australia	81	377
10	Malcolm Marshall	West Indies	81	376

Courtney Walsh made his Test debut in the First Test against Australia at Perth
in 1984–85. A right arm fast bowler, his 519 wickets were achieved with an
average of 24.44 and his best figures of 7–37 were against New Zealand in 1975.
He became the most prolific Test wicket taker against Zimbabwe in 2000.

Top 10 Most runs in a Test career

	Player	Country	Innings	Runs
1	Allan Border	Australia	265	11,174
2	Sunil Gavaskar	India	214	10,122
3	Steve Waugh	Australia	228	9,505
4	Graham Gooch	England	215	8,900
5	Javed Miandad	Pakistan	189	8,832
6	Viv Richards	West Indies	182	8,540
7	David Gower	England	204	8,231
8	Geoff Boycott	England	193	8,114
9	Gary Sobers	West Indies	160	8,032
10	Mark Waugh	Australia	200	7,780

Allan Border made his Test debut in the 1978–79 series against England. In the
final Test, he was relegated to drinks' waiter. That was the last time he missed a
game for Australia as he went on to play a record 153 consecutive Tests, 47 more
than the next-best figure of 106 by Sunil Gavaskar.

- Best First-class batting averages
- Most runs scored off a six-ball over
- Highest individual First-class innings
- Most First-class centuries
- Most sixes in a First-class innings

THE LAST SCORE

On his way to yet another century during a match in 1893, W. G. Grace suddenly announced his team's declaration while he was on 93. When asked why he had declared instead of going on to make another century he replied, "It suddenly dawned on me that 93 was the only score between 0 and 100 I had never made so it was best to put the record straight!"

BATTING GREATS

Top 10 Best First-class batting averages*

	Batsman	Country	Matches	Innings	Not out	Runs	Highest score	Average
1	Don Bradman	Australia	234	338	43	28,067	452#	95.14
2	Vijay Merchant	India	150	234	46	13,470	359#	71.64
3	Ajay Sharma	India	129	166	16	10,120	259#	67.46
4	Bill Ponsford	Australia	162	235	23	13,819	437	65.18
5	Bill Woodfull	Australia	174	245	39	13,388	284	64.99
6	Sachin Tendulkar	India	171	265	28	14,705	233#	62.04
7	Vijay Hazare	India	238	367	46	18,740	316#	58.38
8	Lindsay Hassett	Australia	216	322	32	16,890	232	58.24
9	Ruhal Dravid	India	150	245	35	12,056	215	57.40
10	Alan Kippax	Australia	175	256	33	12,762	315#	57.22

* Minimum qualification: 10,000 runs

\# Not out

The highest-placed English player is Geoff Boycott (11th), with an average of 56.83.

Top 10 Most runs scored off a six-ball over*

	Batsman	Match	Year	Bowler	Runs
1 =	Ravi Shastri	Bombay v Baroda	1984–85	Tilak Raj	36
=	Gary Sobers	Nottinghamshire v Glamorgan	1968	Malcolm Nash	36
3 =	Edwin Alletson	Nottinghamshire v Sussex	1911	Ernest Killick	34
=	Glen Chapple#	Lancashire v Glamorgan	1993	Tony Cottey	34
=	Frank Hayes	Lancashire v Glamorgan	1977	Malcolm Nash	34
=	Matthew Maynard#	Glamorgan v Kent	1992	Steve Marsh	34
=	Barry Touzel#	W. Province B v Griqualand West B	1993–94	Frans Viljoen	34
8 =	Ian Botham	England XI v Central Districts	1983–84	Ian Snook	32
=	Glen Chapple#	Lancashire v Glamorgan	1993	Tony Cottey	32
=	Mark Ealham#	Kent v Gloucestershire	1992	Dean Hodgson	32
=	Clive Inman	Leicestershire v Nottinghamshire	1965	Norman Hill	32
=	Trevor Jesty#	Hampshire v Nottinghamshire	1984	Robin Boyd Moss	32
=	Khalid Mahmood	Gujranwala v Sargodha	2000–01	Naved Latif	32
=	Paul Parker	Sussex v Warwickshire	1982	Alvin Kallicharran	32
=	Ian Redpath	Australia v Orange Free State	1969–70	Neil Rosendorff	32
=	Cyril Smart	Glamorgan v Hampshire	1935	Gerald Hill	32

* Without no-balls

\# Indicates the fielding side deliberately conceded runs in order to manufacture a "result"

During the Canterbury v Wellington Shell Trophy match at Christchurch in the 1989–90 season, an amazing 77 runs were scored off one over when Wellington bowler Robert Vance deliberately bowled 17 no-balls in an effort to produce a positive result from the match. Canterbury's wicketkeeper, Lee Gernon, hit eight sixes and five fours during the amazing over, in his total of 69. In the confusion, the umpires miscalculated and only five official balls were delivered. However, because of the nature of the "record", it cannot be treated as legitimate.

> I couldn't bat for the length of time required to score 500. I'd get bored and fall over.
>
> Denis Compton

Top 10 Highest individual First-class innings

	Batsman	Match	Venue	Year	Score
1	Brian Lara	Warwickshire v Durham	Edgbaston	1994	501*
2	Hanif Mohammad	Karachi v Bahawalpur	Karachi	1958-59	499
3	Don Bradman	New South Wales v Queensland	Sydney	1929-30	452*
4	Bhausahib Nimbalkar	Maharashtra v Kathiawar	Poona	1948-49	443*
5	Bill Ponsford	Victoria v Queensland	Melbourne	1927-28	437
6	Bill Ponsford	Victoria v Tasmania	Melbourne	1922-23	429
7	Aftab Baloch	Sind v Baluchistan	Karachi	1973-74	428
8	Archie MacLaren	Lancashire v Somerset	Taunton	1895	424
9	Graeme Hick	Worcestershire v Somerset	Taunton	1988	405*
10	Javed Latif	Sargodha v Gujranwala	Gujranwala	2000-01	394

* Not out

Top 10 Most First-class centuries

	Batsman	Innings	Centuries
1	Jack Hobbs	1,325	199
2	Patsy Hendren	1,300	170
3	Walter Hammond	1,005	167
4	Philip Mead	1,340	153
5 =	Geoff Boycott	1,014	151
=	Herbert Sutcliffe	1,098	151
7	Frank Woolley	1,530	145
8	Len Hutton	814	129
9	Graham Gooch	990	128
10	W. G. Grace	1,478	124

◄ The West Indies captain and one of the greatest batsmen and most prolific run makers of the modern era, Brian Lara.

Top 10 Most sixes in a First-class innings

	Player	Match	Year	Score	Sixes
1	Andrew Symonds	Gloucestershire v Glamorgan	1995	254	16
2	John Reid	Wellington v Northern Districts	1962-63	296	15
3	Shakti Singh	Himachal Pradesh v Haryana	1990-91	128	14
4 =	Gordon Greenidge	D.H. Robins' XI v Pakistan	1974	273*	13
=	Gordon Greenidge	Hampshire v Sussex	1975	259	13
=	Geoff Humpage	Warwickshire v Lancashire	1982	254	13
=	Majid Khan	Pakistan v Glamorgan	1967	147*	13
=	Ravi Shastri	Bombay v Baroda	1984-85	200*	13
=	Barry Touzel	W Province B v Griqualand West	1993-94	128*	13
10 =	Wasim Akram	Pakistan v Zimbabwe	1996-97	257*	12
=	Ian Botham	Somerset v Warwickshire	1985	138*	12
=	Nisal Fernando	Sinhalese SC v Sebastianites	1990-91	160	12
=	Roger Harper	Northants v Gloucestershire	1986	234	12
=	Dean Jones	Australia v Warwickshire	1989	248	12
=	Gulfraz Khan	Railways v Universities	1976-77	207	12
=	Graham Lloyd	Lancashire v Essex	1996	241	12
=	Dipak Patel	Auckland v Northern Districts	1991-92	204	12
=	Woorkeri Raman	Tamil Nadu v Kerala	1991-92	206	12

* Not out

BOWLING GREATS

- ● Best bowling figures in a First-class match
- ● Best bowling averages in a First-class career
- ● First bowlers to take a hat-trick on their First-class debut
- ● Wicket-takers in a First-class career
- ● Most hat-tricks in a First-class career

> " When you win the toss, bat. If you are in doubt, think about it – then bat. If you have very big doubts, consult a colleague – then bat.
> W. G. Grace "

Top 10 Best bowling figures in a First-class match

	Bowler	Match	Venue	Year	Haul
1	Jim Laker	England v Australia	Manchester	1956	19–90
2	Henry Arkwright	MCC v Gentlemen of Kent	Canterbury	1861	18–96
3	Colin Blythe	Kent v Northamptonshire	Northampton	1907	17–48
4	Charlie Turner	Australia v England XI	Hastings	1888	17–50
5	Bill Howell	Australia v Western Province	Cape Town	1902–03	17–54
6	Charlie Parker	Gloucestershire v Essex	Gloucester	1925	17–56
7	Alfred "Tich" Freeman	Kent v Sussex	Hove	1922	17–67
8 =	W. G. Grace	Gloucestershire v Notts	Cheltenham	1877	17–89
=	Frank Matthews	Nottinghamshire v Northants	Nottingham	1923	17–89
10 =	Harry Dean	Lancashire v Yorkshire	Liverpool	1913	17–91
=	Hedley Verity	Yorkshire v Essex	Leyton	1933	17–91

Top 10 Best bowling averages in a First-class career*

Bowler	Wickets	Average
1 Alfred Shaw	2,028	12.12
2 Tom Emmett	1,571	13.56
3 George Lohmann	1,841	13.74
4 James Southerton	1,681	14.46
5 Hedley Verity	1,956	14.90
6 William Attewell	1,950	15.33
7 Arthur Mold	1,673	15.54
8 Schofield Haigh	2,012	15.95
9 Johnny Briggs	2,221	15.93
10 Robert Peel	1,775	16.20

* Minimum qualification: 1,500 wickets

Wilf Rhodes, cricket's leading wicket-taker with 4,187 victims, is in 12th place with an average of 16.71.

Top 10 First bowlers to take a hat-trick on their First-class debut

Bowler	Match	Venue	Year
1 Henry Hay	South Australia v Lord Hawke's XI	Adelaide	1902–03
2 Herbert Sedgwick	Yorkshire v Worcestershire	Hull	1906
3 Reginald Wooster	Northants v Dublin University	Northampton	1925
4 John Treanor	New South Wales v Queensland	Brisbane	1954–55
5 Vasant Ranjane	Maharashtra v Saurashtra	Poona	1956–57
6 Joginder Rao	Services v Jammu and Kashmir	Delhi	1963–64
7 Norton Fredrick	Ceylon v Madras	Colombo	1963–64
8 Mehboodullah	Uttar Pradesh v Madhya Pradesh	Lucknow	1971–72
9 Rod Estwick	Barbados v Guyana	Bridgetown	1982–83
10 Salil Ankola	Maharashtra v Gujarat	Pune	1988–89

Less than a week after performing this feat, Joginder Rao achieved a hat-trick twice in one match against North Punjab. Remarkably, he took only 21 first-class wickets – a climbing accident cut short his career.

Top 10 Wicket-takers in a First-class career

Bowler	Career	Wickets
1 Wilf Rhodes	1898–1930	4,187
2 Alfred "Tich" Freeman	1914–36	3,776
3 Charlie Parker	1903–35	3,278
4 Jack Hearne	1888–1923	3,061
5 Tom Goddard	1922–52	2,979
6 W. G. Grace	1865–1908	2,876
7 Alex Kennedy	1907–36	2,874
8 Derek Shackleton	1948–69	2,857
9 Tony Lock	1946–71	2,844
10 Fred Titmus	1949–82	2,830

Wilf Rhodes is the oldest man to play Test match cricket. He made his Test debut during W. G. Grace's last Test in 1914, and played his last match in 1930, at the age of 52 years, 165 days.

◀ W. G. Grace played his last game on 25 July 1914 for Eltham against Grove Park. Although aged 66 at the time, he scored 69 runs in his last innings.

Top 10 Most hat-tricks in a First-class career

Bowler/country*	Team(s)	No.
1 Doug Wright	Kent	7
2 = Tom Goddard	Gloucestershire	6
= Charlie Parker	Gloucestershire	6
4 = Schofield Haigh	Yorkshire	5
= Vallance Jupp	Sussex, Northamptonshire	5
= Dusty Rhodes	Derbyshire	5
= F. A. Tarrant	Middlesex	5
8 = Dick Barlow	Lancashire	4
= Arthur "Tich" Freeman	Kent	4
= Jack Hearne	Middlesex	4
= Jim Laker	Surrey	4
= Tony Lock	Surrey, Leicestershire, Western Australia	4
= George Macaulay	Yorkshire	4
= Jimmy Matthews, Australia	Victoria	4
= Mike Procter, South Africa	Gloucestershire	4
= Tom Richardson	Surrey	4
= Frederick Spofforth, Australia	New South Wales	4
= Freddie Trueman	Yorkshire	4

* All UK unless otherwise stated

CRICKET

ALL-ROUNDERS

- ● Best all-rounders in First-class cricket
- ● First players to score a century and perform a hat-trick in the same First-class match
- ● Most catches by an outfielder
- ● Most appearances in First-class matches
- ● Most stumpings in First-class cricket
- ● Most dismissals by a wicketkeeper in First-class cricket

> His first appearance in county cricket was at Old Trafford in June 1906. He was this day born fully fledged; he never improved on the ease and grace of this baptismal innings. It could not be improved on. His cricket was spontaneously and miraculously created. And miracles are not subject to development.
>
> **Neville Cardus** on Frank Woolley

Top 10 Best all-rounders in First-class cricket*

	Player	Country	Runs	HS	Ave	Wkts	BB	Ave	Ratio
1	W. G. Grace	England	54,211	344	39.45	2,809	10–49	18.14	2.174
2	Frank Tarrant	Australia	17,952	250#	36.41	1,512	110–90	17.49	2.082
3	Frank Woolley	England	58,959	305#	40.77	2,066	8–22	19.87	2.052
4	Gary Sobers	West Indies	28,314	365#	54.87	1,043	9–49	27.74	1.978
5	Mike Procter	South Africa	21,936	254	36.01	1,417	9–71	19.53	1.844
6	Wilf Rhodes	England	39,969	267#	30.81	4,204	9–24	16.72	1.842
7	George Hirst	England	36,356	341	34.13	2,742	9–23	18.73	1.822
8	Richard Hadlee	New Zealand	12,052	210#	31.71	1,490	9–52	18.11	1.751
9	Jack Hearne	England	37,252	285#	40.98	1,839	9–61	24.42	1.678
10	Imran Khan	Pakistan	17,771	170	36.79	1,287	8–34	22.32	1.684

* Based on First-class batting average divided by First-class bowling average; minimum qualification: 10,000 runs and 1,000 wickets

\# Not out

Grace's best season was 1871 when he scored 2,739 runs and took 78 wickets. His highest First-class innings was 344 for the MCC against Kent at Canterbury in 1876 and his best bowling was 10–49 for the MCC against Oxford University at Oxford in 1886. He scored 152 on his Test debut, the first century by an Englishman in Test cricket.

Top 10 First players to score a century and perform a hat-trick in the same First-class match

	Bowler	Match	Venue	Date
1	George Giffen	Australia v Lancashire	Manchester	1884
2	William Roller	Surrey v Sussex	The Oval	1885
3	William Burns	Worcestershire v Gloucestershire	Worcester	1913
4	Vallance Jupp	Sussex v Essex	Colchester	1921
5	Bob Wyatt	MCC v Ceylon	Colombo	1926–27
6	Learie Constantine	West Indies v Northamptonshire	Northampton	1928
7	David Davies	Glamorgan v Leicestershire	Leicester	1937
8	Vijay Merchant	Dr C. R. Pereira XI v Sir Homi Mehta XI	Bombay	1946–47
9	Mike Procter	Gloucestershire v Essex	Westcliff-on-Sea	1972
10	Mike Procter	Gloucestershire v Leicestershire	Bristol	1979

Playing for Hampshire against the Indians at Southampton in 1996, Kevan James uniquely scored a century and took four wickets in four balls. South African-born Mike Procter has uniquely scored a century and performed the hat-trick in the same First-class match on two occasions. He has performed the hat-trick four times in First-class cricket and once in the Benson and Hedges Cup. With the bat he has a personal best innings of 254 for Rhodesia against Western Province in 1970–71. He is also one of the few batsmen to have hit six consecutive balls for six, but not in the same over; two off the last two balls of one over and four off the first four balls of the next he faced. Due to South Africa's apartheid policy, he played in only two official Test matches for his country.

Top 10 Most catches by an outfielder

	Fielder*	Years	Catches
1	Frank Woolley	1906–38	1,018
2	W. G. Grace	1865–1908	887
3	Tony Lock	1946–71	830
4	Walter Hammond	1920–51	819
5	Brian Close	1949–86	813
6	John Langridge	1928–55	784
7	Wilf Rhodes	1896–1930	764
8	Arthur Milton	1948–74	758
9	Patsy Hendren	1907–38	754
10	Peter Walker	1956–72	697

* All UK

During his career Frank Woolley scored nearly 60,000 First-class runs for Kent and England and is second only on the all-time list behind Jack Hobbs. Proving himself to be an all-rounder, he also took 2,068 wickets.

Top 10 Most appearances in First-class matches

	Player*	Years	Matches
1	Wilf Rhodes	1898–1930	1,110
2	Frank Woolley	1906–38	978
3	W. G. Grace	1865–1908	870
4	Jack Hobbs	1905–34	834
5	Patsy Hendren	1907–37	833
6	George Hirst	1891–1929	826
7	Philip Mead	1905–36	814
8	Fred Titmus	1949–82	792
9	Ray Illingworth	1951–83	787
10	Brian Close	1949–77	786

* All UK

Top 10 Most stumpings in First-class cricket

	Wicketkeeper	Years	Total
1	Les Ames	1926–51	417
2	Fred Huish	1895–1900	377
3	Edward Pooley	1861–83	358
4	Jack Board	1891–1915	355
5	David Hunter	1888–1909	350
6	George Duckworth	1923–47	343
7	Walter Cornford	1921–47	342
8	Harold Stephenson	1948–64	334
9	Fred Price	1926–47	322
10	Harry Elliott	1920–47	303

* All UK

Top 10 Most dismissals by a wicketkeeper in First-class cricket

	Player*	Years	Matches	Caught	Stumped	Total dismissals
1	Bob Taylor	1960–88	639	1,473	176	1,649
2	John Murray	1952–75	635	1,270	257	1,527
3	Herbert Strudwick	1902–27	674	1,241	254	1,495
4	Alan Knott	1964–85	511	1,211	133	1,344
5	Frederick Huish	1895–1914	497	933	377	1,310
6	Brian Taylor	1949–73	572	1,083	211	1,294
7	David Hunter	1888–1909	552	913	350	1,263
8	Jack Russell	1981–2001	435	1,119	122	1,241
9	Harry Butt	1890–1912	550	953	275	1,228
10	Jack Board	1891–1915	525	851	355	1,206

* All UK

▶ Derbyshire's Bob Taylor played 57 times for England. Had his career not coincided for a large part with that of Alan Knott, he would surely have added to the total.

THE ENGLISH GAME

- Individual First-class innings in England
- Most wickets in an English First-class season
- Most major domestic English titles
- Most runs in an English season
- Highest team totals in the County Championship

Top 10 Individual First-class innings in England

	Batsman	Match	Venue	Year	Score
1	Brian Lara	Warwickshire v Durham	Birmingham	1994	501*
2	Archie MacLaren	Lancashire v Somerset	Taunton	1895	424
3	Graeme Hick	Worcestershire v Somerset	Taunton	1988	405*
4	Neil Fairbrother	Lancashire v Surrey	The Oval	1990	366
5	Len Hutton	England v Australia	The Oval	1938	364
6	Bobby Abel	Surrey v Somerset	The Oval	1899	357*
7	Charlie Macartney	Australia v Nottinghamshire	Nottingham	1921	345
8	W. G. Grace	MCC v Kent	Canterbury	1876	344
9	Percy Perrin	Essex v Derbyshire	Chesterfield	1904	343*
10	George Hirst	Yorkshire v Leicestershire	Leicester	1905	341

* Not out

Brian Lara's record-breaking innings started at 3.28 pm on Friday 3 June 1994. At the close of play, Lara was 111 not out (an unlucky score for batsmen). Play resumed on the Monday and Lara reached 500 in the session after tea when he hit a boundary off the bowling of J. E. Morris.

WOMEN'S CRICKET

The first women's cricket match dates from Friday 26 July 1745 when Hambledon spinsters played Bramley maidens at Gosden Common, near Guildford, Surrey. Hambledon won by 127 notches (runs) to 119.

Top 10 Most wickets in an English First-class season

	Bowler	Year	Wickets
1	Alfred "Tich" Freeman	1928	304
2	Alfred "Tich" Freeman	1933	298
3	Tom Richardson	1895	290
4	Charlie Turner	1888	283
5	Alfred "Tich" Freeman	1931	276
6	Alfred "Tich" Freeman	1930	275
7	Tom Richardson	1897	273
8	Alfred "Tich" Freeman	1929	267
9	Wilf Rhodes	1900	261
10	Jack Hearne	1896	257

Alfred Freeman of Kent was nicknamed "Tich" because he was only 1.57 m (5 ft 2 in) tall. That didn't stop him from taking 3,776 First-class wickets. He was an exponent of leg bowling, which fooled many English batsmen of his day, as his figures testify. Although "Tich" took 200 wickets in a season on no fewer than eight occasions, the sport's most prolific wicket-taker, Wilf Rhodes, performed the feat just three times. The first man to claim more than 200 victims in one season was James Southerton, who took 210 wickets in 1870. Since the reduction of County Championship matches in 1969, the best haul has been 134, by Malcolm Marshall in 1982.

◀ Denis Compton scoring a century against the South Africans in 1947, just one of 18 he scored in his record-breaking season.

Top 10 Most major domestic English titles

	County	County Championship	C & G Trophy*	Benson & Hedges	Norwich Union League	Total
1	Yorkshire	31#	2	1	1	35
2	Lancashire	8*	7	4	5	24
3	Surrey	18#	1	3	1	23
4	Middlesex	12†	4	2	1	19
5	Kent	7#	2	3	5	17
6	Warwickshire	5	5	1	3	14
7	Essex	6	2	2	3	13
8	Worcestershire	5	1	1	3	10
9 =	Hampshire	2	1	2	3	8
=	Leicestershire	3	0	3	2	8

* Formerly Gillette Cup and Nat West Trophy
\# Indicates shared title
† Indicates two shared titles

Top 10 Most runs in an English season

	Batsman	Season	Runs
1	Denis Compton	1947	3,816
2	Bill Edrich	1947	3,539
3	Tom Hayward	1906	3,518
4	Len Hutton	1949	3,429
5	Frank Woolley	1928	3,352
6	Herbert Sutcliffe	1932	3,336
7	Walter Hammond	1933	3,323
8	Patsy Hendren	1928	3,311
9	Bobby Abel	1901	3,309
10	Walter Hammond	1937	3,252

Since the reduction in the number of County Championship matches in 1969, the best total has been 2,746, by Graham Gooch in 1990.

Top 10 Highest team totals in the County Championship

	Match	Venue	Year	Total
1	Yorkshire v Warwickshire	Birmingham	1896	887
2	Lancashire v Surrey	The Oval	1990	863
3	Surrey v Somerset	The Oval	1899	811
4	Warwickshire v Durham	Birmingham	1994	810–4 dec
5	Kent v Essex	Brentwood	1934	803–4 dec
6	Lancashire v Somerset	Taunton	1895	801
7	Northamptonshire v Nottinghamshire	Northampton	1995	781–7 dec
8	Essex v Leicestershire	Chelmsford	1990	761–6 dec
9	Surrey v Hampshire	The Oval	1909	742
10	Nottinghamshire v Sussex	Nottingham	1903	739–7 dec

Glamorgan scored 718 for the loss of only three wickets before declaring against Sussex at Colwyn Bay in 2000. Yorkshire's 887 is well short of the all-time First-class record of 1,107 scored by Victoria against New South Wales at Melbourne in 1926–27. Remarkably, Victoria broke their own world record set four years earlier when they scored 1,059 against Tasmania, also at Melbourne. They are the only two instances of a team scoring four figures in an innings in First-class cricket.

◀ Yorkshire captain David Byas celebrates with team-mates after winning the County Championship for the record 31st time in 2001.

- ● Highest individual First-class innings in Australia
- ● Most runs in women's Test cricket
- ● Best batting averages in the Sheffield Shield and Pura Cup
- ● Best bowling averages in the Sheffield Shield and Pura Cup
- ● Highest individual scores by West Indian batsmen in Test cricket

> We have nothing against man cricketers. Some of them are quite nice people, even though they don't win as often as we do.
> Rachael Heyhoe-Flint

AROUND THE WORLD

Top 10 Highest individual First-class innings in Australia

	Batsman	Match	Venue	Season	Score
1	Don Bradman	New South Wales v Queensland	Sydney	1929–30	452*
2	Bill Ponsford	Victoria v Queensland	Melbourne	1927–28	437
3	Bill Ponsford	Victoria v Tasmania	Melbourne	1922–23	429
4	Charles Gregory	New South Wales v Queensland	Brisbane	1906–07	383
5	Don Bradman	South Australia v Tasmania	Adelaide	1935–36	369
6	Clem Hill	South Australia v New South Wales	Adelaide	1900–01	365*
7	Bobby Simpson	New South Wales v Queensland	Brisbane	1963–64	359
8	Don Bradman	South Australia v Victoria	Melbourne	1935–36	357
9	Barry Richards#	South Australia v Western Australia	Perth	1970–71	356
10	Geoff Marsh	Western Australia v South Australia	Perth	1989–90	355*

* Not out

\# South African, all other players Australian

◀ Don Bradman scored 118 on his debut for New South Wales against South Australia when he was aged just 19.

Top 10 Most runs in women's Test cricket

	Player	Country	Innings	Runs
1	Jeanette Brittin	England	44	1,935
2	Rachael Heyhoe-Flint	England	38	1,594
3	Debbie Hockley	New Zealand	29	1,301
4	Carole Hodges	England	31	1,164
5	Sandiya Agarwal	India	23	1,110
6	Enid Bakewell	England	22	1,078
7	Myrtle Maclagan	England	25	1,007
8	Molly Hide	England	27	872
9	Betty Wilson	Australia	16	862
10	Cecilia Robinson	England	27	829

Jeanette Brittin also scored a record five Test centuries and 11 half centuries. The first century in women's Test cricket was by Myrtle Maclagan (119) for England against Australia at Sydney in the second test of 1934–35. The highest individual innings in women's test cricket is 209 not out by Karen Rolton for Australia against England at Leeds in 2001.

Top 10 Best batting averages in the Sheffield Shield and Pura Cup*

	Batsman	Matches	Innings	Not out	Runs	Average
1	Don Bradman	62	96	15	8,926	110.19
2	Bill Ponsford	43	70	5	5,413	83.27
3	Alan Kippax	61	95	9	6,096	70.88
4	Monty Noble	51	81	9	4,896	68.00
5	Bill Woodfull	39	64	10	3,620	67.03
6	Ricky Ponting	47	87	13	4,749	64.17
7	Arthur Morris	37	58	3	3,517	63.94
8	Lindsay Hassett	58	97	10	5,535	63.62
9	Warren Bardsley	47	77	8	4,171	60.44
10	Jack Badcock	30	47	5	2,473	58.88

* Minimum qualification: 20 innings

Australia's leading inter-state competition, the Sheffield Shield, was inaugurated in 1871–72 when states played for the shield purchased with money donated by the Third Earl of Sheffield. Until 1926–27, when Queensland joined, the Shield was contested by just three states: New South Wales, Victoria, and South Australia.

Top 10 Best bowling averages in the Sheffield Shield and Pura Cup*

	Bowler	Matches	Balls	Maidens	Runs	Wickets	Average
1	Bill O'Reilly	33	10,740	363	3,472	203	17.10
2	Joel Garner#	8	2,419	131	976	55	17.74
3	Geff Noblet	38	11,156	272	3,396	190	17.87
4	Pat Crawford	12	2,517	37	1,104	61	18.09
5	Charlie Turner	14	3,920	202	1,393	73	19.08
6	Clement Hill†	11	2,800	127	693	36	19.25
7	Andrew Newell	12	2,164	123	781	40	19.52
8	Bill Hunt	12	3,156	83	989	48	20.60
9	Tom McKibbin	18	5,726	199	2,855	137	20.83
10	Jack Massie	8	2,282	73	1,108	53	20.90

* Minimum qualification: 2,000 balls bowled

West Indies; all other bowlers Australian

† Not to be confused with Clem Hill

A left-handed batsman and right-handed bowler, Bill O'Reilly, was one of five men to have played Test cricket for Australia both sides of World War II. After his cricketing career was over, O'Reilly wrote for the *Sydney Morning Herald* for 42 years before his retirement in 1988. The Bill O'Reilly Trophy is awarded to the best bowler in the Sheffield Shield each year.

◀ Rachael Heyhoe-Flint's eight-year campaign for women to become MCC members came to fruition in 1999 when she and nine others were accepted.

Top 10 Highest individual scores by West Indian batsmen in Test cricket

	Player	Opponents	Venue	Season	Score
1	Brian Lara	England	St. John's	1993–94	375
2	Gary Sobers	Pakistan	Kingston	1957–58	365*
3	Lawrence Rowe	England	Bridgetown	1973–74	302
4	Viv Richards	England	The Oval	1976	291
5	Brian Lara	Australia	Sydney	1992–93	277
6	George Headley	England	Kingston	1934–35	270*
7	Frank Worrell	England	Nottingham	1950	261
8	Conrad Hunte	Pakistan	Kingston	1957–58	260
9	Seymour Nurse	New Zealand	Christchurch	1968–69	258
10	Rohan Kanhai	India	Calcutta	1958–59	256

* Not out

Brian Lara and Gary Sobers are also first and second on the all-time list of highest individual Test innings. It didn't take Brian Lara long to establish himself on the Test cricket scene. He scored 44 runs in his first Test innings in the Third Test against Pakistan at Lahore in 1990–91. His first Test century was 277 against the Australians in 1992–93 and on the same tour he hit three centuries in five one-day matches. However, his best was to come on home soil in 1993–94 when the West Indies entertained England. Having made 83 in the First Test and 167 in the Third, he saved his best for the Antigua match at St. John's. It was there, on 18 April 1994, that he became a national hero when he surpassed Gary Sobers' 36-year-old record for the highest individual Test innings.

CRICKET

THE ONE-DAY GAME

- Highest individual innings in one-day internationals
- Most appearances in one-day internationals
- Highest totals in one-day internationals
- Most wickets in one-day internationals
- Most wickets in the World Cup
- Most runs in one-day internationals

> If there is a threat to the game of cricket, that threat lies in the First-class arena. One-day cricket, especially day-night cricket, is here to stay.
>
> **Sir Donald Bradman**

Top 10 Highest individual innings in one-day internationals

	Batsman	For-against	Venue	Year	Score
1	Saeed Anwar	Pakistan v India	Chennai	1996–97	194
2 =	Sanath Jayasuriya	Sri Lanka v India	Sharjah	2000–01	189
=	Viv Richards	West Indies v England	Manchester	1984	189*
4	Gary Kirsten	South Africa v United Arab Emirates#	Rawalpindi	1995–96	188*
5	Sachin Tendulkar	India v New Zealand	Hyderabad	1999–00	186*
6	Sourav Ganguly	India v Sri Lanka#	Taunton	1999	183
7	Viv Richards	West Indies v Sri Lanka#	Karachi	1987–88	181
8	Kapil Dev	India v Zimbabwe#	Tunbridge Wells	1983	175*
9	Mark Waugh	Australia v West Indies	Melbourne	2000–01	173
10	Glenn Turner	New Zealand v East Africa#	Birmingham	1975	171*

* Not out

\# World Cup match

Top 10 Most appearances in one-day internationals

	Player	Country	Apps
1	Mohammad Azharuddin	India	334
2	Steve Waugh	Australia	324
3	Wasim Akram	Pakistan	323
4	Sachin Tendulkar	India	284
5	Saleem Malik	Pakistan	283
6	Aravinda de Silva	Sri Lanka	275
7	Allan Border	Australia	273
8	Arjuna Ranatunga	Sri Lanka	269
9	Inzamam-ul-Haq	Pakistan	254
10	Sanath Jayasuriya	Sri Lanka	252

The former Indian captain Mohammad Azharuddin bowed out of the game in shame in December 2000 when he was banned for life following an investigation into match fixing. Prior to that, Azharuddin had distinguished himself as one of the top Indian cricketers of the late-1980s and early-90s, being appointed his country's captain in 1989. He became the first man to play in 300 one-day internationals on 29 October 1999 against Australia at Dhaka.

◀ Sanath Jayasuriya's 189 came off 161 balls and 104 of his runs came from boundaries, as he guided his side to a record 245-run victory.

Top 10 Highest totals in one-day internationals

	Match	Venue	Year	Score
1	Sri Lanka v Kenya	Kandy	1995-96	398-5
2	India v New Zealand	Hyderabad	1999-2000	376-2
3	India v Sri Lanka	Taunton	1999	373-6
4	Pakistan v Sri Lanka	Nairobi	1996-97	371-9
5 =	England v Pakistan	Nottingham	1992	363-7
=	South Africa v Zimbabwe	Bulawayo	2001-02	363-3
7	West Indies v Sri Lanka	Karachi	1987-88	360-4
8	South Africa v Kenya	Cape Town	2001-02	354-3
9	India v Kenya	Paarl	2001-02	351-3
10 =	Australia v New Zealand	Christchurch	1999-2000	349-6
=	New Zealand v India	Rajkot	1999-2000	349-9
=	Sri Lanka v Pakistan	Singapore	1995-96	349-9

Top 10 Most wickets in one-day internationals

	Bowler	Country	Matches	Wickets
1	Wasim Akram	Pakistan	323	446
2	Waqar Younis	Pakistan	223	358
3	Anil Kumble	India	219	288
4	Javagal Srinath	India	202	273
5	Shane Warne	Australia	174	268
6	Muttiah Muralitharan	Sri Lanka	183	267
7	Saqlain Mushtaq	Pakistan	147	262
8	Kapil Dev	India	225	253
9	Allan Donald	South Africa	139	232
10	Courtney Walsh	West Indies	205	227

A left-arm fast bowler, Wasim Akram was the first man to take 400 wickets in both Test matches and one-day internationals. In only his second Test match, he took 10 wickets to indicate what a great new bowling talent had been unearthed by Pakistan. He made his one-day international debut against New Zealand at Faisalabad in 1984–85. His best one-day haul is 5–15.

Top 10 Most wickets in the World Cup

	Player	Country	Matches	Wickets
1	Wasim Akram	Pakistan	32	43
2	Allan Donald	South Africa	22	37
3	Imran Khan	Pakistan	28	34
4	Shane Warne	Australia	17	32
5 =	Ian Botham	England	22	30
=	Chris Harris	New Zealand	22	30
7	Phil DeFreitas	England	22	29
8 =	Kapil Dev	India	26	28
=	Javagal Srinath	India	23	28
10 =	Craig McDermott	Australia	17	27
=	Courtney Walsh	West Indies	17	27
=	Steve Waugh	Australia	33	27

Shane Warne, with 32 wickets from just 17 matches, represents the best average haul amongst the above players. Outstanding performances against South Africa in the semi-finals and Pakistan in the final of the 1999 World Cup earned him back-to-back Man of the Match awards. His wicket haul from those two matches alone was eight (4–29 and 4–33 respectively) and his tally for the tournament that year was 20 at an average of 18.05. His other 12 wickets were taken in the 1996 tournament, including 4–36 against West Indies in the semi-finals.

◀ Despite taking 14 wickets prior to the final of the 1999 World Cup, Wasim Akram of Pakistan could not prevent Australia winning the trophy.

Top 10 Most runs in one-day internationals

	Batsman	Country	Innings	Runs
1	Sachin Tendulkar	India	276	11,039
2	Mohammad Azharuddin	India	308	9,378
3	Desmond Haynes	West Indies	237	8,648
4	Mark Waugh	Australia	234	8,445
5	Aravinda de Silva	Sri Lanka	266	8,430
6	Saeed Anwar	Pakistan	227	8,348
7	Inzamam-ul-Haq	Pakistan	239	8,218
8	Steve Waugh	Australia	286	7,520
9	Arjuna Ranatunga	Sri Lanka	255	7,456
10	Javed Miandad	Pakistan	218	7,381

Born in 1973, Sachin Tendulkar made his one-day international debut at Gujranwala against Pakistan in 1989–90 at the age of 16, facing the bowling of Wasim Akram and Waqar Younis. He also made his Test debut at the same age. Despite his diminutive stature (he is just 5 ft 4 in tall) he has played First-class cricket for Bombay, Yorkshire and his home country, India.

RUGBY

At the Start

According to a legend of dubious origin, rugby started in 1823 at Rugby School in Warwickshire, when William Webb Ellis picked up a football and ran with it. However, various football games played in medieval Britain and Europe allowed handling of the ball, while a type of football similar to today's Australian Rules was played at Rugby almost 100 years before Webb Ellis. The first rules were drawn up in 1848. Scotland, Wales, and Ireland adopted the game in the 1850s, and the first overseas clubs were formed in the ensuing decades. The Rugby Football Union was formed by Edwin Ash in 1871, when the laws of the game were codified, and in 1876 the number of players was reduced from 20 to 15. Rugby League dates from 1895 when 22 northern teams broke away from the RFU to form the Northern Union.

RUGBY

INTERNATIONAL RUGBY UNION

- Most capped internationals
- Most capped English internationals
- Most capped Irish internationals
- Most capped Scottish internationals
- Most capped Welsh internationals
- Most points in an international match by a team
- Most tries in Test matches

Top 10 Most capped internationals*

	Player/country	Career	Caps#
1	Philippe Sella, France	1982–95	111
2	Jason Leonard, England	1990–2002	102(5)
3	David Campese, Australia	1982–96	101
4	Serge Blanco, France	1980–91	93
5	Shaun Fitzpatrick, New Zealand	1987–97	92
6	Rory Underwood, England	1984–96	91(6)
7	Neil Jenkins, Wales	1991–2001	88(4)
8	John Eales, Australia	1991–2001	86
9	Mike Gibson, Ireland	1964–79	81(12)
10 =	Tim Horam, Australia	1989–2000	80
=	Willie John McBride, Ireland	1962–75	80(17)

* As at 8 April 2002

\# Figures in brackets indicate number of appearances for the British Lions

Source: International Rugby Board (IRB)

Top 10 Most capped English internationals*

	Player	Career	Caps
1	Jason Leonard	1990–2002	97
2	Rory Underwood	1984–96	85
3	Will Carling	1988–97	72
4	Rob Andrew	1985–97	71
5	Martin Johnson	1993–2002	67
6	Jeremy Guscott	1989–99	65
7	Brian Moore	1987–95	64
8	Peter Winterbottom	1982–93	58
9	Mike Catt	1994–2002	56
10	Wade Dooley	1985–93	55

* As at 8 April 2002

Source: International Rugby Board (IRB)

Jason Leonard made his England debut in the 25–12 defeat by Argentina in 1990. He played in the second Test and in the next 40 consecutive internationals.

THE SIX NATIONS

In 1884, England, Ireland, Scotland, and Wales contested the very first International Championship. France joined to make it a "Five Nations" tournament in 1910, but the next change did not occur until 2000, when Italy joined to make it the "Six Nations" event.

◄ With 97 caps, England's most capped player, prop forward Jason Leonard.

Top 10 Most capped Irish internationals*

	Player	Career	Caps
1	Mike Gibson	1964–79	69
2	Willie John McBride	1962–75	63
3	Fergus Slattery	1970–84	61
4	Paddy Johns	1990–2000	59
5	Phil Orr	1976–87	58
6	Brendan Mullin	1984–95	55
7 =	Peter Clohessy	1993–2002	54
=	Tom Kiernan	1960–73	54
9	Donal Lenihan	1981–92	52
10	Moss Keane	1974–84	51

* As at 8 April 2002

Source: International Rugby Board (IRB)

In addition to his 63 Ireland appearances, Willie John McBride played a record 17 times for the British Lions. He was also voted Pipesmoker of the Year in 1998!

Top 10 Most capped Scottish internationals*

	Player	Career	Caps
1	Gregor Townsend	1993–2002	66
2	Scott Hastings	1986–97	65
3 =	Gavin Hastings	1986–95	61
=	Dodie Weir	1990–2000	61
5	Craig Chalmers	1989–99	60
6	Kenny Logan	1992–2001	53
7 =	Paul Burnell	1989–99	52
=	Colin Deans	1978–87	52
=	Jim Renwick	1972–84	52
=	Tony Stanger	1989–98	52

* As at 8 April 2002

Source: International Rugby Board (IRB)

Gavin and Scott Hastings both played a major part in Scotland's Grand Slam season in 1990. Gavin captained both his country and the British Lions.

Top 10 Most capped Welsh internationals*

	Player	Career	Caps
1	Neil Jenkins	1991–2001	84
2	Ieuan Evans	1987–98	72
3	Gareth Llewellyn	1989–2001	65
4	Rob Howley	1996–2002	59
5	Garin Jenkins	1991–2000	58
6	Gareth Thomas	1995–2002	57
7	J. P. R. Williams	1969–81	55
8	Robert Jones	1986–95	54
9 =	Gareth Edwards	1967–78	53
=	Scott Gibbs	1991–2001	53

* As at 8 April 2002

Source: International Rugby Board (IRB)

Playing against France on 17 March 2001, Neil Jenkins scored 28 points in Wales' 43–35 victory, becoming the first man to surpass 1,000 points in international rugby.

Top 10 Most points in an international match by a team*

	Country/opponent	Venue	Year	Points scored
1	New Zealand v Japan	Bloemfontein	1995	145
2 =	Japan v Chinese Taipei	Singapore	1998	134
=	England v Romania	Twickenham	2001	134
4	Argentina v Brazil	Sao Paulo	1993	114
5	England v Netherlands	Huddersfield	1998	110
6	Argentina v Brazil	Santiago	1979	109
7	England v United States	Twickenham	1999	106
8	Italy v Czech Republic	Viadana	1994	104
9 =	Argentina v Brazil	Montevideo	1989	103
=	Argentina v Paraguay	Asuncion	1995	103

* As at 8 April 2002

Source: International Rugby Board (IRB)

England's 134–0 demolition of Romania at Twickenham in November 2001 is the biggest winning margin in international rugby. Despite scoring a record 145 points against Japan in 1995, the losers managed to score 17 points to make the winning margin 128 points.

Top 10 Most tries in Test matches*

	Player/country	Tests#	Career	Tries#
1	David Campese, Australia	101	1982–96	64
2	Rory Underwood, England/Lions	91(6)	1984–96	50(1)
3	Jeff Wilson, New Zealand	60	1993–2001	44
4	Christian Cullen, New Zealand	52	1996–2001	42
5	Serge Blanco, France	93	1980–91	38
6	John Kirwan, New Zealand	63	1984–94	35
=	Joost van der Westhuizen, South Africa	75	1993–2002	35
8 =	Ieuan Evans, Wales/Lions	79(7)	1987–98	34(1)
=	Jonah Lomu, New Zealand	52	1994–2002	34
10	Philippe Saint-Andre, France	69	1990–97	32

* As at 8 April 2002

\# Figures in brackets indicate appearances and tries for the British Lions

Source: International Rugby Board (IRB)

On 23 October 1996, David Campese played his 100th international to become the first southern hemisphere player to reach this milestone. He retired from all rugby in 1999.

◄ Will Carling, prolific centre and captain of England a record 59 times.

RUGBY

INDIVIDUAL RUGBY LEAGUE RECORDS

- Appearances in a Rugby League career
- Goalscorers in a Rugby League career
- Try scorers in a Rugby League career
- Goalscorers in a Super League season
- Try scorers in a Super League season

COSTLY MISS

One of sport's most memorable mishaps occurred in the 1968 Rugby League Challenge Cup final at Wembley. Don Fox of Wakefield Trinity had already been crowned "Man of the Match" as the game went into its closing stages. Leeds led 11–10 when Fox had the simplest of kicks in front of the posts to win the Cup. He toe-poked it, and the ball shot wide.

Top 10 Appearances in a Rugby League career

	Player	Club(s)	Years	Apps*
1	Jim Sullivan	Wigan	1921–46	928
2	Gus Risman	Salford, Workington Town, Batley	1929–54	873
3	Neil Fox	Wakefield Trinity, Bradford Northern, Hull K.R., York, Bramley, Huddersfield	1956–79	828 (28)
4	Jeff Grayson	Dewsbury, Bradford Northern, Leeds, Featherstone Rovers, Batley	1969–95	776 (57)
5	Graham Idle	Bramley, Wakefield Trinity, Bradford Northern, Hunslet, Rochdale Hornets, Sheffield Eagles, Doncaster, Nottingham, Sheffield Eagles, Doncaster, Nottingham City, Highfield	1969–93	740 (46)
6	Colin Dixon	Halifax, Salford, Hull K.R.	1961–81	738 (25)
7	Paul Charlton	Workington Town, Salford, Blackpool Borough	1961–81	727 (9)
8	Keith Mumby	Bradford Northern, Sheffield Eagles, Keighley, Ryedale-York, Wakefield Trinity	1973–95	695 (26)
9	Ernie Ashcroft	Wigan, Huddersfield, Warrington	1942–62	691 (1)
10	Brian Bevan	Warrington, Blackpool Borough	1945–64	688

* Figures in brackets indicate appearances as substitute

Jim Sullivan, the son of a Cardiff butcher, moved to Wigan as a 17-year-old in June 1921 and stayed for 31 years as a player and then coach.

Top 10 Goalscorers in a Rugby League career

	Player	Club(s)	Years	Goals*
1	Jim Sullivan	Wigan	1921–46	2,867
2	Neil Fox	Wakefield Trinity, Bradford Northern, Hull K.R., York, Bramley, Huddersfield	1956–79	2,575
3	Cyril Kellett	Hull K.R., Featherstone Rovers	1956–74	1,768
4	Kel Coslett	St. Helens, Rochdale Hornets	1962–79	1,698
5	Gus Risman	Salford, Workington Town, Batley	1929–54	1,677
6	John Woods	Leigh, Bradford Northern, Warrington, Rochdale Hornets	1976–92	1,591
7	Steve Quinn	York, Featherstone Rovers	1970–88	1,578
8	Jim Ledgard	Leeds, Dewsbury, Leigh	1944–61	1,560
9	Lewis Jones	Leeds	1952–64	1,478
10	Mike Fletcher	Hull K.R., Hunslet Hawks	1985–2000	1,406

* Including drop goals

Before he moved North to join Wigan, Jim Sullivan, one of the game's greatest players, had set his sights on a career in golf and had also represented Wales at baseball. However, he was persuaded by the Wigan directors that his future lay in Rugby League – and they were right! Having already played Union for Cardiff, he also turned his back on an international career in the 15-a-side game.

◀ In the Ashes Series first Test, Great Britain's Andy Farrell breaks through the tackle of Australia's Brad Fittler.

Top 10 Try scorers in a Rugby League career

	Player	Club(s)	Years	Tries
1	Brian Bevan	Warrington, Blackpool Borough	1945–64	796
2	Billy Boston	Wigan, Blackpool Borough	1953–70	571
3	Martin Offiah	Widnes, Wigan, London Broncos, Salford City Reds	1987–2001	481
4	Alf Ellaby	St. Helens, Wigan	1926–39	446
5	Eric Batten	Wakefield Trinity, Hunslet, Bradford Northern, Featherstone Rovers	1933–54	443
6	Lionel Cooper	Huddersfield	1947–55	441
7	Ellery Hanley	Bradford Northern, Wigan, Leeds	1978–95	428
8	Johnny Ring	Wigan, Rochdale Hornets	1922–33	415
9	Clive Sullivan	Hull, Hull K.R., Oldham, Doncaster	1961–85	406
10	John Atkinson	Leeds, Carlisle	1966–83	401

Brian Bevan arrived on British shores in 1945 while serving with the Australian Navy. He wrote to Leeds asking for a trial. They gave him one but were not impressed, so he joined Warrington instead, where he stayed 17 years – a costly error by Leeds. He ended his career at the age of 39 on 22 February 1964, with Blackpool Borough.

Top 10 Goalscorers in a Super League season

	Player/club	Season	Goals
1	Henry Paul, Bradford Bulls	2001	168
2	Andrew Farrell, Wigan Warriors	2001	164
3	Andrew Farrell, Wigan Warriors	2000	151
4	Henry Paul, Bradford Bulls	2000	142
5	Sean Long, St. Helens	2000	136
6	Iestyn Harris, Leeds Rhinos	1999	129
7	Bobbie Goulding, St. Helens	1996	120
8	Andrew Farrell, Wigan Warriors	1998	115
9	Andrew Farrell, Wigan Warriors	1997	109
10	Ian Herron, Gateshead Thunder	1999	105

Bobbie Goulding (1996), Andy Farrell (1998), Sean Long (2000), and Henry Paul (2001) all played for the Super League champions in the same season. Loose-forward Andy Farrell joined Wigan from local amateur side Orrell St. James as a 16-year-old in 1991, and has gone on to captain his club and country. One of the game's great players, he has won the Man of Steel and Harry Sunderland trophies, and is currently fifth on the all-time Wigan points-scoring list.

Top 10 Try scorers in a Super League season

	Player/club	Season	Tries
1	Paul Newlove, St. Helens	1996	28
2	Kris Radlinski, Wigan Warriors	2001	27
3 =	Matt Daylight, Gateshead Thunder	1999	25
=	Toa Kohe-Love, Warrington Wolves	1999	25
5 =	Jason Robinson, Wigan	1996	24
=	Anthony Sullivan, St. Helens	1999	24
7 =	Francis Cummins, Leeds Rhinos	1999	23
=	Greg Fleming, London Broncos	1999	23
9 =	Tonie Carroll, Leeds Rhinos	2001	22
=	Tevita Vaikona, Bradford Bulls	2001	22
=	Michael Withers, Bradford Bulls	2001	22

◀ Iestyn Harris (right) of Leeds tries to avoid the tackle of Bradford's David Boyle in the 2000 Challenge Cup final, which the Bulls won 24–18.

AMERICAN SPORTS

At the Start

It is probable that baseball derived from medieval European ball games, and the game of "base-ball" is even mentioned in Jane Austen's *Northanger Abbey*, which she wrote almost 50 years before the game was first played in the United States. American football began in the early 19th century as a college game with close affinities to British rugby, while ice hockey, played informally in Europe in the 17th century, acquired its first rules in Montreal, Canada, in the 1870s. The origin of the game of basketball can be unusually precisely stated: Dr. James Naismith invented it at the International YMCA College at Springfield, Massachusetts, in December 1891 – although it may have been influenced by ball and hoop games played by Aztec and other Central and South American peoples.

- Largest-winning margins in the Super Bowl

- Most points in NFL history

- Most Super Bowl appearances

- Most AFL-AFC Championships

- Most NFL-NFC Championships

AMERICAN FOOTBALL – TEAM RECORDS

Top 10 Largest-winning margins in the Super Bowl

	Winners	Runners-up	Year	Score	Margin
1	San Francisco 49ers	Denver Broncos	1990	55–10	45
2	Chicago Bears	New England Patriots	1986	46–10	36
3	Dallas Cowboys	Buffalo Bills	1993	52–17	35
4	Washington Redskins	Denver Broncos	1988	42–10	32
5	Los Angeles Raiders	Washington Redskins	1984	38–9	29
6	Baltimore Ravens	New York Giants	2001	34–7	27
7	Green Bay Packers	Kansas City Chiefs	1967	35–10	25
8	San Francisco 49ers	San Diego Chargers	1995	49–26	23
9	San Francisco 49ers	Miami Dolphins	1985	38–16	22
10	Dallas Cowboys	Miami Dolphins	1972	24–3	21

Source: National Football League

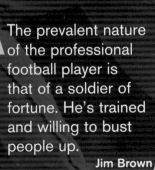

"The prevalent nature of the professional football player is that of a soldier of fortune. He's trained and willing to bust people up.

Jim Brown "

◄ The Green Bay Packers discussing tactics.
The Green Bay Packers have won more NFL-NFC
Championships than any other team.

The 10 Most points in NFL history*

	Team	Points
1	Green Bay Packers	19,725
2	Chicago Bears	19,512
3	Washington Redskins	19,414
4	St. Louis Rams	18,554
5	New York Giants	18,443
6	Detroit Lions	18,316
7	San Francisco 49ers	17,934
8	Philadelphia Eagles	17,804
9	Pittsburgh Steelers	17,681
10	Arizona Cardinals	16,764

* In a regular season, from 1933–2001

Top 10 Most Super Bowl appearances

	Team	Wins	Losses	Apps
1	Dallas Cowboys	5	3	8
2	Denver Broncos	2	4	6
3 =	Miami Dolphins	2	3	5
=	Pittsburgh Steelers	4	1	5
=	San Francisco 49ers	5	0	5
=	Washington Redskins	3	2	5
7 =	Buffalo Bills	0	4	4
=	Green Bay Packers	3	1	4
=	Minnesota Vikings	0	4	4
=	Oakland/Los Angeles Raiders	3	1	4

Top 10 Most AFL-AFC Championships*

	Team	Years	Titles
1 =	Buffalo Bills	1964–92	6
=	Denver Broncos	1977–98	6
3 =	Miami Dolphins	1971–84	5
=	Pittsburgh Steelers	1974–95	5
5	Los Angeles/Oakland Raiders	1967–83	4
6 =	Dallas Texans/Kansas City Chiefs	1962–69	3
=	Houston Oilers#	1960–61	3
=	New England Patriots	1985–2001	3
9 =	Cincinnati Bengals	1981–88	2
=	San Diego Chargers	1963–94	2

* 1960–69 for the AFL Championship and since 1970 for the AFC Championship following the merger of the NFL and the AFL at the end of the 1969 season

\# Now the Tennessee Titans

Top 10 Most NFL-NFC Championships*

	Team	Years	Titles
1	Green Bay Packers	1936–97	10
2	Dallas Cowboys	1970–95	8
3 =	Chicago Bears	1933–85	7
=	Washington Redskins	1937–91	7
5	New York Giants	1934–2000	6
6 =	Cleveland/Los Angeles/St. Louis Rams	1946–2001	5
=	San Francisco 49ers	1981–94	5
8 =	Cleveland Browns	1950–64	4
=	Detroit Lions	1935–57	4
=	Minnesota Vikings	1969–76	4
=	Philadelphia Eagles	1948–80	4

* 1933–69 for the NFL Championship and since 1970 for the NFC Championship following the merger of the NFL and the AFL at the end of the 1969 season

The New York Giants have appeared in a record 17 NFL–NFC Championship games.

◄ Dallas Cowboys' running-back Emmitt Smith,
who headed the NFC rushing list four times in
five years, from 1991–95.

AMERICAN FOOTBALL – INDIVIDUAL RECORDS

- ● Most points in a Super Bowl career
- ● Most points in a single NFL game
- ● Most touchdowns in a season
- ● Most points in a season
- ● Most points in a career

HOW DID IT BEGIN?

American Football began on 6 November 1869 with a match between Rutgers and Princeton at New Brunswick. Both teams were pioneering their own versions of "American Football" rules, which were adaptations of the London Football Association rules of soccer. Rutgers won that historic first match 6–4.

Top 10 Most points in a Super Bowl career

	Player/team	Games	Touchdowns	Field goals	PAT*	Points
1	Jerry Rice, San Francisco 49ers	3	7	0	0	42
2	Emmitt Smith, Dallas Cowboys	3	5	0	0	30
3 =	Roger Craig, San Francisco 49ers	3	4	0	0	24
=	John Elway, Denver Broncos	5	4	0	0	24
=	Franco Harris, Pittsburgh Steelers	4	4	0	0	24
=	Thurman Thomas, Buffalo Bills	4	4	0	0	24
7	Ray Wersching, San Francisco 49ers	2	0	5	7	22
8	Don Chandler, Green Bay Packers	2	0	4	8	20
9 =	Cliff Branch, Los Angeles Raiders	3	3	0	0	18
=	Terrell Davis, Denver Broncos	2	3	0	0	18
=	Antonio Freeman, Green Bay Packers	2	3	0	0	18
=	John Stallworth, Pittsburgh Steelers	4	3	0	0	18
=	Lynn Swann, Pittsburgh Steelers	4	3	0	0	18
=	Ricky Watters, San Francisco 49ers	1	3	0	0	18

* Point after touchdown

This list also represents all the players who have scored three or more touchdowns in a Super Bowl career.

Top 10 Most points in a single NFL game

	Player	Match	Date	Points
1	Ernie Nevers	Chicago Cardinals v Chicago Bears	28 Nov 1929	40
2 =	Dub Jones	Cleveland Browns v Chicago Bears	25 Nov 1951	36
=	Gale Sayers	Chicago Bears v San Francisco 49ers	12 Dec 1965	36
4	Paul Hornung	Green Bay Packers v Baltimore Colts	10 Aug 1961	33
5 =	Jim Brown	Cleveland Browns v Baltimore Colts	1 Nov 1959	30
=	Billy Cannon	Houston Oilers v New York Titans	12 Oct 1961	30
=	Cookie Gilchrist	Buffalo Bills v New York Jets	12 Aug 1963	30
=	Abner Haynes	Dallas Texans v Oakland Raiders	26 Nov 1961	30
=	Jerry Rice	San Francisco 49ers v Atlanta Falcons	14 Oct 1990	30
=	Bob Shaw	Chicago Cards v Baltimore Colts	11 Jan 1959	30
=	James Stewart	Jacksonville Jaguars v Philadelphia Eagles	12 Oct 1997	30
=	Kellen Winslow	San Diego Chargers v Oakland Raiders	22 Nov 1981	30

Ernie Nevers' record-breaking achievement was accomplished at Comiskey Park in the annual Thanksgiving Day match between the Cardinals and the Bears. He scored all 40 of his team's points in a 40–6 win. Nevers was only brought out of retirement by the Cardinals' new owner Dr. David Jones midway through the 1929 season. Nevers also played Major League Baseball with the St. Louis Browns for three years.

◀ In 1998, Minnesota Vikings' kicker Gary Anderson became the first player in 15 years to score 150 points in a season in the NFL.

Top 10 Most touchdowns in a season

	Player/team	Season	Touchdowns
1	Marshall Faulk, St. Louis Rams	2000	26
2	Emmitt Smith, Dallas Cowboys	1995	25
3	John Riggins, Washington Redskins	1983	24
4 =	Terrell Davis, Denver Broncos	1998	23
=	Jerry Rice, San Francisco 49ers	1987	23
=	O. J. Simpson, Buffalo Bills	1975	23
7 =	Chuck Foreman, Minnesota Vikings	1975	22
=	Gale Sayers, Chicago Bears	1966	22
=	Emmitt Smith, Dallas Cowboys	1994	22
10 =	Terry Allen, Washington Redskins	1996	21
=	Jim Brown, Cleveland Browns	1965	21
=	Marshall Faulk, St. Louis Rams	2001	21
=	Joe Morris, New York Giants	1985	21

Top 10 Most points in a season

	Player/team	Season	Points
1	Paul Hornung, Green Bay Packers	1960	176
2	Gary Anderson, Minnnesota Vikings	1998	164
3	Mark Moseley, Washington Redskins	1983	161
4	Marshall Faulk, St. Louis Rams	2000	160
5	Gino Cappelletti, Boston Patriots	1964	155
6	Emmitt Smith, Dallas Cowboys	1995	150
7	Chip Lohmiller, Washington Redskins	1991	149
8	Gino Cappen, Green Bay Packers	1961	146
9 =	John Kasay, Carolina Panthers	1996	145
=	Jim Turner, New York Jets	1968	145
=	Mike Vanderjagt, Indianapolis Colts	1999	145

Top 10 Most points in a career

	Player	Points
1	Gary Anderson*	2,133
2	Morten Andersen*	2,036
3	George Blanda	2,002
4	Norm Johnson	1,736
5	Nick Lowery	1,711
6	Jan Stenerud	1,699
7	Eddie Murray	1,594
8	Al Del Greco	1,584
9	Pat Leahy	1,470
10	Jim Turner	1,439

* Active during 2001 season

▶ After 16 successful seasons with the 49ers, Super Bowl hero Jerry Rice moved to the Oakland Raiders for the 2001 season.

BASEBALL

- Biggest single game wins in the World Series
- Players with the most MLB career strikeouts
- Players with the most home runs in an MLB career
- Most World Series wins
- Most appearances in the World Series
- Largest Major League ballparks

> Ruth must have admired records because he created so many of them.
>
> **Red Smith,** sportswriter on Babe Ruth

Top 10 Biggest single game wins in the World Series

	Teams (winners first)/game	Date	Score
1	New York Yankees v New York Giants (Game 2)	2 Oct 1936	18–4
2 =	Arizona Diamondbacks v New York Yankees (Game 6)	3 Nov 2001	15–2
=	New York Yankees v Pittsburgh Pirates (Game 2)	6 Oct 1960	16–3
4 =	Detroit Tigers v St. Louis Cardinals (Game 6)	9 Oct 1968	13–1
=	New York Yankees v Milwaukee Brewers (Game 6)	19 Oct 1982	13–1
=	New York Yankees v New York Giants (Game 5)	9 Oct 1951	13–1
=	New York Yankees v Pittsburgh Pirates (Game 6)	12 Oct 1960	12–0
8 =	Atlanta Braves v New York Yankees (Game 1)	20 Oct 1996	12–1
=	Chicago White Sox v Los Angeles Dodgers (Game 1)	1 Oct 1959	11–0
=	Kansas City Royals v St. Louis Cardinals (Game 7)	27 Oct 1985	11–0
=	New York Yankees v Philadelphia Athletics (Game 6)	26 Oct 1911	13–2
=	St. Louis Cardinals v Detroit Tigers (Game 7)	9 Oct 1934	11–0

Source: Major League Baseball

Top 10 Players with the most MLB career strikeouts

	Pitcher	Strikeouts
1	Nolan Ryan	5,714
2	Steve Carlton	4,136
3	Roger Clemens*	3,717
4	Bert Blyleven	3,701
5	Tom Seaver	3,640
6	Don Sutton	3,574
7	Gaylord Perry	3,534
8	Walter Johnson	3,508
9	Randy Johnson*	3,412
10	Phil Niekro	3,342

* Active in 2001
Source: Major League Baseball

Nolan Ryan was known as the "Babe Ruth of strikeout pitchers", pitching faster (a record 101 mph/162.5 km/h) and longer (27 seasons – 1966 and 1968–93) than any previous player. As well as his 5,714 strikeouts, including 383 in one season, he walked 2,795 batters and allowed the fewest hits (6.55) per nine innings.

Top 10 Players with the most home runs in an MLB career

	Player	Home runs
1	Hank Aaron	755
2	Babe Ruth	714
3	Willie Mays	660
4	Frank Robinson	586
5	Mark McGwire*	583
6	Harmon Killebrew	573
7	Barry Bonds*	567
8	Reggie Jackson	563
9	Mike Schmidt	548
10	Mickey Mantle	536

* Active in 2001
Source: Major League Baseball

George Herman "Babe" Ruth set a home run record in 1919 by hitting 29, breaking it the next season by hitting 54. His career (1914–35) total of 714 came from 8,399 "at bats", which represents an average of 8.5 per cent – considerably better than the next man in the averages, Harmon Killebrew, who averages at 7.0 per cent.

Top 10 Most World Series wins

	Team	Total wins
1	New York Yankees	26
2 =	Philadelphia/Oakland Athletics	9
=	St. Louis Cardinals	9
4	Brooklyn/Los Angeles Dodgers	6
5 =	Boston Red Sox	5
=	Cincinnati Reds	5
=	New York Giants	5
=	Pittsburgh Pirates	5
9	Detroit Tigers	4
10 =	Baltimore Orioles	3
=	Boston/Milwaukee/Atlanta Braves	3
=	Washington Senators/Minnesota Twins	3

The World Series was first contested in 1903 when Pittsburgh, the champions of the National League, invited Boston Red Sox, the champions of the newer American League, to play them to decide the world champions. The Red Sox won the best-of-nine series 5–3.

Top 10 Most appearances in the World Series

	Teams wins	Wins	Losses	Apps
1	New York Yankees	26	12	38
2	Brooklyn/Los Angeles Dodgers	6	12	18
3	New York/San Francisco Giants	5	11	16
4	St. Louis Cardinals	9	6	15
5	Philadelphia/Kansas City/Oakland Athletics	9	5	14
6	Chicago Cubs	2	8	10
7 =	Boston/Milwaukee/Atlanta Braves	3	6	9
=	Boston Red Sox	5	4	9
=	Cincinnati Reds	5	4	9
=	Detroit Tigers	4	5	9

The Toronto Blue Jays is the only team to have appeared in two World Series and not lost, whilst the San Diego Padres is the only team to have appeared in two Series and not won. The Yankees appeared in 15 of the 18 World Series held between 1947 and 1964, winning 10 and losing five. That streak included a record five straight wins 1949–53.

◀ Luke Prokopec (No. 57) in action for the Los Angeles Dodgers of the National League at the Dodgers Stadium against the Texas Rangers of the American League during the 2001 season.

Top 10 Largest Major League ballparks*

	Stadium	Home team	Capacity
1	Qualcomm Stadium	San Diego Padres	66,307
2	Veterans Stadium	Philadelphia Phillies	62,418
3	Yankee Stadium	New York Yankees	57,746
4	Shea Stadium	New York Mets	56,516
5	Dodger Stadium	Los Angeles Dodgers	56,000
6	SkyDome	Toronto Blue Jays	50,516
7	Coors Field	Colorado Rockies	50,449
8	Turner Field	Atlanta Braves	50,062
9	Busch Stadium	St. Louis Cardinals	49,738
10	The Ballpark in Arlington	Texas Rangers	49,115

* By capacity
Source: Major League Baseball

Stadium capacities vary constantly, some being adjusted according to the event: Veterans Stadium, for example, holds fewer for baseball games (62,418) than for football matches (65,356). The Colorado Rockies formerly played at the Mile High Stadium, Denver, Colorado, which holds 76,125, but now play at Coors Field, which has a capacity of only 50,449.

AMERICAN SPORTS

ICE HOCKEY

- Most Benson & Hedges Cup wins
- Most British Championships
- Most goals in an NHL career
- Goaltenders in an NHL career
- Point scorers in an NHL career
- Medal-winning countries at the men's World Championships
- Most Stanley Cup wins

> Some people skate to the puck. I skate to where the puck is going to be.
>
> **Wayne Gretzky**

Top 10 Most Benson & Hedges Cup wins

	Team	Wins
1	Murrayfield Racers	9
2	Nottingham Panthers	6
3 =	Brighton Tigers	4
=	Durham Wasps	4
=	Fife Flyers	4
=	Harringay Racers	4
7	Streatham	3
8	Sheffield Steelers	2
9 =	Ayr Scottish Eagles	1
=	Cardiff Devils	1
=	Dundee Rockets	1
=	Manchester Storm	1
=	Paisley Mohawks	1
=	Wembley Lions	1
=	Wembley Monarchs	1
=	Whitley Warriors	1

The Benson & Hedges Cup was inaugurated in the 1946–47 season as the English Autumn Cup, but became the British Autumn Cup in 1954. From 1983, it has been a sponsored event; the current sponsors took over in 1992.

Top 10 Most British Championships

	Team	Wins
1	Murrayfield Racers	7
2 =	Cardiff Devils	4
=	Durham Wasps	4
=	Sheffield Steelers	4
5	Dundee Rockets	3
6	Whitley Warriors	2
7 =	Ayr Scottish Eagles	1
=	Brighton Tigers	1
=	Fife Flyers	1
=	Glasgow Dynamos	1
=	London Knights	1
=	London Lions	1
=	Nottingham Panthers	1
=	Paisley Mohawks	1

The British Championships were first held in 1930, and then at occasional intervals until 1966, when it became an annual event.

Top 10 Most goals in an NHL career

	Player	Years	Games	Goals
1	Wayne Gretzky	20	1,487	894
2	Gordie Howe	26	1,767	801
3	Marcel Dionne	18	1,348	731
4	Phil Esposito	18	1,282	717
5	Mark Gartner	19	1,432	708
6	Mark Messier*	22	1,561	651
7	Brett Hull*	16	1,019	649
8	Mario Lemieux*	13	788	648
9	Steve Yzerman*	18	1,310	645
10	Bobby Hull	16	1,063	610

* Active during 2000–01 season

Gordie Howe, who holds the record for the most games and seasons played in the NHL, retired in 1971 but returned to play alongside his sons Mark and Marty for Houston in the newly formed World Hockey Association.

Top 10 Goaltenders in an NHL career

	Player	Years	Games	Wins
1	Patrick Roy*	17	903	484
2	Terry Sawchuk	21	971	447
3	Jacques Plante	18	837	434
4	Tony Esposito	16	886	423
5	Glenn Hall	18	906	407
6	Grant Fuhr	19	868	403
7	Mike Vernon*	18	763	383
8 =	Andy Moog	18	713	372
=	John Vanbiesbrouck*	19	877	372
10	Rogie Vachon	16	795	355

* Active during 2000–01 season

The first of Patrick Roy's 484 career wins was in the 1985 season when he came on for one period for the Montreal Canadiens against Winnipeg Jets. He faced just two shots but got a credit for the win.

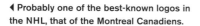
◀ Probably one of the best-known logos in the NHL, that of the Montreal Canadiens.

Top 10 Point scorers in an NHL career

	Player	Years	Games	Goals	Assists	Points
1	Wayne Gretzky	20	1,487	894	1,963	2,857
2	Gordie Howe	26	1,767	801	1,049	1,850
3	Mark Messier*	22	1,561	651	1,130	1,781
4	Marcel Dionne	18	1,348	731	1,040	1,771
5	Ron Francis*	20	1,489	487	1,137	1,624
6	Steve Yzerman*	18	1,310	645	969	1,614
7	Phil Esposito	18	1,282	717	873	1,590
8	Ray Bourque*	22	1,612	410	1,169	1,579
9	Mario Lemieux*	13	788	648	922	1,570
10	Paul Coffey*	21	1,409	396	1,135	1,531

* Active during 2001 season

◀ When people talk of ice hockey records the name of one man crops up time and time again – Wayne Gretzky of the Los Angeles Kings – the game's greatest player.

Top 10 Medal-winning countries at the men's World Championships

	Country	Gold	Silver	Bronze	Total
1	Czechoslovakia/Czech Republic	10	12	19	41
2	Canada	21	10	9	40
3	Sweden	7	16	13	36
4	USSR/Russia	23	7	5	35
5	USA	2	9	4	15
6	Switzerland	0	1	8	9
7	Finland	1	5	1	7
8	UK	1	2	2	5
9	Germany	0	2	2	4
10	Austria	0	0	2	2

The World Championship for men has been contested since 1930, although the Olympic Champions of 1920, 1924, and 1928 were also deemed to be World Champions. Between 1932 and 1968, the Olympic Champions were also declared World Champions and in the Olympic years of 1972, 1976, and 1992 the International Ice Hockey Federation (IIHF) ran its own World Championships, but there were no championships in the Olympic years of 1980, 1984, and 1988. The only other country to have won a medal is Slovakia, with one bronze.

Top 10 Most Stanley Cup wins

	Team	Years	Wins
1	Montreal Canadiens	1916–93	24
2	Toronto Maple Leafs	1918–67	13
3	Detroit Red Wings	1936–98	9
4 =	Boston Bruins	1929–72	5
=	Edmonton Oilers	1984–90	5
6 =	Montreal Victorias	1895–98	4
=	Montreal Wanderers	1906–10	4
=	New York Islanders	1980–83	4
=	New York Rangers	1933–94	4
=	Ottawa Senators	1920–27	4

The Stanley Cup was originally a challenge trophy whereby any amateur team in Canada could challenge for the trophy over a single match. This was later changed to a best-of-three series. Following the formation of the professional National Hockey Association in 1910–11, the trophy was presented to their first champions, but challenges were still eligible to be made from any other team. Following the formation of a new league, the Pacific Coast Hockey Association (PCHA) in 1912–13, there began the first end-of-season series of games between the champions of the respective leagues.

MOTOR SPORTS

At the Start

In 1878, a 33-hour contest between two steam wagons over the 323 kilometres (201 miles) from Green Bay to Madison, Wisconsin, USA, marks the world's first motor race. Sixteen years later, in 1894, 25 cars competed in a race from Paris to Rouen, with the Comte de Dion as victor. In the United States the following year, Frank Duryea won the 87-km (54-mile) round-trip race between Chicago and Evanston, Illinois with an average speed of 12km/h (7.5mph). Road races were progressively replaced by those on tracks, the first of which took place on a harness racetrack in Cranston, Rhode Island, in 1896. The first Grand Prix was the French Grand Prix, which was held in 1906.

NASCAR, CART & INDY 500 RECORDS

- Most wins in a NASCAR season
- NASCAR career money winners
- CART career money winners
- Drivers with the most wins in CART races 1909–2001
- Fastest winning speeds of the Indianapolis 500
- Drivers with the most wins in the Indianapolis 500

A. J. FOYT

A. J. Foyt is the only man in history to win the big four auto races: 12 Hours of Sebring, Indianapolis 500, Daytona 500, and the Le Mans 24 Hours. He completed a record 12,272.5 miles in his 35 Indianapolis 500 races during his career, a race which earned him $2,640,576. His last Indy 500 was in 1992.

Top 10 Most wins in a NASCAR season

	Driver*	Season	Wins
1	Richard Petty	1967	27
2	Richard Petty	1971	21
3 =	Tim Flock	1955	18
=	Richard Petty	1970	18
5	Bobby Isaac	1969	17
6 =	David Pearson	1968	16
=	Richard Petty	1968	16
8 =	Ned Jarrett	1964	15
=	David Pearson	1966	15
10 =	Buck Baker	1956	14
=	Richard Petty	1963	14

* All USA

Source: NASCAR

All these wins were in the Grand National Series. The best total since the launch of the Winston Cup Series in 1972 is 13 by Richard Petty in 1975 and Jeff Gordon in 1998.

Top 10 NASCAR career money winners*

	Driver	Career winnings ($)
1	Jeff Gordon	45,748,580
2	Dale Earnhardt	41,742,384
3	Dale Jarrett	33,274,832
4	Rusty Wallace	29,657,719
5	Mark Martin	29,165,332
6	Bill Elliott	27,306,174
7	Terry Labonte	26,536,692
8	Bobby Labonte	25,953,024
9	Ricky Rudd	24,530,223
10	Jeff Burton	22,958,499

* To end of 2001 season

Source: NASCAR

All drivers are from the USA and were active in 2001. Dale Earnhardt sadly lost his life in a tragic accident during the 2001 Daytona 500.

Top 10 CART career money winners*

	Driver#	Career winnings ($)
1	Al Unser Jr.	18,828,406
2	Michael Andretti	17,409,368
3	Bobby Rahal	16,344,008
4	Emerson Fittipaldi, Brazil	14,293,625
5	Mario Andretti	11,552,154
6	Rick Mears	11,050,807
7	Jimmy Vasser	10,124,994
8	Danny Sullivan	8,884,126
9	Paul Tracy, Canada	8,331,520
10	Arie Luyendyk, Netherlands	7,732,188

* As at 31 December 2001

All USA unless otherwise stated

Source: Championship Auto Racing Teams

Michael Andretti is the only current driver on this list. He, like Unser, comes from a famous racing family – his father Mario was not only a successful CART driver but was, in 1978, only the second driver from the USA to win the Formula One world title. Michael's 15-year-old son Marco, currently enjoying a Karting career, looks set to follow in the footsteps of his famous father and grandfather.

Top 10 Drivers with the most wins in CART races 1909–2001*

	Driver	Career	Wins
1	A. J. Foyt	1960–81	67
2	Mario Andretti	1965–93	52
3	Michael Andretti	1986–2001	41
4	Al Unser	1965–87	39
5	Bobby Unser	1966–81	35
6	Al Unser Jr.	1984–95	31
7	Rick Mears	1978–91	29
8	Johnny Rutherford	1965–86	27
9	Rodger Ward	1953–66	26
10	Gordon Johncock	1965–83	25

* Since the start of the AAA (American Automobile Association) series in 1909, later the USAC (United States Auto Club) series, and, since 1979, the CART (Championship Auto Racing Teams) Series

Source: Championship Auto Racing Teams

The Unser family dominate the CART scene: Al and Bobby are brothers, while Al's son, Al Jr., also makes a showing here and as all-time money winner. In 1998, after pursuing other auto sports, Bobby's son Robby also entered Indy car racing. Michael Andretti, who started his CART career in 1983, is the only current driver in this list.

> A gigantic, grimy lawn party, a monstrous holiday compounded of dust and danger and noise, the world's biggest carnival.
>
> **Red Smith**, sportswriter, on the Indianapolis 500

Top 10 Fastest winning speeds of the Indianapolis 500

	Driver/country*	Car	Year	Speed (km/h)	Speed (mph)
1	Arie Luyendyk, Netherlands	Lola-Chevrolet	1990	299.307	185.981
2	Rick Mears	Chevrolet-Lumina	1991	283.980	176.457
3	Bobby Rahal	March-Cosworth	1986	274.750	170.722
4	Juan Montoya, Colombia	G Force-Aurora	2000	269.730	167.607
5	Emerson Fittipaldi, Brazil	Penske-Chevrolet	1989	269.695	167.581
6	Rick Mears	March-Cosworth	1984	263.308	163.612
7	Mark Donohue	McLaren-Offenhauser	1972	262.619	162.962
8	Al Unser	March-Cosworth	1987	260.995	162.175
9	Tom Sneva	March-Cosworth	1983	260.902	162.117
10	Gordon Johncock	Wildcat-Cosworth	1982	260.760	162.029

* All USA unless otherwise stated

Source: Indianapolis Motor Speedway

The first Indianapolis 500, known affectionately as the "Indy", was held on Memorial Day, 30 May 1911, and was won by Ray Harroun, driving a bright yellow 447-cubic inch six-cylinder Marmon Wasp at an average speed of 74.59 mph (120.04 km/h). The race takes place over 200 laps of the 2.5-mile (4-km) Indianapolis Raceway, which was owned by First World War flying ace Eddie Rickenbacker from 1927 to 1945. Over the years, the speed has steadily increased: Harroun's race took 6 hours 42 minutes 6 seconds to complete, while Arie Luyendyk's record-breaking win was achieved in just 2 hours 18 minutes 18.248 seconds. He also holds the track record of 237.498 mph (382.20 km/h) set in 1996.

Top 10 Drivers with the most wins in the Indianapolis 500

	Driver*	Years	Wins
1 =	A. J. Foyt	1961, 1964, 1967, 1977	4
=	Rick Mears	1979, 1984, 1988, 1991	4
=	Al Unser	1970–71, 1978, 1987	4
4	Louie Meyer	1928, 1933, 1936	3
=	Mauri Rose	1941, 1947–48	3
=	Johnny Rutherford	1974, 1976, 1980	3
=	Wilbur Shaw	1937, 1939–40	3
=	Bobby Unser	1968, 1975, 1981	3
9 =	Emerson Fittipaldi, Brazil	1989, 1993	2
=	Gordon Johncock	1973, 1982	2
=	Arie Luyendyk, Netherlands	1990, 1997	2
=	Tommy Milton	1921, 1923	2
=	Al Unser Jr.	1992, 1994	2
=	Bill Vukovich	1953–54	2
=	Rodger Ward	1959, 1962	2

* All USA unless otherwise stated

Source: Indianapolis Motor Speedway

▼ Richard Petty, seven-time winner of the Winston Cup series, a record he holds with the late Dale Earnhardt.

CIRCUITS & RACES

- Countries with the most Formula One circuits

- Countries to host the most Grand Prix races

- Countries with the most Grand Prix wins

- First Formula One World Championship races

- Longest current Formula One circuits

Top 10 Countries with the most Formula One circuits*

	Country	Circuits	Total
1	USA	Indianapolis Motor Speedway, Sebring International Raceway, Riverside, Watkins Glen International, Long Beach/USA West, Caesars Palace, Detroit, Fair Park, Phoenix	9
2	France	Reims, Rouen Les Essarts-Ferrand, Le Mans (Bugatti), Paul Ricard, Dijon-Prenois, Nevers-Magny Cours	7
3	Spain	Pedralbes, Járama, Montjuich, Jeréz, Catalunya (Montmelo)	5
4	UK	Silverstone, Aintree, Brands Hatch, Donington Park	4
5 =	Austria	Zeltweg, Osterreichring, A1-Ring	3
=	Belgium	Spa-Francorchamps, Nivelles, Zolder	3
=	Canada	Mosport, Mont-Tremblant, Gilles Villeneuve	3
=	Germany	Nürburgring, Avus, Hockenheimring	3
=	Italy	Monza, Pescara, Imola	3
=	Japan	Fuji, Suzuka, Aida	3
=	Portugal	Oporto, Monsanto, Estoril	3

* Used for Formula One World Championship races

The Nürburgring in Germany is one of most notorious and testing of racetracks. The 17.6-mile circuit was built around the village of Nürburg in the Eifel area of the country, set amongst forest land, and opened in 1927. The first German Grand Prix at the Nürburgring was in 1927. The "Ring" was reduced to just 2.8 miles in the 1970s, and in 1984 it returned to the Grand Prix calendar after an eight-year absence.

> There's no secret. You just press the accelerator to the floor and steer left.
> **Bill Vukovich, Sr.,** on the Indianapolis 500 – in which he was killed in 1955

Top 10 Countries to host the most Grand Prix races*

	Country/Grand Prix	First/last races	Total races
1	Italy (Italian GP 52; San Marino GP 21; Pescara GP 1)	1950–2001	74
2	USA (United States GP 27; Indianapolis 500 11; Detroit GP 7; United States GP (West) 8; Las Vegas GP 2; Indianapolis GP 2; Dallas GP 1)	1950–2001	58
3	Germany (German GP 49; European GP 6; Luxembourg GP 2)	1951–2001	57
4	UK (British GP 52; European GP 3)	1950–2001	55
5	France (French GP 51; Swiss GP 1)	1950–2001	52
6 =	Belgium	1950–2001	48
=	Monaco	1950–2001	48
8 =	Canada	1967–2001	33
=	Spain (Spanish GP 31; European GP 2)	1951–2001	33
10	Netherlands	1952–85	30

* For Formula One World Championship races; as at 1 March 2002

Since the launch of the Formula One World Championship in 1950, one race each year has been designated the Grand Prix d'Europe – the European Grand Prix. The first race to carry such a title – but no extra points – was the inaugural race at Silverstone on 13 May 1950. The first separate European Grand Prix was raced at Brands Hatch in 1983 and won by Nelson Piquet (Brazil) in a Brabham–BMW.

Top 10 Countries with the most Grand Prix wins*

	Country	Wins
1	UK	187
2	Brazil	80
3	France	79
4	Germany	63
5	Austria	41
6	Italy	39
7	Argentina	36
8	USA	33
9	Australia	26
10	Finland	25

* As at 10 January 2002

The first UK driver to win a World Championship Grand Prix race was Mike Hawthorn, on 5 July 1953, when he won the 500-km (311-mile) French Grand Prix at Reims in a Ferrari at an average speed of 182.86 km/h (113.65 mph).

Top 10 First Formula One World Championship races

	Grand Prix	Venue	Winner/country	Date
1	British GP	Silverstone	Giuseppe Farina, Italy	13 May 1950
2	Monaco GP	Monte Carlo	Juan Manuel Fangio, Argentina	21 May 1950
3	Indianapolis 500*	Indianapolis	Johnnie Parsons, USA	30 May 1950
4	Swiss GP	Bremgarten	Giuseppe Farina, Italy	4 June 1950
5	Belgian GP	Spa	Juan Manuel Fangio, Argentina	18 June 1950
6	French GP	Reims	Juan Manuel Fangio, Argentina	2 July 1950
7	Italian GP	Monza	Giuseppe Farina, Italy	3 Sep 1950
8	Swiss GP	Bremgarten	Juan Manuel Fangio, Argentina	27 May 1951
9	Indianapolis 500*	Indianapolis	Lee Wallard, USA	30 May 1951
10	Belgian GP	Spa	Giuseppe Farina, Italy	11 June 1951

* Between 1950 and 1960, the Indianapolis 500 formed a round of the Formula One World Championship

Italian drivers dominated the first World Championship Grand Prix at Silverstone in 1950, with Luigi Fagioli following his compatriot Giuseppe Farina in second place. Both men were driving Alfa Romeos, as was the third-placed driver, Britain's Reg Parnell. Farina started the race from pole position and also recorded the fastest lap. The race was attended by King George VI.

Top 10 Longest current Formula One circuits*

	Circuit/country	km	miles
1	Spa-Francorchamps, Belgium	6.968	4.33
2	Hockenheimring, Germany	6.825	4.24
3	Suzuka, Japan	5.864	3.64
4	Monza, Italy	5.793	3.60
5	Sepang, Kuala Lumpur	5.543	3.44
6	Albert Park, Melbourne, Australia	5.303	3.30
7	Silverstone, UK	5.141	3.19
8	Autodromo Enzo e Dino Ferrari, Imola, Italy	4.933	3.07
9	Circuit de Catalunya, Spain	4.730	2.94
10	Nürburgring, Germany	4.556	2.83

* During the 2002 season

Monaco, at 3.37 kilometres (2.09 miles), is the shortest Formula One circuit. The longest Formula One circuit ever was the Pescara track, used for the one and only Pescara Grand Prix in 1957. It measured 25.579 km (15.9 miles).

◀ The sight all racing drivers long to see – the chequered flag at the finish.

FORMULA ONE CONSTRUCTORS' RECORDS

> Ferrari is the greatest name in motor sport and I deem it a privilege to be able to drive for them.
>
> **Nigel Mansell**

Top 10 Constructors with the most titles

	Constructor	First/last title	Titles
1	Ferrari	1961–2001	11
2	Williams	1980–97	9
3	McLaren	1974–98	8
4	Lotus	1963–78	7
5 =	Brabham	1966–67	2
=	Cooper	1959–60	2
7 =	Benetton	1995	1
=	BRM	1962	1
=	Matra	1969	1
=	Tyrrell	1971	1
=	Vanwall	1958	1

While the World Championship for drivers was launched in 1950, the first championship for constructors was not initiated until 1958.

Top 10 Most wins in a season by a constructor

	Constructor	Year	Wins
1	McLaren	1988	15
2 =	McLaren	1984	12
=	Williams	1996	12
4	Benetton	1995	11
5 =	Ferrari	2000	10
=	McLaren	1989	10
=	Williams	1992	10
=	Williams	1993	10
9 =	Ferrari	2001	9
=	McLaren	1998	9
=	Williams	1986	9
=	Williams	1987	9

The only race McLaren did not win in the 1988 season was the Italian Grand Prix at Monza, which was won by Gerhard Berger of Austria in a Ferrari.

Top 10 Constructors with the most Formula One Grand Prix wins*

	Constructor	First/last win	Wins
1	Ferrari	1951–2001	144
2	McLaren	1968–2001	134
3	Williams	1979–2001	107
4	Lotus	1960–87	79
5	Brabham	1964–85	35
6	Benetton	1986–97	27
7	Tyrrell	1971–83	23
8	BRM	1959–72	17
9	Cooper	1958–67	16
10	Renault	1979–83	15

* As at 1 March 2002

Having finished second in two races (the Monaco Grand Prix and Italian Grand Prix) in the inaugural World Championship season, Ferrari eventually registered their first win in the fifth race of the 1951 season, the British Grand Prix at Silverstone on 14 July. José Froilan Gonzalez of Argentina was the driver.

Top 10 Most points in a season by a constructor

	Constructor	Year	Points
1	McLaren	1988	199
2	Ferrari	2001	179
3	Williams	1996	175
4	Ferrari	2000	170
5	Williams	1993	168
6	Williams	1992	164
7	McLaren	2000	162
8	McLaren	1998	156
9	Benetton	1995	147
10	McLaren	1995	144

During their record-breaking season in 1988, the Honda-powered McLaren finished first and second in 10 of the 16 races. They won the constructors' titles by 134 points from second-placed Ferrari. Ayrton Senna drove eight of the team's 15 wins, Alain Prost the other seven.

Top 10 Constructors with the most starts*

Constructor	Starts
1 Ferrari	654
2 McLaren	527
3 Lotus	491
4 Tyrrell	431
5 Williams	396
6 Brabham	394
7 Ligier	326
8 Arrows	281
9 Minardi	272
10 Benetton	260

* As at 1 March 2002

Ferrari's first participation in a Formula One championship race was at Monaco on 21 May 1950. They entered four cars, but only three started the race and two finished, their best placed being Alberto Ascari of Italy in second position.

Top 10 Constructors with the most starts without a win*

Constructor	Starts
1 Arrows	281
2 Minardi	272
3 Lola	148
4 Sauber	147
5 Osella	133
6 Surtees	118
7 Fittipaldi	103
8 Ensign	99
9 Footwork	91
10 ATS	90

* As at 1 March 2002

The Arrows racing team was founded in 1977. Their first Grand Prix was in Brazil in 1978 and, to date, their best finishes have been seconds in Sweden (1978), USA (1980), San Marino (1981 and 1985), and Hungary (1997).

The 10 First World Championships for Ferrari

Driver/country	Year
1 Alberto Ascari, Italy	1952
2 Alberto Ascari, Italy	1953
3 Juan Manuel Fangio, Argentina	1956
4 Mike Hawthorn, UK	1958
5 Phil Hill, USA	1961
6 John Surtees, UK	1964
7 Niki Lauda, Austria	1975
8 Niki Lauda, Austria	1977
9 Jody Scheckter, South Africa	1979
10 Michael Schumacher, Germany	2000

Top 10 Constructors finishing first and second most often

Constructor	First & second finishes
1 Ferrari	25
2 Williams	18
3 = Lotus	17
= McLaren	17
5 = Benetton	6
= Brabham	6
7 Alfa Romeo	4
8 = BRM	3
= Cooper	3
= Maserati	3
= Tyrrell	3

Ten of McLaren's 17 first and seconds came in the 1988 season when they won 15 of the 16 championship races.

▶ Races can often be won and lost on the speed of wheel changes. Anything over 10 seconds is deemed to be slow – and that's for all four wheels!

FORMULA ONE DRIVERS

- Formula One drivers with the most wins in a season
- Formula One drivers with the most career wins
- Formula One drivers with the most career points
- Formula One drivers to compete in most Grands Prix
- Formula One drivers with the most World titles
- British drivers with the most Formula One wins

> The best classroom of all times was about two car lengths behind Juan Manuel Fangio.
> **Stirling Moss**

Top 10 Formula One drivers with the most wins in a season

	Driver/country	Year	Wins
1 =	Nigel Mansell, UK	1992	9
=	Michael Schumacher, Germany	1995	9
=	Michael Schumacher, Germany	2000	9
=	Michael Schumacher, Germany	2001	9
5 =	Mika Häkkinen, Finland	1998	8
=	Damon Hill, UK	1996	8
=	Michael Schumacher, Germany	1994	8
=	Ayrton Senna, Brazil	1988	8
9 =	Jim Clark, UK	1963	7
=	Alain Prost, France	1984	7
=	Alain Prost, France	1988	7
=	Alain Prost, France	1993	7
=	Ayrton Senna, Brazil	1991	7
=	Jacques Villeneuve, Canada	1997	7

Top 10 Formula One drivers with the most career wins

	Driver/country	Career	Wins*
1	Michael Schumacher, Germany	1991–	53
2	Alain Prost, France	1980-93	51
3	Ayrton Senna, Brazil	1984-94	41
4	Nigel Mansell, UK	1980-95	31
5	Jackie Stewart, UK	1965-73	27
6 =	Jim Clark, UK	1960-68	25
=	Niki Lauda, Austria	1971-85	25
8	Juan Manuel Fangio, Argentina	1950-58	24
9	Nelson Piquet, Brazil	1978-91	23
10	Damon Hill, UK	1992-99	22

* As at 1 March 2002

Michael Schumacher started his Formula One career with Jordan in 1991, but after one race moved to Benetton. He won his first Grand Prix, the 1992 Belgian Grand Prix, in his first full season.

Top 10 Formula One drivers with the most career points*

	Driver/country	Points
1	Michael Schumacher#, Germany	801
2	Alain Prost, France	798.5
3	Ayrton Senna, Brazil	614
4	Nelson Piquet, Brazil	485.5
5	Nigel Mansell, UK	482
6	Niki Lauda, Austria	420.5
7	Mika Häkkinen, Finland	420
8	Gerhard Berger, Austria	385
9 =	Damon Hill, UK	360
=	Jackie Stewart, UK	360

* As at 1 March 2002

\# Active in the 2001 season

When he won the Japanese Grand Prix at Fuji on 14 October 2001, Michael Schumacher overtook Alain Prost's eight-year-old record for most points in a career. The 10 points Schumacher collected made him the first man to register 800 in a career.

Top 10 Formula One drivers to compete in most Grands Prix*

	Driver/country	Starts
1	Riccardo Patrese, Italy	256
2	Gerhard Berger, Austria	210
3	Andrea de Cesaris, Italy	208
4	Nelson Piquet, Brazil	204
5	Jean Alesi, France	201
6	Alain Prost, France	199
7	Michele Alboreto, Italy	194
8	Nigel Mansell, UK	187
9 =	Graham Hill, UK	176
=	Jacques Laffite, France	176

* As at 1 March 2002

Riccardo Patrese started his career with the Shadow team in 1977 and picked up one point for finishing sixth in the season's final race, the Japanese Grand Prix. His final season was in 1993, the year after his best finish in the Drivers' Championship, when he finished second to the UK's Nigel Mansell.

◀ Brazilian driver Ayrton Senna, one of the most talented drivers ever in Formula One.

Top 10 Formula One drivers with the most World titles

	Driver/country	Years	Races won	World titles
1	Juan Manuel Fangio, Argentina	1951–57	24	5
2 =	Alain Prost, France	1985–93	51	4
=	Michael Schumacher, Germany	1994–2001	53	4
4 =	Jack Brabham, Australia	1959–60	14	3
=	Niki Lauda, Austria	1975–84	25	3
=	Nelson Piquet, Brazil	1981–87	23	3
=	Ayrton Senna, Brazil	1988–91	41	3
=	Jackie Stewart, UK	1969–71	27	3
9 =	Alberto Ascari, Italy	1952–53	13	2
=	Jim Clark, UK	1963–65	25	2
=	Emerson Fittipaldi, Brazil	1972–74	14	2
=	Mika Häkkinen, Finland	1998–99	20	2
=	Graham Hill, UK	1962–68	14	2

Top 10 British drivers with the most Formula One wins*

	Driver	Wins
1	Nigel Mansell	31
2	Jackie Stewart	27
3	Jim Clark	25
4	Damon Hill	22
5	Stirling Moss	16
6	Graham Hill	14
7	David Coulthard#	11
8	James Hunt	10
9 =	Tony Brooks	6
=	John Surtees	6

* As at 1 March 2002

\# Active in the 2001 season

The first of Nigel Mansell's 31 wins was in 1985, on home soil at Brands Hatch, when he won the European Grand Prix in a Williams-Honda ahead of Brazil's Ayrton Senna.

▼ The man who put Ferrari back on the Formula One map in the 1990s, Germany's Michael Schumacher.

ENDURANCE RACES & RALLYING

- Most wins in the 24 Hours of Daytona
- Most wins in the Le Mans 24 Hours
- Constructors in the World Rally Championships
- Car models in the World Rally Championships
- Drivers in the World Rally Championships

JACKY ICKX

Six-time Le Mans winner Jacky Ickx was also a talented Formula One driver, winning eight World Championship races in 116 drives between 1966 and 1979. He was twice runner-up in the World Drivers' Dhampionship: to Jackie Stewart (UK) in 1969 and to the posthumous winner of the title, Jochen Rindt (Austria) in 1970.

Top 10 Most wins in the 24 Hours of Daytona

	Driver*	First/last win	Total
1	Hurley Haywood	1973–91	5
2 =	Peter Gregg	1973–78	4
=	Pedro Rodriguez	1963–71	4
=	Bob Wollek, France	1983–91	4
5 =	Derek Bell, UK	1986–89	3
=	Butch Leitzinger	1994–99	3
=	Rolf Stommelen, Germany	1978–82	3
8 =	Mauro Baldi, Italy	1998–2001	2
=	Elliott Forbes-Robinson	1987–89	2
=	A. J. Foyt	1983–85	2
=	Al Holbert	1986–87	2
=	Ken Miles	1965–66	2
=	Brian Redman, UK	1976–81	2
=	Lloyd Ruby	1965–66	2
=	Didier Theys, Belgium	1998–2001	2
=	Al Unser Jr.	1986–87	2
=	Andy Wallace, UK	1997–99	2

* All USA unless otherwise stated

First held as a three-hour race in 1962 and won by Dan Gurney in a Lotus Ford, this event has changed format over the years. Since 1973, it has been a 24-hour race. There was no race in 1974 as a result of a national energy crisis.

Top 10 Most wins in the Le Mans 24 Hours

	Driver/country	First/last win	Wins
1	Jacky Ickx, Belgium	1969–82	6
2	Derek Bell, UK	1975–87	5
3 =	Yannick Dalmas, France	1992–99	4
=	Olivier Gendebien, Belgium	1958–62	4
=	Henri Pescarolo, France	1972–84	4
6 =	Woolf Barnato, UK	1928–30	3
=	Luigi Chinetti, Italy/USA	1932–49	3
=	Hurley Haywood, USA	1977–94	3
=	Phil Hill, USA	1958–62	3
=	Al Holbert, USA	1983–87	3
=	Tom Kristensen, Norway	1997–2001	3
=	Klaus Ludwig, West Germany	1979–85	3

The first Le Mans endurance race was held on 26–27 May 1923 and won by André Lagache and René Leonard in a Chenard & Walcker at an average speed of 92.07 km/h (57.21 mph). The record-winning speed is 222.30 km/h (138.13 mph), set in 1971 by Gijs van Lennep (Netherlands) and Helmut Marko, (Austria) in a Porsche 917. The original Le Mans circuit measured 17.26 kilometres (10.73 miles).

Top 10 Constructors in the World Rally Championships*

	Constructor	Wins
1	Lancia	74
2	Toyota	43
3	Ford	40
4 =	Mitsubishi	34
=	Peugeot	34
=	Subaru	34
7	Audi	24
8	Fiat	21
9	Nissan/Datsun	9
10 =	Opel	6
=	Renault	6
=	Renault-Alpine	6

* As at 1 March 2002

The first Lancia driver to win the World Rally Championships was Juha Kankkunen in 1987. The first Lancia to win the manufacturers' title was in 1972.

Top 10 Car models in the World Rally Championships*

	Model	Wins
1	Subaru Impreza WRC	22
2	Audi Quattro	21
3	Fiat 131 Abarth	18
4 =	Ford Escort RS	17
=	Lancia Stratos	17
6	Toyota Celica Turbo 4wd	16
7	Peugeot 206 WRC	15
8	Lancia Delta Integrale	14
9 =	Lancia Delta Integrale 16V	13
=	Toyota Celica GT-Four	13

* As at 1 March 2002

Subaru's 34 championship wins have come with just three cars: the Impreza WRC, Impreza 555 (11 wins), and the Legacy RS (one win). They won the constructors' title in 1997 with the WRC, and in 1995 and 1996 with the 555.

Top 10 Drivers in the World Rally Championships*

	Driver/country	Wins
1	Tommi Mäkinen, Finland	24
2 =	Juha Kankkunen, Finland	23
=	Colin McRae, UK	23
=	Carlos Sainz, Spain	23
5	Didier Auriol, France	20
6	Markku Alen, Finland	19
7	Hannu Mikkola, Finland	18
8	Massimo Biasion, Italy	17
9	Bjorn Waldegaard, Sweden	16
10	Walter Röhrl, Germany	14

* As at 1 January 2002

Launched in 1977 under the aegis of the Féderation International de l'Automobile (FIA), the World Rally Championship begins each year in January with the Monte Carlo Rally, after which a further 13 rallies are held across the world. Kankkunen (1986–87, 1991, 1993) and Mäkinen (1996–99) have each won the World Rally Driver's Championship a record four times. There have been two UK winners of the title – Colin McRae in 1995 and Richard Burns in 2001.

◄ Spain's leading rally driver, Carlos Sainz, in his Lancia during the 1993 Monte Carlo Rally.

ON TWO WHEELS

- Fastest-ever Daytona 200 races
- Most World Motor Cycling titles
- Most Isle of Man TT wins
- Most consecutive World Motor Cycling titles
- Most World Trials Championship titles

Top 10 Fastest-ever Daytona 200 races

	Rider*	Bike	Year	Average speed (km/h)	Average speed (mph)
1	Matt Mladin, Australia	Suzuki	2000	182.87	113.63
2	Miguel Duhamel, Canada	Honda	1999	182.61	113.47
3	Kenny Roberts	Yamaha	1984	182.08	113.14
4	Scott Russell	Yamaha	1998	179.89	111.78
5	Kenny Roberts	Yamaha	1983	178.52	110.93
6	Scott Russell	Kawasaki	1992	178.11	110.67
7	Graeme Crosby, New Zealand	Yamaha	1982	175.58	109.10
8	Steve Baker	Yamaha	1977	175.18	108.85
9	Miguel Duhamel, Canada	Honda	1996	175.13	108.82
10	Johnny Cecotto, Venezuela	Yamaha	1976	175.05	108.77

* All USA unless otherwise stated

The Daytona 200, which was first held in 1937, forms a round in the AMA (American Motorcyclist Association) Grand National Dirt Track series. It is raced over 57 laps of the 5.73-kilometre (3.56-mile) Daytona International Speedway. In addition to those riders named here, the only other non-United States winners have been: Billy Matthews (Canada) 1941, 1950; Jaarno Saarinen (Finland) 1973; Giacomo Agostini (Italy) 1974; and Patrick Pons (France) 1980.

> In 500, you have more advantage with a new tyre than with a new bike.
> **Valentino Rossi,** Italy's former 125cc and 250cc champion, who became 500cc champion in 2001, winning 11 of 16 races

▼ Italy's Giacomo Agostini in action during the British Grand Prix (500cc), which he won five years in succession, from 1968–72.

Top 10 Most World Motor Cycling titles*

	Rider/country	Title	500cc	350cc	250cc	125cc	50/80cc	Total
1	Giacomo Agostini, Italy	1966–75	8	7	0	0	0	15
2	Angel Nieto, Spain	1969–84	0	0	0	7	6	13
3 =	Mike Hailwood, UK	1961–67	4	2	3	0	0	9
=	Carlo Ubbiali, Italy	1951–60	0	0	3	6	0	9
5 =	Phil Read, UK	1964–74	2	0	4	1	0	7
=	John Surtees, UK	1956–60	4	3	0	0	0	7
7 =	Geoff Duke, UK	1951–55	4	2	0	0	0	6
=	Jim Redman, Southern Rhodesia	1962–65	0	4	2	0	0	6
9 =	Michael Doohan, Australia	1994–98	5	0	0	0	0	5
=	Anton Mang, West Germany	1980–87	0	2	3	0	0	5

* Solo classes only

The first World Road Race Championship season was in 1949, and the British Grand Prix on the Isle of Man was the very first race. Harold Daniell (UK) won the 500cc race, Freddie Frith (UK) the 350cc, and Manliff Barrington (Ireland) the 250cc. After six rounds, the inaugural world champions were: 500cc: Leslie Graham (UK) on an AJS; 350cc: Freddie Frith (UK) on a Velocette; 250cc: Bruno Ruffo (Italy) on a Guzzi; 125cc: Nello Pagani (Italy) on a Mondial; Sidecar: Eric Oliver (UK) on a Norton. AJS won the inaugural manufacturers' title.

Top 10 Most Isle of Man TT wins

	Rider/country*	First/last wins	Wins
1	Joey Dunlop	1977–2000	26
2	Mike Hailwood	1961–79	14
3 =	Steve Hislop	1987–94	11
=	Phillip McCallen	1992–97	11
5 =	Giacomo Agostini, Italy	1966–75	10
=	Stanley Woods	1923–39	10
7 =	Mick Boddice#	1983–89	9
=	Dave Saville#	1985–90	9
=	Siegfried Schauzu#, West Germany	1967–75	9
10 =	Rob Fisher#	1994–2000	8
=	Charles Mortimer	1970–78	8
=	Phil Read	1961–77	8

* All UK unless otherwise stated
# Wins in sidecar class

Top 10 Most consecutive World Motor Cycling titles*

	Rider/country	Class	Years	Consecutive wins
1	Giacomo Agostini, Italy	500cc	1966–72	7
=	Giacomo Agostini, Italy	350cc	1968–74	7
3	Michael Doohan, Australia	500cc	1994–98	5
4 =	Max Biaggi, Italy	250cc	1994–97	4
=	Stefan Dorflinger, Switzerland	50/80cc	1982–85	4
=	Mike Hailwood, UK	500cc	1962–65	4
=	Angel Nieto, Spain	125cc	1981–84	4
=	Jim Redman, Southern Rhodesia	350cc	1962–65	4
9 =	Hans Georg Anscheidt, West Germany	50cc	1966–68	3
=	Jorge Martínez Aspar, Spain	80cc	1986–88	3
=	Angel Nieto, Spain	50cc	1975–77	3
=	Walter Villa, Italy	50cc	1974–76	3
=	Carlo Ubbiali, Italy	125cc	1958–60	3

* Solo classes only

Giacomo Agostini's reign as World 500cc champion was ended by Phil Read (UK) in 1973. Agostini finished third that year and was fourth in 1974, when Read won again. However, Agostini claimed his eighth 500cc title in 1975 when he beat Read into second place by just eight points.

Top 10 Most World Trials Championship titles

	Rider/country	First/last title	Wins
1	Jordi Tarrés, Spain	1987–95	7
2	Doug Lampkin, UK	1997–2001	5
3 =	Eddy Lejeune, Belgium	1982–84	3
=	Thierry Michaud, France	1985–88	3
=	Yrjo Vesterinen, Finland	1976–78	3
6 =	Tommi Ahvala, Finland	1992	1
=	Gilles Burgat, France	1981	1
=	Marc Colomer, Spain	1996	1
=	Ulf Karlson, Sweden	1980	1
=	Martin Lampkin, UK	1975	1
=	Bernie Schreiber, USA	1979	1

The World Trials Championship evolved from the famous Scottish Six-Day Trial, which was launched in 1909. An International Six-Day Trial was first held in 1913, but it was not until 1973 that the World Championship was launched.

OLYMPICS

At the Start

The Olympic Games, which were part of a religious festival held every four years, may have been staged even earlier, but the first on record took place in 776 BC. Originally, running was the only event, but in successive Games, jumping, discus and javelin throwing, wrestling, boxing, and chariot-racing were added, making a total of 23 events. In AD 393, the Games were banned as a pagan ritual by order of the Christian emperor Theodosius I. Various revivals were mooted, and an Olympic festival was first held in Much Wenlock, England, in 1849. This event encouraged French sports enthusiast Baron Pierre de Coubertin to launch the modern Olympic movement, which led, in 1896, to the revival of the Games.

OLYMPIC CHAMPIONS

- Men with the most Olympic medals
- Women with the most Olympic medals
- All-time medal-winning countries
- Individual gold medal winners at the Summer Olympics
- First athletes to win medals at five or more Summer Olympics

> I've had an incredible career, and it's time to stop. To be able to end your career with an Olympic gold medal... is a dream. I feel like I've been blessed.
>
> **Carl Lewis,** after winning his 9th Olympic gold medal, 1992

Top 10 Men with the most Olympic medals*

	Athlete/country	Sport	Years	G	S	B	Total
1	Nikolai Andrianov, USSR	Gymnastics	1972–80	7	5	3	15
2 =	Edoardo Mangiarotti, Italy	Fencing	1936–60	6	5	2	13
=	Takashi Ono, Japan	Gymnastics	1952–64	5	4	4	13
=	Boris Shakhlin, USSR	Gymnastics	1956–64	7	4	2	13
5 =	Sawao Kato, Japan	Gymnastics	1968–76	8	3	1	12
=	Alexei Nemov, Russia	Gymnastics	1996–2000	4	2	6	12
=	Paavo Nurmi, Finland	Athletics	1920–28	9	3	0	12
8 =	Matt Biondi, USA	Swimming	1984–92	8	2	1	11
=	Viktor Chukarin, USSR	Gymnastics	1952–56	7	3	1	11
=	Carl Osburn, USA	Shooting	1912–24	5	4	2	11
=	Mark Spitz, USA	Swimming	1968–72	9	1	1	11

* At the Summer Olympics 1896–2000˙

G – gold medals, S – silver medals, B – bronze medals

Top 10 Women with the most Olympic medals*

	Athlete/country	Sport	Years	G	S	B	Total
1	Larissa Latynina, USSR	Gymnastics	1956–64	9	5	4	18
2	Vera Cáslavská, Czechoslovakia	Gymnastics	1960–68	7	4	0	11
3 =	Polina Astakhova, USSR	Gymnastics	1956–64	5	2	3	10
=	Birgit Fischer-Schmidt, East Germany	Canoeing	1980–2000	7	3	0	10
=	Agnes Keleti, Hungary	Gymnastics	1952–56	5	3	2	10
=	Jenny Thompson, USA	Swimming	1992–2000	8	1	1	10
7 =	Nadia Comaneci, Romania	Gymnastics	1976–80	5	3	1	9
=	Dara Torres, USA	Swimming	1984–2000	4	1	4	9
=	Lyudmila Turishcheva, USSR	Gymnastics	1968–76	4	3	2	9
10 =	Shirley Babashoff, USA	Swimming	1972–76	2	6	0	8
=	Kornelia Ender, East Germany	Swimming	1972–76	4	4	0	8
=	Dawn Fraser, Australia	Swimming	1956–64	4	4	0	8
=	Sofia Muratova, USSR	Gymnastics	1956–60	2	2	4	8

* At the Summer Olympics 1896–2000

G – gold medals, S – silver medals, B – bronze medals

▶ Larissa Latynina of Russia in action during the women's compulsory exercises in the gymnastics event at the 1964 Olympic Games in Tokyo.

◀ The official logo of the 2000 Sydney Olympics. Logos have been used since the 1932 Los Angeles Games.

Top 10 All-time medal-winning countries

	Country	Gold	Silver	Bronze	Total
1	USA	872	658	586	2,116
2	Russia*	498	409	371	1,278
3	Germany#	214	242	280	736
4	United Kingdom	180	233	225	638
5	France	188	193	217	598
6	Italy	179	143	157	479
7	Sweden	136	156	177	469
8	East Germany	159	150	136	445
9	Hungary	150	135	158	443
10	Australia	102	110	138	350

* Including USSR (1952–88) and Unified Team (1992)

\# Including West Germany (1968–88)

Top 10 Individual gold medal winners at the Summer Olympics

	Athlete/country	Sport	Years	Gold medals
1	Ray Ewry, USA	Athletics	1900–08	10
2 =	Larissa Latynina, USSR	Gymnastics	1956–64	9
=	Carl Lewis, USA	Athletics	1984–96	9
=	Paavo Nurmi, Finland	Athletics	1920–28	9
=	Mark Spitz, USA	Swimming	1968–72	9
6 =	Matt Biondi, USA	Swimming	1984–92	8
=	Sawao Kato, Japan	Gymnastics	1968–76	8
=	Jenny Thompson, USA	Swimming	1992–2000	8
9 =	Nikolai Andrianov, USSR	Gymnastics	1972–80	7
=	Vera Cáslavská, Czechoslovakia	Gymnastics	1964–68	7
=	Viktor Chukarin, USSR	Gymnastics	1952–56	7
=	Birgit Fischer-Schmidt, East Germany	Canoeing	1980–2000	7
=	Aladár Gerevich, Hungary	Fencing	1932–60	7
=	Boris Shakhlin, USSR	Gymnastics	1956–64	7

All Ewry's golds were in the standing jumps – long jump, high jump, and triple jump – that once formed part of the track and field competition. Born in 1873, Ewry contracted polio as a boy and seemed destined to be confined to a wheelchair for life, but through a determined effort to overcome his handicap, he exercised and developed his legs to such a remarkable degree that he went on to become an outstanding athlete. Spitz's seven gold medals in 1972 is a record number for medals won at one celebration.

Top 10 First athletes to win medals at five or more Summer Olympics

	Athlete/country	Sport	Years
1	Heikki Ilmari Savolainen, Finland	Gymnastics	1928–52
2	Aladár Gerevich*, Hungary	Fencing	1932–56
3	Edoardo Mangiarotti, Italy	Fencing	1936–60
4	Gustav Fischer, Switzerland	Dressage	1952–68
5	Hans Günther Winkler#, West Germany	Show jumping	1956–72
6	Ildikó Ságiné-Rejtö (née Uljaki-Rejtö), Hungary	Fencing	1960–76
7	John Michael Plumb, USA	Three-day event	1964–84
8	Reiner Klimke, West Germany	Dressage	1964–88
9 =	Teresa Edwards, USA	Basketball	1984–2000
=	Birgit Fischer-Schmidt, East Germany	Canoeing	1980–2000
=	Stephen Redgrave, UK	Rowing	1984–2000

* Also won medal at the 1960 Games

\# Also won medal at the 1976 Games

MEDAL-WINNING COUNTRIES 1896–1928

IN TWO COUNTRIES

The 12-foot dinghy sailing event at the 1920 Olympics is the only event in Olympic history to have been staged in two countries. The first race was in Belgium but, because the only two competitors were Dutch, the last two races took place in the Netherlands.

Top 10 Countries at the 1896 Olympic Games

	Country	G	S	B	Total
1	Greece*	10	19	18	47
2	USA	11	6	2	19
3	Germany	7	5	3	15
4	France	5	4	2	11
5 =	Denmark	1	2	4	7
=	UK	3	3	1	7
7	Hungary	2	1	3	6
8	Austria	2	0	3	5
9	Switzerland	1	2	0	3
10	Australia	2	0	0	2

* Host country

G – gold medals, S – silver medals, B – bronze medals

The first modern Olympic champion was James Connolly (USA) in the hop, step, and jump (now the triple jump) on 6 April 1896. Connolly was the first Olympic champion since the ancient Games of 369 AD.

Top 10 Countries at the 1900 Olympic Games

	Country	G	S	B	Total
1	France*	26	37	32	95
2	USA	18	14	15	47
3	UK	16	6	8	30
4	Belgium	6	5	5	16
5	Switzerland	6	1	1	8
6	Germany	3	2	2	7
7 =	Australia	2	0	4	6
=	Austria	0	3	3	6
=	Denmark	1	3	2	6
=	Hungary	1	3	2	6
=	Netherlands	1	2	3	6

* Host country

G – gold medals, S – silver medals, B – bronze medals

Women competed for the first time in 1900, and the first women's Olympic champion was Charlotte Cooper (UK) in the singles lawn tennis event.

Top 10 Countries at the 1904 Olympic Games

	Country	G	S	B	Total
1	USA*	79	84	82	245
2	Germany	4	4	4	12
3	Canada	4	1	1	6
4 =	Cuba	4	0	0	4
=	Hungary	2	1	1	4
6	Austria	1	1	1	3
7 =	Greece	1	0	1	2
=	UK	0	1	1	2
=	Switzerland	1	0	1	2
10	Ireland	1	0	0	1

* Host country

G – gold medals, S – silver medals, B – bronze medals

One of the most remarkable competitors at the 1904 St. Louis Olympics was the American gymnast George Eyser. He won six medals despite having a wooden leg.

Top 10 Countries at the 1906 Olympic Games

	Country	G	S	B	Total
1	France	15	9	16	40
2	Greece*	8	13	12	33
3 =	UK	8	11	5	24
=	USA	12	6	6	24
5	Italy	7	6	3	16
6 =	Germany	4	6	5	15
=	Switzerland	5	6	4	15
8	Sweden	2	5	7	14
9	Hungary	2	5	3	10
10	Austria	3	3	2	8

* Host country

G – gold medals, S – silver medals, B – bronze medals

The 1906 Olympics were Intercalated Games in Greece to celebrate the 10th anniversary of the founding of the modern Olympics.

> The important thing in the Olympic Games is not to win but to take part, just as the most important thing in life is not the triumph but the struggle.
>
> **Pierre de Coubertin,** the founder of the modern Olympics at the 1908 Games

Top 10 Countries at the 1908 Olympic Games

	Country	G	S	B	Total
1	UK*	54	46	38	138
2	USA	23	12	12	47
3	Sweden	8	6	11	25
4	France	5	5	9	19
5	Canada	3	3	10	16
6	Germany	3	5	5	13
7	Hungary	3	4	2	9
8 =	Belgium	1	5	2	8
=	Norway	2	3	3	8
10 =	Australia	1	2	2	5
=	Denmark	0	2	3	5
=	Finland	1	1	3	5

* Host country

G – gold medals, S – silver medals, B – bronze medals

Top 10 Countries at the 1912 Olympic Games

	Country	G	S	B	Total
1	Sweden*	23	24	17	64
2	USA	25	18	20	63
3	UK	10	15	16	41
4	Finland	9	8	9	26
5	Germany	5	13	7	25
6	France	7	4	3	14
7	Denmark	1	6	5	12
8	Norway	3	2	5	10
9 =	Canada	3	2	3	8
=	Hungary	3	2	3	8

* Host country

G – gold medals, S – silver medals, B – bronze medals

The cycling road race in the 1912 Stockholm Olympics was 320 kilometres (199 miles) in length and is the longest race of any kind in Olympic history.

Top 10 Countries at the 1920 Olympic Games

	Country	G	S	B	Total
1	USA	41	27	27	95
2	Sweden	19	20	25	64
3	UK	14	15	13	42
4	France	9	19	13	41
5	Belgium*	13	11	11	35
6	Finland	15	10	9	34
7	Norway	13	9	9	31
8	Italy	13	5	5	23
9	Denmark	3	9	1	13
10 =	Netherlands	4	2	5	11
=	Switzerland	2	2	7	11

* Host country

G – gold medals, S – silver medals, B – bronze medals

Victor Boin became the first man to swear the athletes' Olympic Oath when it was introduced in 1920.

Top 10 Countries at the 1924 Olympic Games

	Country	G	S	B	Total
1	USA	45	27	27	99
2	France*	13	15	10	38
3	Finland	14	13	10	37
4	UK	9	13	12	34
5	Sweden	4	13	12	29
6	Switzerland	7	8	10	25
7	Italy	8	3	5	16
8	Belgium	3	7	3	13
9 =	Czechoslovakia	1	4	5	10
=	Netherlands	4	1	5	10
=	Norway	5	2	3	10

* Host country

G – gold medals, S – silver medals, B – bronze medals

The Olympic motto of "Citius, Altius, Fortius" (Swifter, Higher, Stronger) was introduced in 1924, as was the closing ceremony ritual of raising the flag of the IOC host country alongside that of the next host country.

Top 10 Countries at the 1928 Olympic Games

	Country	G	S	B	Total
1	USA	22	18	16	56
2	Germany	10	7	14	31
3 =	Finland	8	8	9	25
=	Sweden	7	6	12	25
5	France	6	10	5	21
6	UK	3	10	7	20
7 =	Italy	7	5	7	19
=	Netherlands*	6	9	4	19
9 =	Canada	4	4	7	15
=	Switzerland	7	4	4	15

* Host country

G – gold medals, S – silver medals, B – bronze medals

The now-standard practice of Greece leading the parade of athletes at the opening ceremony with the host country bringing up the rear was first adopted at the 1928 Games.

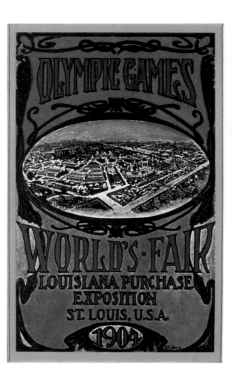

▲ The official poster from the 1904 Olympic Games, held in St. Louis, Missouri, USA.

OLYMPICS

MEDAL-WINNING COUNTRIES 1932–1968

- Countries at the 1932 Olympic Games
- Countries at the 1936 Olympic Games
- Countries at the 1948 Olympic Games
- Countries at the 1952 Olympic Games
- Countries at the 1956 Olympic Games
- Countries at the 1960 Olympic Games
- Countries at the 1964 Olympic Games
- Countries at the 1968 Olympic Games

THE OLYMPIC TORCH

The Olympic torch relay was introduced for the 1936 Olympic Games. It was the idea of Dr. Carl Diem. The first relay saw the torch make its 3,000-km (1,864-mile) journey from Olympia through seven countries: Greece, Bulgaria, Yugoslavia, Hungary, Czechoslovakia, Austria, and Germany.

Top 10 Countries at the 1932 Olympic Games

	Country	G	S	B	Total
1	USA*	41	32	30	103
2	Italy	12	12	12	36
3	Finland	5	8	12	25
4	Sweden	9	5	9	23
5	Germany	3	12	5	20
6	France	10	5	4	19
7	Japan	7	7	4	18
8	UK	4	7	5	16
9 =	Canada	2	5	8	15
=	Hungary	6	4	5	15

* Host country
G – gold medals, S – silver medals, B – bronze medals

The 1932 Olympics lasted just 16 days. Previously no Summer Games had lasted less than 79 days. Since 1932 all subsequent Games have lasted between 15 and 18 days.

Top 10 Countries at the 1936 Olympic Games

	Country	G	S	B	Total
1	Germany*	33	26	30	89
2	USA	24	20	12	56
3	Italy	8	9	5	22
4	Sweden	6	5	9	20
5 =	Finland	7	6	6	19
=	France	7	6	6	19
7	Japan	6	4	8	18
8	Netherlands	6	4	7	17
9	Hungary	10	1	5	16
10	Switzerland	1	9	5	15

* Host country
G – gold medals, S – silver medals, B – bronze medals

As a result of the UK's dropping out of the Top 10 (in 11th place with 14 medals), the United States is the only country to have appeared in the Top 10 every year since the launch of the Games in 1896.

Top 10 Countries at the 1948 Olympic Games

	Country	G	S	B	Total
1	USA	38	27	19	84
2	Sweden	16	11	17	44
3 =	France	10	6	13	29
=	Italy	8	12	9	29
5	Hungary	10	5	12	27
6	UK*	3	14	6	23
7 =	Denmark	5	7	8	20
=	Finland	8	7	5	20
=	Switzerland	5	10	5	20
10	Netherlands	5	2	9	16

* Host country
G – gold medals, S – silver medals, B – bronze medals

USA athlete Bob Mathias won the decathlon in 1948 at the age of 17, just four months after taking up the event. He is the youngest male athlete to win a track and field event in Olympic history.

Top 10 Countries at the 1952 Olympic Games

	Country	G	S	B	Total
1	USA	40	19	17	76
2	Soviet Union	22	30	18	70
3	Hungary	16	10	16	42
4	Sweden	12	13	10	35
5	Germany	0	7	17	24
6	Finland*	6	3	13	22
7	Italy	8	9	4	21
8	France	6	6	6	18
9	Switzerland	2	6	6	14
10	Czechoslovakia	7	3	3	13

* Host country
G – gold medals, S – silver medals, B – bronze medals

Germany's 5th position is the highest-ever position by a country not winning a gold medal, and is the biggest medal haul without a gold among the total.

◄ Germany's Konrad Frey, winner of the parallel bars and pommel horse events at the 1936 Berlin Olympic Games.

Top 10 Countries at the 1956 Olympic Games

	Country	G	S	B	Total
1	USSR	37	29	32	98
2	USA	32	25	17	74
3	Australia*	13	8	14	35
4	Hungary	9	10	7	26
5	Italy	8	8	9	25
6	UK	6	7	11	24
7	West Germany	5	9	6	20
8 =	Japan	4	10	5	19
=	Sweden	8	5	6	19
10	Finland	3	1	11	15

* Host country
G – gold medals, S – silver medals, B – bronze medals

Due to quarantine restrictions in Australia, the equestrian events in 1956 were held in Sweden five months before the opening of the Games in Melbourne – the first Games to be held in the Southern Hemisphere.

Top 10 Countries at the 1960 Olympic Games

	Country	G	S	B	Total
1	USSR	43	29	31	103
2	USA	34	21	16	71
3	Italy*	13	10	13	36
4	West Germany	10	10	6	26
5	Australia	8	8	6	22
6 =	Hungary	6	8	7	21
=	Poland	4	6	11	21
8	UK	2	6	12	20
9	East Germany	3	9	7	19
10	Japan	4	7	7	18

* Host country
G – gold medals, S – silver medals, B – bronze medals

Top 10 Countries at the 1964 Olympic Games

	Country	G	S	B	Total
1	USA	36	26	28	90
2	USSR	30	31	25	86
3	West Germany	7	14	14	35
4	Japan*	16	5	8	29
5	Italy	10	10	7	27
6	Poland	7	6	10	23
7	Hungary	10	7	5	22
8	East Germany	3	11	5	19
9 =	Australia	6	2	10	18
=	UK	4	12	2	18

* Host country
G – gold medals, S – silver medals, B – bronze medals

Top 10 Countries at the 1968 Olympic Games

	Country	G	S	B	Total
1	USA	45	28	34	107
2	USSR	29	32	30	91
3	Hungary	10	10	12	32
4 =	East Germany	9	9	7	25
=	Japan	11	7	7	25
=	West Germany	5	10	10	25
7	Poland	5	2	11	18
8	Australia	5	7	5	17
9	Italy	3	4	9	16
10 =	France	7	3	5	15
=	Romania	4	6	5	15

G – gold medals, S – silver medals, B – bronze medals

Mexico, the host country, finished in joint 13th place with nine medals (three gold, three silver, three bronze). They were the first hosts not to finish in the Top 10.

▶ Jesse Owens starting off in the 200 metres at the 1936 Berlin Games. It was to be one of four events Owens won at those Olympics.

MEDAL-WINNING COUNTRIES 1972–2000

> I'm looking forward to gloating over the performances of the US athletes.
>
> **Larry Ellis,** US men's coach, before the 1984 Los Angeles Olympics

Top 10 Countries at the 1972 Olympic Games

	Country	G	S	B	Total
1	USSR	50	27	22	99
2	USA	33	31	30	94
3	East Germany	20	23	23	66
4	West Germany*	13	11	16	40
5	Hungary	6	13	16	35
6	Japan	13	8	8	29
7 =	Bulgaria	6	10	5	21
=	Poland	7	5	9	21
9 =	Italy	5	3	10	18
=	UK	4	5	9	18

* Host country

G – gold medals, S – silver medals, B – bronze medals

The 1972 Olympics were marred by events on 5 September when eight Palestinian terrorists broke into the Olympic village and killed two members of the Israeli team. The also took nine members of the team hostage, and, in a bloody battle, they too were all killed, along with five of the terrorists and one policeman. It was the blackest day in Olympic history.

Top 10 Countries at the 1976 Olympic Games

	Country	G	S	B	Total
1	USSR	49	41	35	125
2	USA	34	35	25	94
3	East Germany	40	25	25	90
4	West Germany	10	12	17	39
5	Romania	4	9	14	27
6	Poland	7	6	13	26
7	Japan	9	6	10	25
8 =	Bulgaria	6	9	7	22
=	Hungary	4	5	13	22
10 =	Cuba	6	4	3	13
=	Italy	2	7	4	13
=	UK	3	5	5	13

* Host country

G – gold medals, S – silver medals, B – bronze medals

Canada finished in 13th place with 11 medals (five silver, six bronze). They are the only host country not to win a gold medal. Following a tour by the New Zealand All Blacks rugby team to South Africa in 1976, 32 countries boycotted the Olympics because the IOC would not bar New Zealand from the Games.

Top 10 Countries at the 1980 Olympic Games

	Country	G	S	B	Total
1	USSR*	80	69	46	195
2	East Germany	47	37	42	126
3	Bulgaria	8	16	17	41
4 =	Hungary	7	10	15	32
=	Poland	3	14	15	32
6	Romania	6	6	13	25
7	UK	5	7	9	21
8	Cuba	8	7	5	20
9	Italy	8	3	4	15
10 =	Czechoslovakia	2	3	9	14
=	France	6	5	3	14

* Host country

G – gold medals, S – silver medals, B – bronze medals

The United States and 63 other countries boycotted the 1980 Olympic Games because of the USSR's invasion of Afghanistan on 27 December 1979.

Top 10 Countries at the 1984 Olympic Games

	Country	G	S	B	Total
1	USA*	83	61	30	174
2	West Germany	17	19	23	59
3	Romania	20	16	17	53
4	Canada	10	18	16	44
5	UK	5	11	21	37
6 =	China	15	8	9	32
=	Italy	14	6	12	32
=	Japan	10	8	14	32
9	France	5	7	16	28
10	Australia	4	8	12	24

* Host country

G – gold medals, S – silver medals, B – bronze medals

The Soviet Union and 13 other Eastern Bloc countries did not attend the Games, choosing to boycott them in retaliation for the American boycott of the 1980 Games.

◄ American shot-putter Randy Barnes in action during the 1988 Seoul Olympics, where he won silver. He won the gold medal at Atlanta in 1996.

Top 10 Countries at the 1988 Olympic Games

	Country	G	S	B	Total
1	USSR	55	31	46	132
2	East Germany	37	35	30	102
3	USA	36	31	27	94
4	West Germany	11	14	15	40
5	Bulgaria	10	12	13	35
6	South Korea*	12	10	11	33
7	China	5	11	12	28
8 =	UK	5	10	9	24
=	Romania	7	11	6	24
10	Hungary	11	6	6	23

* Host country

G – gold medals, S – silver medals, B – bronze medals

Top 10 Countries at the 1992 Olympic Games

	Country	G	S	B	Total
1	Unified Team	45	38	29	112
2	USA	37	34	37	108
3	Germany	33	21	28	82
4	China	16	22	16	54
5	Cuba	14	6	11	31
6	Hungary	11	12	7	30
7 =	France	8	5	16	29
=	South Korea	12	5	12	29
9	Australia	7	9	11	27
10 =	Japan	3	8	11	22
=	Spain*	13	7	2	22

* Host country

G – gold medals, S – silver medals, B – bronze medals

Top 10 Countries at the 1996 Olympic Games

	Country	G	S	B	Total
1	Unified Team	45	38	29	112
2	USA*	44	32	25	101
3	Germany	20	18	27	65
4	Russia	26	21	16	63
5	China	16	22	12	50
6	Australia	9	9	23	41
7	France	15	7	15	37
8	Italy	13	10	12	35
9	South Korea	7	15	5	27
10	Cuba	9	8	8	25

* Host country

G – gold medals, S – silver medals, B – bronze medals

Top 10 Countries at the 2000 Olympic Games

	Country	G	S	B	Total
1	USA	39	25	33	97
2	Russia	32	28	28	88
3	China	28	16	15	59
4	Australia*	16	25	17	58
5	Germany	14	17	26	57
6	France	13	14	11	38
7	Italy	13	8	13	34
8	Cuba	11	11	7	29
9 =	UK	11	10	7	28
=	Korea	8	9	11	28

* Host country

G – gold medals, S – silver medals, B – bronze medals

The Sydney Olympics were the biggest to date, with 10,651 athletes (6,582 men and 4,069 women) competing in 300 events. The Games were opened by Sir William Deane, Governor General of Australia, and the Olympic flame was lit by Australian track star Cathy Freeman.

▶ China's Linghui Kong in action in the Table Tennis Men's Singles Final on his way to a gold medal at the 2000 Sydney Olympics.

WINTER GAMES

- Most medals won by men at the Winter Olympics

- Most medals won by women at the Winter Olympics

- Medal-winning countries at the Winter Olympics

- Sports at which the USA has won the most Winter Olympic medals

EARLY EVENTS

The Winter Olympics did not start until 1924, but figure skating was included in the Summer programme in 1908 and 1920, while ice hockey was part of the 1920 Antwerp Olympics.

Top 10 Most medals won by men at the Winter Olympics

	Athlete/country	Event	G	S	B	Total
1	Bjorn Dählie, Norway	Cross-country	8	4	0	12
2	Sixten Jernberg, Sweden	Cross-country	4	3	2	9
3 =	Kjetil André Aamodt, Norway	Alpine skiing	3	2	2	7
=	Peter Angerer, Germany/West Germany	Biathlon	3	2	2	7
=	Ivar Ballangrud, Norway	Speed skating	4	2	1	7
=	Rico Gross, Germany	Biathlon	3	3	1	7
=	Veikko Hakulinen, Finland	Cross-country	3	3	1	7
=	Eero Mäntyranta, Finland	Cross-country	3	2	2	7
=	Bogdan Musiol, Germany/East Germany	Bobsled	1	5	1	7
=	Clas Thunberg, Finland	Speed skating	5	1	1	7

G – gold medals, S – silver medals, B – bronze medals

Norway's Bjorn Dählie won his 12 Olympic medals in the three Games between 1992 and 1998. He was just 30 when he won his last medal, but injury forced him to retire at the age of 33 in March 2001. He was nicknamed the "Nannestad Express" after his home town.

Top 10 Most medals won by women at the Winter Olympics

	Athlete/country	Event	G	S	B	Total
1	Raisa Smetanina, USSR/Unified Team	Cross-country	4	5	1	10
2 =	Stefania Belmondo, Italy	Cross-country	2	3	4	9
=	Lyubov Egorova, Unified Team/Russia	Cross-country	6	3	0	9
=	Larissa Lazutina, Unified Team/Russia	Cross-country	5	3	1	9
5 =	Karin Kania (née Enke), East Germany	Speed skating	3	4	1	8
=	Galina Kulakova, USSR	Cross-country	4	2	2	8
=	Gunda Neimann-Stirnemann, Germany	Speed skating	3	4	1	8
7 =	Andrea Ehrig (née Mitscherlich, formerly Schöne), East Germany	Speed skating	1	5	1	7
=	Marja-Liisa Kirvesniemi (née Hämäläinen), Finland	Cross-country	3	0	4	7
=	Claudia Pechstein, Germany	Speed skating	4	1	2	7
=	Elena Valbe, Unified Team/Russia	Cross-country	3	0	4	7

G – gold medals, S – silver medals, B – bronze medals

Born on 29 February 1952, Russia's Raisa Smetanina appeared in five Olympics for the Soviet Union and the Unified Team in 1992. Her first medal was silver in the 5-km cross-country in Innsbruck in 1976. She came away from those Games with two golds and a silver, and won silver and gold in 1980, two silvers in 1984, a bronze and silver in 1988, and her 10th and last medal, a gold in the 4 x 5-km relay in 1992.

◀ The most successful athlete in Winter Olympic history, Bjorn Dählie of Norway.

Top 10 Medal-winning countries at the Winter Olympics*

Country	G	S	B	Total
1 Russia/USSR/Unified Team	113	82	78	273
2 Norway	94	93	73	260
3 USA	70	70	51	191
4 Germany/West Germany	68	67	52	187
5 Austria	41	57	66	164
6 Finland	41	51	49	141
7 East Germany	39	37	35	111
8 Sweden	36	28	38	102
9 Switzerland	32	33	36	101
10 Canada	30	28	37	95

G – gold medals, S – silver medals, B – bronze medals

* Includes medals won in figure skating and ice hockey in the Summer Games prior to the launch of the Winter Olympics in 1924

Top 10 Sports at which the USA has won the most Winter Olympic medals*

Sport	G	S	B	Total
1 Speed skating	26	16	14	56
2 Figure skating	13	13	15	41
3 Alpine skiing	10	15	4	29
4 Bobsleigh	6	5	6	17
5 Ice hockey	3	7	1	11
6 = Freestyle skiing	4	4	1	9
= Short track speed skating	3	3	3	9
8 Snowboarding	2	1	4	7
9 Skeleton	3	3	0	6
10 Luge	0	2	2	4

G – gold medals, S – silver medals, B – bronze medals

* Includes medals won in figure skating and ice hockey in the Summer Games prior to the launch of the Winter Olympics in 1924

▲ Apolo Anton "Chunky" Ohno, gold medal winner in the 1,500 metres speed skating event at Salt Lake City 2002. He was 14 when he won his first US title.

OLYMPICS

- ● Paralympics with the most competitors
- ● Medal-winning countries at the Summer Paralympics
- ● Medal-winning countries at the Winter Paralympics
- ● Medal-winning countries at the 2000 Sydney Summer Paralympics
- ● Medal-winning countries at the 2002 Salt Lake City Winter Paralympics

SIR LUDWIG GUTTMAN

Four years prior to the first international Games in Stoke Mandeville in 1952, Sir Ludwig Guttmann, a neurosurgeon, organized a sports competition there involving World War II veterans with spinal cord injuries. This was the forerunner to the now very popular Paralympics. Guttmann, who was Jewish, had fled Germany during the war.

PARALYMPICS

Top 10 Paralympics with the most competitors

Venue/country	Year	Countries	Competitors
1 Stoke Mandeville, England/New York, USA	1984	42	4,080
2 Sydney, Australia	2000	127	3,843
3 Atlanta, USA	1996	103	3,193
4 Seoul, Korea	1988	61	3,053
5 Barcelona, Spain	1992	82	3,020
6 Arnhem, Netherlands	1980	42	2,500
7 Toronto, Canada	1976	42	1,600
8 Heidelberg, Germany	1972	44	1,000
9 Tel Aviv, Israel	1968	29	750
10 Rome, Italy	1960	23	400

The 1984 Games were split, with one group of athletes competing in New York in June and the wheelchair athletes competing in Stoke Mandeville in July and August. President Reagan led the opening ceremony in New York and HRH Prince Charles led the Stoke Mandeville opening ceremony.

◀ The UK's Tanni Grey-Thompson has amassed nine golds, four silvers, and a bronze medal in her Paralympic career. She has also won five London Marathons.

> Participating in the Sydney Games has been all along my dream. Not only do I wish to meet top athletes from all over the world, I am also determined to win medals.
>
> **Chun-lai Yu (China)**, cerebral palsy track athlete, at the Sydney 2000 Paralympics

Top 10 Medal-winning countries at the Summer Paralympics*

	Country	Gold medals	Silver medals	Bronze medals	Total
1	USA	576	523	522	1,621
2	UK	389	401	387	1,177
3	Germany/West Germany	404	385	361	1,150
4	Canada	311	250	262	823
5	France	279	264	241	784
6	Australia	240	248	228	716
7	Netherlands	219	179	153	551
8	Poland	194	184	148	526
9	Sweden	197	190	135	522
10	Spain	156	137	152	445

* Excluding medals won at the 1960 Rome and 1968 Tel Aviv Games – the International Paralympic Committee has not maintained records of medals won at these Games

The first international Games for the disabled were held in Stoke Mandeville, England, in 1952, when 130 athletes from just two countries competed. The first Paralympics to take place at the same venue as the Olympic Games was in Rome in 1960. Since then, the Paralympics have been held every four years, and, since Seoul in 1988, at the same venue as the Summer Olympics. Four hundred athletes from 23 countries took part in 1960. In Sydney in 2000, a total of 3,843 athletes from 127 nations competed. The most medals won at one Games is 388 by the United States in the "dual" Paralympics of 1984. Their total of 131 gold medals is also a record for one Games.

Top 10 Medal-winning countries at the Winter Paralympics

	Country	Gold medals	Silver medals	Bronze medals	Total
1	Austria	103	102	96	301
2	Germany/West Germany	101	97	93	291
3	Norway	118	84	68	270
4	USA	89	92	62	243
5	Finland	75	45	55	175
6	Switzerland	48	56	51	155
7	France	39	40	41	120
8	Russia	39	39	27	105
9	Canada	22	33	36	91
10	Sweden	24	32	34	90

The first Winter Paralympics were held in Örnsköldsvik, Sweden, in 1976, when Austria was the leading country with 35 medals. West Germany and Switzerland were the leading gold-medal countries, with nine each. The most medals won at one Games is 82, by Austria in Innsbruck in 1984, and their tally of 41 golds is also a Games record.

Top 10 Medal-winning countries at the 2000 Sydney Summer Paralympics

	Country	Gold medals	Silver medals	Bronze medals	Total
1	Australia	63	39	47	149
2	UK	41	43	47	131
3	USA	36	39	34	109
4	Spain	39	30	38	107
5	Canada	38	33	25	96
6	Germany	15	42	38	95
7	France	30	28	28	86
8	China	34	22	16	72
9	Poland	19	22	12	53
10	Czech Republic	15	15	13	43

A staggering 300 World and Paralympic records were broken in the 18 events at the Sydney Games. There were outstanding performances from the United Kingdom's Tanni Grey-Thompson, who won gold medals in the 100-, 200-, 400-, and 800-metre races, and from US swimmer Jason Wening, who won his third consecutive gold medal in the 400-metre freestyle, breaking his own world record at the same time. He returned from the Games with his undefeated record in the 400 metres, stretching back to 1991, still intact.

Top 10 Medal-winning countries at the 2002 Salt Lake City Winter Paralympics

	Country	Gold medals	Silver medals	Bronze medals	Total
1	USA	10	22	11	43
2	Germany	17	1	15	33
3	Austria	9	10	10	29
4	Russia	7	9	5	21
5 =	France	2	11	6	19
=	Norway	10	3	6	19
7	Canada	6	4	5	15
8 =	Switzerland	6	4	2	12
=	Ukraine	0	6	6	12
10 =	Italy	3	3	3	9
=	Slovakia	0	3	6	9
=	Sweden	0	6	3	9

More than 500 athletes from 35 countries competed in the VIIIth Paralympic Winter Games in Salt Lake City, Utah, USA, from 7–16 March 2002.

WATER SPORTS

At the Start

Competitive swimming and diving have been practiced since early times – the Romans built swimming baths and included the sport as part of every boy's education. Swimming was also highly regarded in Imperial Japan. The first organized swimming events took place in 1837 in London, where the Amateur Swimming Association was founded in 1869. In the United States, swimming as a sport dates from 1888. Sailing competitions were recorded as early as 1661, while rowing has a similarly long history, and has been considered a competitive sport since the early 18th century, with the addition in relatively modern times of such pursuits as water skiing.

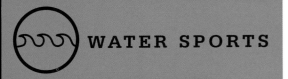

OLYMPIC SWIMMING GREATS

- Most Olympic medals in men's swimming events
- Most Olympic medals in women's swimming events
- Longest-standing Olympic swimming records
- Fastest-ever men's 100-metre freestyle in the Olympics

THE FIRST OLYMPICS

Swimming was featured at the first modern Olympics in 1896 and has been included ever since. In the inaugural Games, the races took place in open waters in the Bay of Zea at Phaleron and were watched by around 40,000 spectators on the shore. There were only four swimming events in 1896, including the 100-metre freestyle for sailors, which was restricted to members of the Greek Navy.

Top 10 Most Olympic medals in men's swimming events

Swimmer/country	Gold medals	Silver medals	Bronze medals	Total
1 = Matt Biondi, USA	8	2	1	11
= Mark Spitz, USA	9	1	1	11
3 = Zoltán Halmay, Hungary	3	5	1	9
= Alexander Popov, Unified Team/Russia	4	5	0	9
5 = Charles Daniels, USA	5	1	2	8
= Gary Hall Jr., USA	4	3	1	8
= Roland Matthes, East Germany	4	2	2	8
= Henry Taylor, UK	4	1	3	8
9 Tom Jager, USA	5	1	1	7
10 = Frank Beaurepaire, Australia	0	3	3	6
= Michael Gross, West Germany	3	2	1	6
= John Jarvis, UK	3	1	2	6
= Murray Rose, Australia	4	1	1	6
= Don Schollander, USA	5	1	0	6
= Johnny Weissmuller*, USA	5	0	1	6

* Total includes one medal at water polo

Top 10 Most Olympic medals in women's swimming events

Swimmer/country	Gold medals	Silver medals	Bronze medals	Total
1 Jenny Thompson, USA	8	1	1	10
2 = Shirley Babashoff, USA	2	6	0	8
= Kornelia Ender, East Germany	4	4	0	8
= Dawn Fraser, Australia	4	4	0	8
= Dagmar Hase, Germany	2	5	1	8
= Susie O'Neill, Australia	2	4	2	8
= Dara Torres, USA	4	0	4	8
= Franziska van Almsick, Germany	0	4	4	8
9 Krisztina Egerszegi, Hungary	5	1	1	7
10 = Daniela Hunger, East Germany/Germany	3	1	2	6
= Angel Martino, USA	3	0	3	6
= Kristin Otto, East Germany	6	0	0	6
= Andrea Pollack, East Germany	3	3	0	6
= Amy van Dyken, USA	6	0	0	6

The 10 Longest-standing Olympic swimming records

	Event	Time (min:sec)	Swimmer/country	Date
1	200-metre freestyle (women)	1:57.65	Heike Friedrich, East Germany	21 Sep 1988
2	400-metre freestyle (women)	4:03.85	Janet Evans, USA	22 Sep 1988
3	200-metre breaststroke (men)	2:10.16	Mike Barrowman, USA	29 July 1992
4	50-metre freestyle (men)	0:21.91	Alexander Popov, Unified Team	30 July 1992
5	200-metre backstroke (women)	2:07.06	Krisztina Egerszegi, Hungary	31 July 1992
6	1,500-metre freestyle (men)	14:43.48	Kieren Perkins, Australia	31 July 1992
7	100-metre breaststroke (women)	1:07.02	Penny Heyns, South Africa	21 July 1996
8	400-metre freestyle (men)	3:40.59	Ian Thorpe, Australia	16 Sep 2000
9	4 x 100-metre freestyle relay (men)	3:13.67	Australia	16 Sep 2000
10	400-metre individual medley (women)	4:33.59	Yana Klochkova, Ukraine	16 Sep 2000

The women's 400-metre freestyle final at the Seoul Olympics was a showdown between Heike Friedrich and Janet Evans. Friedrich had won 13 consecutive major finals, including five golds at the 1985 European Championships as a 15-year-old, and four golds at the 1986 World Championships. She had won the 200-metres freestyle in Seoul in a new Olympic record time, which still stands, but in the 400 metres she was about to meet her match in diminutive US swimmer Janet Evans. Evans was pushed all the way by Friedrich and her German compatriot Anke Möhring but, with two laps to go, Evans pulled away and won in a world record time, and two seconds clear of her rival. Amazingly, she swam the second half of the race faster than the first.

▼ Matt Biondi (below) and fellow American Mark Spitz are the most decorated Olympic swimmers.

Top 10 Fastest-ever men's 100-metre freestyle in the Olympics

	Swimmer/country	Year	Time (sec)
1	Pieter van den Hoogenband, Netherlands	2000	47.84
2	Pieter van den Hoogenband, Netherlands	2000	48.30
3	Matt Biondi, USA	1988	48.63
4	Pieter van den Hoogenband, Netherlands	2000	48.64
5	Alexander Popov, Russia	2000	48.69
6	Gary Hall Jr., USA	2000	48.73
7 =	Michael Klim, Australia	2000	48.74
=	Alexander Popov, Russia	1996	48.74
9 =	Michael Klim, Australia	2000	48.80
10	Gary Hall Jr., USA	1996	48.81

Gary Hall Jr., who makes two appearances in this list, comes from a family of swimmers. His grandfather, Charles Keating, was an All-America swimmer at the University of Cincinnati, and his uncle, Charles Keating Jr. was a member of the 1976 US Olympic team, while his father, Gary Hall Sr., won silver medals at the 1968 and 1972 Olympics and a bronze in the 1976 Olympics.

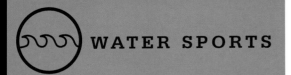
WORLD CHAMPIONS & RECORD HOLDERS

- Longest-standing men's world swimming records
- Longest-standing women's world swimming records
- Women's medal-winning countries at the World Swimming Championships
- Men's medal-winning countries at the World Swimming Championships
- Most men's gold medals at the World Championships

CHAMPIONSHIP VENUES

The swimming World Championships were first held in Belgrade, Yugoslavia, in 1973 and have generally been held sporadically since then. Championship venues have been: Cali, Colombia (1975); Berlin, West Germany (1978); Guayaquil, Ecuador (1982); Madrid, Spain (1986); Perth, Australia (1991); Rome, Italy (1994); Perth, Australia (1998); Fukuoka, Japan (2001). The 2003 venue is Barcelona, Spain.

The 10 Longest-standing men's world swimming records*

	Swimmer/country	Event	Time (min:secs)	Date
1	Mike Barrowman, USA	200-metre breaststroke	2:10.16	29 July 1992
2	Jani Sievinen, Finland	200-metre individual medley	1:58.16	11 Sep 1994
3	Lenny Krayzelburg, USA	100-metre backstroke	0:53.60	24 Aug 1999
4	Lenny Krayzelburg, USA	200-metre backstroke	1:55.87	27 Aug 1999
5	Lenny Krayzelburg, USA	50-metre backstroke	0:24.99	28 Aug 1999
6	Michael Klim, Australia	100-metre butterfly	0:51.81	12 Dec 1999
7	Alexander Popov, Russia	50-metre freestyle	0:21.64	16 June 2000
8	Australia	400-metre freestyle relay	3:13.67	16 Sep 2000
9	Tom Dolan, USA	400-metre individual medley	4:11.76	17 Sep 2000
10	Pieter van den Hoogenband, Netherlands	100-metre freestyle	0:47.84	19 Sep 2000

* Long course world records set in a 50-metre pool

Mike Barrowman's long-standing record in the 200-metre breaststroke is also the longest-standing men's Olympic record. Barrowman went into the final with the five fastest times in the event under his belt. He came out with the sixth, and a gold medal, with a 1.7-second margin of victory over Hungary's Norbert Rósza.

The 10 Longest-standing women's world swimming records*

	Swimmer/country	Event	Time (min:sec)	Date
1	East Germany	800-metre freestyle relay	7:55.47	18 Aug 1987
2	Janet Evans, USA	1,500-metre freestyle	15:52.10	26 Mar 1988
3	Janet Evans, USA	400-metre freestyle	4:03.85	22 Sep 1988
4	Janet Evans, USA	800-metre freestyle	8:16.22	20 Aug 1989
5	Krisztina Egerszegi, Hungary	200-metre backstroke	2:06.62	25 Aug 1991
6	Franziska van Almsick, Germany	200-metre freestyle	1:56.78	6 Sep 1994
7	Cihnong He, China	100-metre backstroke	1:00.16	10 Sep 1994
8	Yanyan Wu, China	200-metre individual medley	2:09.72	17 Oct 1997
9	Penelope Heyns, South Africa	100-metre breaststroke	1:06.52	23 Aug 1999
10	Penelope Heyns, South Africa	50-metre breaststroke	0:30.83	28 Aug 1999

* Long course world records set in a 50-metre pool

Janet Simpson's career has seen her win four Olympic golds and a silver in three Games (1988–96), plus three World Championship golds and a silver. She has set world records in three events and set six US national records. Her 45 national titles is a record second only to that of Tracy Caulkins, who has three more. Simpson won the coveted Sullivan Award as the top US athlete in 1989.

◀ East Germany's Kornelia Ender, who won four Olympic and a record eight World Championship gold medals.

Women's medal-winning countries at the World Swimming Championships*

	Country	Gold medals	Silver medals	Bronze medals	Total
1	USA	37	44	34	115
2	East Germany	44	32	15	91
3	China	21	10	7	38
4	Germany/West Germany	6	12	14	32
5	Australia	12	10	8	30
6	Netherlands	4	5	12	21
7	USSR/Russia	4	6	7	17
8	Canada	0	2	10	12
9	Japan	0	3	7	10
10	Hungary	4	2	2	8

* Excluding the long distance events – 5 km and 25 km

The UK is equal 11th, with 1 gold, 2 silvers, and 4 bronzes.

Men's medal-winning countries at the World Swimming Championships

	Country	Gold medals	Silver medals	Bronze medals	Total
1	USA	60	40	28	128
2	USSR/Russia	13	22	21	56
3	Germany/West Germany	11	15	18	44
4	Australia	18	10	8	36
5	Hungary	12	4	9	25
6	East Germany	6	8	10	24
7	UK	3	3	14	20
8	Italy	3	7	7	17
9	Sweden	3	5	8	16
10	Canada	4	6	4	14

▼ Australia's Ian Thorpe in action on the opening day of the swimming events at Homebush Bay during the 2000 Sydney Olympics. He won three golds to add to the eight he had collected in the World Championships.

Most men's gold medals at the World Championships*

	Swimmer/country	Years	Gold medals
1	Ian Thorpe, Australia	1998–2001	8
2	Jim Montgomery, USA	1973–75	7
3 =	Matt Biondi, USA	1986–91	6
=	Michael Klim, Australia	1998–2001	6
5 =	Rowdy Gaines, USA	1978–82	5
=	Michael Gross, West Germany	1982–90	5
7 =	Joe Bottom, USA	1978	4
=	Tamas Darnyi, Hungary	1986–91	4
=	Grant Hackett, Australia	1998–2001	4
=	Tom Jager, USA	1986–91	4
=	David McCagg, USA	1978–82	4
=	Vladimir Salnikov, Russia	1978–82	4
=	Tim Shaw, USA	1975	4

* Long course championships; diving not included

The most golds won by a woman is also eight, by Kornelia Ender (East Germany), 1973–75.

YACHTING & WATER SKIING

- Most Olympic yachting medals
- Medal-winning countries in yachting at the Olympic Games
- Men's World water-skiing titles
- Women's World water-skiing titles

Top 10 Most Olympic yachting medals

	Competitor/country	Years	G	S	B	Total
1 =	Paul Elvström, Denmark	1948–60	4	0	0	4
=	Torben Grael, Brazil	1984–2000	1	1	2	4
=	Valentyn Mankin, Russia	1968–80	3	1	0	4
=	Jochen Schümann, East Germany/Germany	1976–2000	3	1	0	4
5 =	Jesper Bank, Denmark	1988–2000	2	0	1	3
=	Léon Huybrechts, Belgium	1908–24	1	2	0	3
=	Poul Jensen, Denmark	1968–80	2	1	0	3
=	Barbara Kendall, New Zealand	1992–2000	1	1	1	3
=	Rodney Pattisson, UK	1968–76	2	1	0	3
=	Mark Reynolds, USA	1988–2000	2	1	0	3

G – gold medals, S – silver medals, B – bronze medals

Valentyn Mankin is the only person to win gold medals in three different classes: Finn, Tempest, and Star.

Paul Elvström didn't have the best of starts to his Olympic career in the Finn class at the 1948 Olympics, when he failed to finish the first race on day one. However, he clawed his way back to capture the first of his four Olympic gold medals, going on to become the first man to win gold medals at four consecutive Games.

ALL-ROUND WINNERS

The United States bronze medallists in the Tempest Class at the 1976 Montreal Olympics both had other claims to fame. Conn Findlay had previously won two golds and a bronze medal in coxed pair rowing events in 1956–64, while his skipper Dennis Conner won the America's Cup in 1980, 1987, and 1988.

Top 10 Medal-winning countries in yachting at the Olympic Games

	Country	Gold medals	Silver medals	Bronze medals	Total
1	USA	17	21	16	54
2	UK	18	12	8	38
3	Sweden	9	12	10	31
4	Norway	16	11	3	30
5	France	11	7	9	27
6	Denmark	11	8	4	23
7	Germany/West Germany	5	6	7	18
8 =	Australia	5	3	8	16
=	Netherlands	4	5	7	16
10 =	New Zealand	6	4	5	15
=	USSR/Unified Team/Russia	4	6	5	15

The United States' first Olympic yachting gold medal was in the Star class at the 1932 Los Angeles Games, when *Jupiter*, skippered by Gilbert Gray of New Orleans, won five of the seven races to win by 11 points from the United Kingdom team. It is appropriate that their first gold medal should come in the Star class because the Star was a 6.9-metre boat designed by Francis Sweisguth of New York in 1910.

▶ Action from Rushcutter's Bay, venue for the yachting events at the 2000 Sydney Olympic Games.

Top 10 Men's World water-skiing titles

	Skier/country	Overall	Slalom	Tricks	Jumps	Total
1	Patrice Martin, France	6	0	4	0	10
2 =	Sammy Duval, USA	4	0	0	2	6
=	Andy Mapple, UK	0	6	0	0	6
4 =	Bob La Point, USA	0	4	1	0	5
=	Jaret Llewellyn, Canada	1	0	1	3	5
=	Alfredo Mendoza, Mexico	2	1	0	2	5
=	Mike Suyderhoud, USA	2	1	0	2	5
8 =	George Athans, Canada	2	1	0	0	3
=	Guy de Clercq, Belgium	1	0	0	2	3
=	Wayne Grimditch, USA	0	0	2	1	3
=	Mike Hazelwood, UK	1	0	0	2	3
=	Ricky McCormick, USA	0	0	1	2	3
=	Billy Spencer, USA	1	1	1	0	3

Born in Nantes, France in 1964, Patrice Martin won the first of his 10 world titles (Tricks) in 1979. He won his tenth and last title 20 years later. His long career also saw him win 32 European titles and 13 Masters Tricks titles of the USA, France, and England. A bank accountant by occupation, he started water skiing at the age of two and first competed when he was eight.

Top 10 Women's World water-skiing titles

	Skier/country	Overall	Slalom	Tricks	Jumps	Total
1	Liz Shetter (née Allen), USA	3	3	1	4	11
2	Willa McGuire (née Worthington), USA	3	2	1	2	8
3	Cindy Todd, USA	2	3	0	2	7
4	Deena Mapple (née Brush), USA	2	0	0	4	6
5	Yelena Milakova, Russia	3	0	0	2	5
6 =	Marina Doria, Switzerland	1	1	2	0	4
=	Tawn Hahn (née Larsen), USA	0	0	4	0	4
=	Helena Kjellander, Sweden	0	4	0	0	4
=	Natalya Ponomaryeva (née Rumyantseva), USSR	1	0	3	0	4
10 =	Maria Victoria Carrasco, Venezuela	0	0	3	0	3
=	Britt Larsen, USA	0	0	3	0	3

Liz Shetter won two events at the US National Championships in 1962, at the age of 11. She went on to win 42 National titles in 13 seasons. In 1969, she set a record by winning all three events – slalom, tricks, and jumps – at the Nationals, the World Championships, and the Masters. She began water skiing at the age of five, after her family moved to Florida in 1955 from West Germany, where her father has been stationed prior to his retirement from the army. Shetter retired in 1975, much to the relief of her rivals.

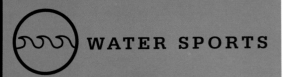
CANOEING & ROWING

- Most medals in Olympic canoeing
- Medal-winning countries in men's rowing in the Olympics
- Medal-winning countries in women's rowing in the Olympics
- Medal-winning countries in men's canoeing in the Olympics
- Medal-winning countries in women's canoeing in the Olympics

Top 10 Most medals in Olympic canoeing

	Competitor/country	Years	G	S	B	Total
1	Birgit Schmidt* (née Fischer), East Germany/Germany	1980–2000	7	3	0	10
2	Gert Fredriksson, Sweden	1948–60	6	1	1	8
3 =	Agneta Andersson*, Sweden	1984–96	3	2	2	7
=	Ivan Patzaichin, Romania	1968–84	4	3	0	7
5 =	Rüdiger Helm, East Germany	1978–80	3	0	3	6
=	Knut Holman, Norway	1992–2000	3	2	1	6
=	Rita Köbán*, Hungary	1988–2000	2	3	1	6
8 =	Kay Bluhm*, Germany	1992–96	3	1	1	5
=	Ian Ferguson, New Zealand	1984–88	4	1	0	5
=	Olaf Heukrodt, East Germany/Germany	1988–92	1	2	2	5
=	Paul MacDonald, New Zealand	1984–88	3	1	1	5
=	Ramona Portwich*, Germany	1992–96	3	2	0	5

G – gold medals, S – silver medals, B – bronze medals

* Female competitor

> "Always remember, there's more to life than rowing – but not much.
> **Donald Beer**, Olympic rowing medallist"

Top 10 Medal-winning countries in men's rowing in the Olympics

	Country	Gold medals	Silver medals	Bronze medals	Total
1	USA	28	22	17	67
2	Germany/West Germany	20	15	15	50
3	UK	21	15	7	43
4	Italy	14	13	10	37
5 =	France	6	14	12	32
=	USSR/Unified Team/Russia	11	14	7	32
7	East Germany	20	4	7	31
8	Switzerland	6	8	9	23
9 =	Australia	6	7	8	21
=	Canada	4	8	9	21

Rowing dates to the 1900 Paris Olympics for men, but as recently as 1976 for women. Some of the discontinued men's rowing events have included: Four-oared Inriggers with Coxswain, Six-man Naval Rowing Boat, and the Seventeen-man Naval Rowing Boat event. The latter two were part of the 1906 Intercalated Games in Athens, when Greece won four of the six medals.

Top 10 Medal-winning countries in women's rowing in the Olympics

	Country	Gold medals	Silver medals	Bronze medals	Total
1	Romania	13	6	5	24
2	East Germany	13	3	1	17
3	USSR/Unified Team/Russia	1	6	6	13
4 =	Canada	4	4	4	12
=	Germany/West Germany	5	2	5	12
=	USA	1	7	4	12
7	Bulgaria	2	4	4	10
8	Netherlands	0	3	2	5
9 =	Australia	1	1	2	4
=	China	0	2	2	4

One of the most touching of Olympic stories was at Barcelona in 1992 when Canada's Silken Laumann took bronze in the single sculls. Less than three months before the Olympics her leg was severely damaged in a freak rowing accident. She was told that she needed at least six months' recovery time, but insisted on making the Olympics, despite being able to walk only with the aid of a stick.

Top 10 Medal-winning countries in men's canoeing in the Olympics

	Country	Gold medals	Silver medals	Bronze medals	Total
1	Hungary	12	19	17	48
2	Germany/West Germany	17	11	17	45
3	USSR/Unified Team/Russia	22	13	7	42
4	Romania	9	9	10	28
5	France	4	6	16	26
6	Sweden	11	9	2	22
7	East Germany	8	5	8	21
8	Czechoslovakia/Czech Republic	10	8	2	20
9	Bulgaria	3	3	7	13
10	Canada	3	5	4	12

A Kayak singles race was contested at the 1906 Intercalated Games in Athens, but it was not until 1936 that canoeing became a regular Olympic sport. Sweden has Gerd Fredriksson to thank for its high rank on the all-time canoeing list because he won six gold medals, one silver, and one bronze between 1948 and 1960. He won the K-1 1,000-metre event at three successive Games. Between 1942 and his retirement in 1964, he won 71 National championships.

◀ Birgit Fischer (front) with Katrina Wagner after winning the K2 final at the 2000 Sydney Olympics. It was Fischer's seventh Olympic gold medal over a 20-year career.

Top 10 Medal-winning countries in women's canoeing in the Olympics

	Country	Gold medals	Silver medals	Bronze medals	Total
1	Germany/West Germany	8	8	2	18
2	Hungary	2	6	6	14
3	USSR/Unified Team/Russia	8	2	3	13
4	East Germany	6	2	1	9
5	Romania	1	2	4	7
6	Sweden	3	2	1	6
7 =	Bulgaria	1	2	1	4
=	Canada	0	3	1	4
=	Netherlands	0	2	2	4
=	Poland	0	0	4	4

Women's canoeing was first included in the 1948 London Olympics.

Birgit Fischer of Germany (formerly East Germany) is not only the only woman to win 10 Olympic canoeing medals, but also the only woman to win Olympic medals 20 years apart. When she won her first Olympic gold, in the Kayak singles in 1980, she became the youngest Olympic canoe champion at the age of 18. Had East Germany not boycotted the 1984 Los Angeles Games, she would surely have increased her medal tally.

HORSE RACING

At the Start

Horse racing developed in ancient times from the use of horses in combat and hunting. Horse and chariot racing were introduced into the Olympic Games and remained popular throughout the Roman Empire. There are records of organized horse races from the Middle Ages, and in England annual race meetings were held in York from 1530 and at Chester, Britain's oldest racecourse, from 1540. The Jockey Club was founded in 1750, and the Derby first run in 1780, followed by other races, many of which remain part of the racing calendar. In the United States, such notable races as the Belmont Stakes, Preakness Stakes, and Kentucky Derby date from the 1860s and 1870s. Harness racing with sulkies was first seen in 1829.

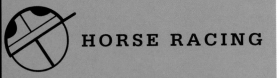
THE CLASSICS

CLASSIC FIRST

When Ma Biche won the 1,000 Guineas, she was trained by the French trainer Criquette Head-Maraak, who thus became the first woman to train a Classic winner in England.

Top 10 Jockeys in the English Classics

	Jockey	First/last wins	1,000 Guineas	2,000 Guineas	Derby	Oaks	St. Leger	Total
1	Lester Piggott	1954–92	2	5	9	6	8	30
2	Frank Buckle	1792–1827	6	5	5	9	2	27
3	Jem Robinson	1817–48	5	9	6	2	2	24
4	Fred Archer	1874–86	2	4	5	4	6	21
5 =	Bill Scott	1821–46	0	3	4	3	9	19
=	Jack Watts	1883–97	4	2	4	4	5	19
7	Willie Carson	1972–94	2	4	4	4	3	17
8 =	John Day	1826–41	5	4	0	5	2	16
=	George Fordham	1859–83	7	3	1	5	0	16
10	Joe Childs	1912–33	2	2	3	4	4	15

Lester Piggott's first Classic winner was Never Say Die at the age of 18, when he partnered the horse to victory in the Derby. His 30th and last win came seven years after his 29th, when he rode Rodrigo de Triano in the 1992 2,000 Guineas.

Top 10 Jockeys in the 1,000 Guineas

	Jockey	First win	Last win	Total
1	George Fordham	1859	1883	7
2	Frank Buckle	1818	1827	6
3 =	John Day	1826	1840	5
=	Jem Robinson	1824	1844	5
5 =	Charlie Elliott	1924	1944	4
=	Fred Rickaby Jr.	1913	1917	4
=	Jack Watts	1886	1897	4
8 =	Bill Arnull	1817	1832	3
=	Tom Cannon	1866	1884	3
=	Nat Flatman	1835	1857	3
=	Rae Johnstone	1935	1950	3
=	Dick Perryman	1926	1941	3
=	Gordon Richards	1942	1951	3
=	Walter Swinburn	1989	1993	3
=	Charlie Wood	1880	1887	3
=	Harry Wragg	1934	1945	3

First run in 1814, the 1,000 Guineas is a one-mile race for three-year-old fillies and is run over the Newmarket course.

Top 10 Jockeys in the 2,000 Guineas

	Jockey	First win	Last win	Total
1	Jem Robinson	1825	1848	9
2	John Osborne	1857	1888	6
3 =	Frank Buckle	1810	1827	5
=	Charlie Elliott	1923	1949	5
=	Lester Piggott	1957	1992	5
6 =	Fred Archer	1874	1885	4
=	Tom Cannon	1878	1889	4
=	Willie Carson	1972	1989	4
=	John Day	1826	1841	4
=	Herbert Jones	1900	1909	4

With the 1,000 Guineas, this is the other early-season Classic. First run in 1809, the 2000 Guineas is held over one mile at Newmarket and is open to three-year-old colts and fillies. The 2,000 Guineas' top jockey, Jem Robinson, rode Enamel, his first winner of the race, in 1825. Between 1833 and 1836, Robinson won the race four years in succession riding, respectively, Clearwell, Glencoe, Ibrahim, and Bay Middleton. Bay Middleton was the only one of his seven winners that did not have a single-word name.

▶ The five English Classics are held at just three courses – Epsom, Newmarket, and Doncaster.

Top 10 Jockeys in the Epsom Derby

	Jockey	First win	Last win	Total
1	Lester Piggott	1954	1983	9
2 =	Steve Donoghue	1915	1925	6
=	Jem Robinson	1817	1836	6
4 =	Fred Archer	1877	1886	5
=	John Arnull	1784	1799	5
=	Frank Buckle	1792	1823	5
=	Bill Clift	1793	1819	5
8 =	Sam Arnull	1780	1798	4
=	Willie Carson	1979	1994	4
=	Tom Goodison	1809	1822	4
=	Bill Scott	1832	1843	4
=	Charlie Smirke	1934	1958	4
=	Jack Watts	1887	1896	4

The most prestigious of all English Classics, the Derby is run over one-and-a-half miles at Epsom Downs. It takes place during the first week in June and is for three-year-old colts and fillies. One of Lester Piggott's nine Derby wins was on Nijinsky in 1970. Together, they won the Triple Crown of Derby, 2,000 Guineas, and St. Leger that year.

Top 10 Jockeys in the Oaks

	Jockey	First win	Last win	Total
1	Frank Buckle	1797	1823	9
2 =	Frank Butler	1843	1852	6
=	Lester Piggott	1957	1984	6
4 =	Sam Chifney Jr.	1807	1825	5
=	John Day	1828	1840	5
=	George Fordham	1859	1881	5
7 =	Fred Archer	1875	1885	4
=	Tom Cannon	1869	1884	4
=	Willie Carson	1978	1990	4
=	Sam Chifney Sr.	1782	1790	4
=	Joe Childs	1912	1921	4
=	Dennis Fitzpatrick	1787	1800	4
=	Jack Watts	1883	1893	4
=	Harry Wragg	1938	1946	4

Run in the same week as the Derby and over the same one-and-a-half mile course at Epsom, the Oaks was first run in 1779 and is named after the Epsom home of the 12th Earl of Derby. The race is for three-year-old fillies.

Top 10 Jockeys in the St. Leger

	Jockey	First win	Last win	Total
1	Bill Scott	1821	1846	9
2 =	John Jackson	1791	1822	8
=	Lester Piggott	1960	1984	8
4 =	Fred Archer	1877	1886	6
=	Ben Smith	1803	1824	6
6 =	Tom Challoner	1861	1875	5
=	John Mangle	1780	1792	5
=	Gordon Richards	1930	1944	5
=	Jack Watts	1883	1896	5
10 =	Joe Childs	1918	1926	4
=	Pat Eddery	1986	1997	4
=	Bob Johnson	1812	1820	4
=	Joe Mercer	1965	1981	4
=	Charlie Smirke	1934	1954	4

The oldest of the five English Classics, the St. Leger was first run in 1776 and is held over one mile six furlongs and 132 yards at Doncaster. It is open to three-year-old colts and fillies.

BREEDERS' CUP & TRIPLE CROWN

- Fastest winning times of the Kentucky Derby
- Trainers with the most Kentucky Derby runners
- Jockeys in the Breeders' Cup
- Money-winning jockeys in the Breeders' Cup
- Biggest winning margins in Breeders' Cup races
- Latest Triple Crown-winning horses

> "A horse gallops with his lungs, perseveres with his heart, and wins with his character."
>
> Federico Tesio, racehorse breeder

Top 10 Fastest winning times of the Kentucky Derby

	Horse	Year	Time (min:sec)
1	Secretariat	1973	1:59.2
2	Monarchos	2001	1:59.4
3	Northern Dancer	1964	2:00.0
4	Spend a Buck	1985	2:00.2
5	Decidedly	1962	2:00.4
6	Proud Clarion	1967	2:00.6
7	Grindstone	1996	2:01.0
8 =	Affirmed	1978	2:01.2
=	Fusaichi Pegasus	2000	2:01.2
=	Lucky Debonair	1965	2:01.2
=	Thunder Gulch	1995	2:01.2

Source: The Jockey Club

The Kentucky Derby is held on the first Saturday in May at Churchill Downs, Louisville, Kentucky. The first leg of the Triple Crown, it was first raced in 1875 over a distance of one mile four furlongs, but after 1896 was reduced to one mile two furlongs.

Top 10 Trainers with the most Kentucky Derby runners

	Trainer	Career	Runners
1	D. Wayne Lukas	1981–2000	38
2	Dick Thompson	1920–37	24
3	James Rowe Sr.	1881*–1925	18
4 =	Max Hirsch	1915–51	14
=	Woody Stephens	1949–88	14
6	LeRoy Jolley	1962–92	13
7	Nick Zito	1990–2001	12
8 =	Bob Baffert	1996–2001	11
=	Sunny Jim Fitzsimmons	1930–57	11
=	Ben Jones	1938–52	11

* Year of Rowe's first winner, Hindoo; year of first race unrecorded

In 1995, former high school basketball coach D. Wayne Lukas became the first man to train the winner of all three Triple Crown races – with different horses: Thunder Gulch (Derby and Belmont Stakes) and Timber Country (Preakness).

Top 10 Jockeys in the Breeders' Cup

	Jockey	Years	Wins
1 =	Jerry Bailey	1991–2001	12
=	Pat Day	1984–2001	12
3	Chris McCarron	1985–2001	9
4 =	Mike Smith	1992–97	8
=	Gary Stevens	1990–2000	8
6 =	Eddie Delahoussaye	1984–93	7
=	Laffit Pincay Jr.	1985–93	7
8 =	Jose Santos	1986–97	6
=	Pat Valenzuela	1986–92	6
10	Corey Nakatani	1996–99	5

Source: The Breeders' Cup

Held at a different venue each year, the Breeders' Cup is an end-of-season gathering with eight races run during the day, with the season's best thoroughbreds competing in each category. Staged in October or November, there was nearly $13,000,000 prize money on offer in 2001, with over $2,000,000 going to the winner of the day's senior race, the Classic.

Top 10 Money-winning jockeys in the Breeders' Cup

	Jockey	Career winnings ($)
1	Pat Day	21,717,800
2	Chris McCarron	17,669,520
3	Jerry Bailey	13,691,000
4	Gary Stevens	13,324,720
5	Mike Smith	8,194,200
6	Eddie Delahoussaye	7,775,000
7	Laffit Pincay Jr.	6,811,000
8	Corey Nakatani	6,440,360
9	Angel Cordero Jr.	6,020,000
10	Jose Santos	5,828,800

In 2001, Pat Day became only the third jockey, after Bill Shoemaker and Laffit Pincay Jr., to win 8,000 races. Day was born in 1953, and rode his first winner at age 20. His record money winnings in the Breeders' Cup have been aided by a record 12 wins, including four in the Classic, in 1984 on Wild Again, in 1990 on Unbridled, on Awesome Again in 1998, and Cat Thief in 1999.

Top 10 Biggest winning margins in Breeders' Cup races

	Winning horse	Runner-up	Year/race	Winning distance (lengths)
1	Inside Information	Heavenly Prize	1995 Distaff	13½
2	Countess Diana	Career Collection	1997 Juvenile Fillies	8½
3	Princess Rooney	Life's Magic	1984 Distaff	7
4	Bayakoa (Argentina)	Colonial Waters	1990 Distaff	6¾
5	Life's Magic	Lady's Secret	1985 Distaff	6¼
6	Skip Away	Deputy Commander	1997 Classic	6
7 =	Banks Hill (UK)	Sook Express	2001 Filly and Mare Turf	5½
=	Brave Raj	Tappiano	1986 Juvenile Fillies	5½
=	Favorite Trick	Dawson's Legacy	1997 Juvenile	5½
10 =	Arazi	Bertrando	1991 Juvenile	5
=	Brocco	Blumin Affair	1993 Juvenile	5
=	Meadow Star	Private Treasure	1990 Juvenile Fillies	5

▼ Pat Day celebrates winning his third Preakness on Tabasco Cat at Pimlico in 1994.

The 10 Latest Triple Crown-winning horses*

	Horse	Year
1	Affirmed	1978
2	Seattle Slew	1977
3	Secretariat	1973
4	Citation	1948
5	Assault	1946
6	Count Fleet	1943
7	Whirlaway	1941
8	War Admiral	1937
9	Omaha	1935
10	Gallant Fox	1930

* Horses that have won the Kentucky Derby, the Preakness, and Belmont Stakes in the same season

Since 1875, the only horse other than those in the above list to have won all three races in one season was Sir Barton, in 1919. Since Affirmed's victory in 1978, three horses have come close to winning the Triple Crown, but missed out by finishing second in one race. They were: Sunday Silence (1989), Silver Charm (1997), and Real Quiet (1998).

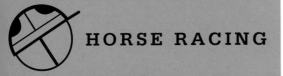

HORSE RACING

CHAMPION JOCKEYS

- Jockeys of all time in the UK
- Jockeys in a UK flat-racing season
- Most flat race Jockeys' Championships in the UK
- Most wins in a season by the annual money leader in the US
- Money-winning North American jockeys
- US jockeys with most wins in a career

> "Mother always told me my day was coming, but I never realized I'd end up being the shortest knight of the year.
> **Gordon Richards,** jockey, on being knighted, 1953

Top 10 Jockeys of all time in the UK

	Jockey	Years	Wins
1	Gordon Richards	1921–54	4,870
2	Lester Piggott	1948–95	4,513
3	Pat Eddery	1969–2001	4,476
4	Willie Carson	1962–96	3,828
5	Doug Smith	1931–67	3,111
6	Joe Mercer	1950–85	2,810
7	Fred Archer	1870–86	2,748
8	Edward Hide	1951–85	2,591
9	George Fordham	1850–84	2,587
10	Eph Smith	1930–65	2,313

When Pat Eddery rode Silver Partriarch to victory in the St. Leger at Doncaster on 13 September 1997, he became only the third member of the elite "4,000 Club" – jockeys who have won more than 4,000 races.

Top 10 Jockeys in a UK flat-racing season

	Jockey	Year	Wins
1	Gordon Richards	1947	269
2	Gordon Richards	1949	261
3	Gordon Richards	1933	259
4	Fred Archer	1885	246
5	Fred Archer	1884	241
6	Frankie Dettori	1994	233
7	Fred Archer	1883	232
8	Gordon Richards	1952	231
9	Fred Archer	1878	229
10	Gordon Richards	1951	227

Richards rode over 200 winners in a season 12 times, while Archer did so on eight occasions. The only other men to reach double centuries are Tommy Loates (1893), Pat Eddery (1990), Michael Roberts (1992), Frankie Dettori (1995), and Kieren Fallon (1997, 1998, and 1999).

Top 10 Most flat race Jockeys' Championships in the UK

	Jockey	First title	Last title	Total
1	Gordon Richards	1925	1953	26
2	George Fordham	1855	1871	14
3 =	Fred Archer	1874	1886	13
=	Elnathan "Nat" Flatman	1840	1852	13
5 =	Pat Eddery	1974	1996	11
=	Lester Piggott	1960	1982	11
7	Steve Donoghue	1914	1923	10
8	Morny Cannon	1891	1897	6
9 =	Willie Carson	1972	1983	5
=	Doug Smith	1954	1959	5

Apart from Pat Eddery (No. 5=), the best total of other current jockeys is four wins by Kieren Fallon, between 1997 and 2001. Sir Gordon Richards' last jockeys' title was in 1953, the year he eventually won the Derby on Pinza, when he beat the Queen's horse Auriole into second place – shortly after the Queen had knighted him. It was with some irony that Sir Gordon's career came to an end the following year after an accident on one of the Queen's horses.

▶ Bill Shoemaker on Ferdinand edges out Chris McCarron on Alysheba to win the 1987 Breeders' Cup Classic.

◄ Britain's most successful jockey Sir Gordon Richards, winner of the most races in a career, jockeys' titles, and races in a flat-racing season.

Top 10 Most wins in a season by the annual money leader in the US

	Jockey	Year	Wins
1	Steve Cauthen	1977	487
2	Bill Shoemaker	1953	485
3	Laffit Pincay Jr.	1979	420
4	Chris McCarron	1980	405
5	Angel Cordero Jr.	1982	397
6 =	Laffit Pincay Jr.	1971	380
=	Bill Shoemaker	1954	380
8	Darrel McHargue	1978	375
9	Jose Santos	1988	370
10	Angel Cordero Jr.	1983	362

Steve Cauthen rode his first winner just two weeks after his 16th birthday. He was still under 18 when he rode 487 winners in 1977. He won the Triple Crown at 18, and in 1979 moved to England where he went on to win 10 Classics, including the Derby twice (1985 and 1987).

Top 10 Money-winning North American jockeys*

	Jockey	Prize money ($)
1	Chris McCarron	260,239,073
2	Pat Day	256,418,663
3	Laffit Pincay Jr.	226,071,563
4	Jerry Bailey	218,820,137
5	Gary Stevens	202,224,804
6	Eddie Delahoussaye	190,427,188
7	Angel Cordero Jr.	164,561,227
8	Kent Desormeaux	148,784,542
9	Jose Santos	143,494,382
10	Alexis Solis	143,394,762

* Up to and including 2001 season

Source: NTRA Communications

Chris McCarron has won the Breeders' Cup Classic five times, each of the US Triple Crown races twice, and, in 2000, came close to winning the Epsom Derby when he finished fourth on Best of the Bests.

Top 10 US jockeys with most wins in a career*

	Jockey	Years riding	Wins
1	Laffit Pincay Jr.	38	9,291
2	Bill Shoemaker	42	8,833
3	Pat Day	29	8,146
4	Russell Baze	28	7,658
5	David Gall	43	7,396
6	Chris McCarron	27	7,089
7	Angel Cordero Jr.	35	7,057
8	Jorge Velasquez	33	6,795
9	Sandy Hawley	31	6,449
10	Larry Snyder	35	6,388

* As at end of 2001 season

Source: NTRA Communications

Laffit Pincay Jr. was born in Panama in 1946 and rode his first winner in the USA in 1966. He overtook Bill Shoemaker's all-time record on 10 December 1999 when, at the age of 52, he rode Irish Nip to victory at Hollywood Park. It was his 8,834th career win.

NATIONAL HUNT RECORDS

- Jockeys in the Grand National
- Fastest winning times of the Grand National
- First 20th century favourites to win the Grand National
- National Hunt jockeys with most wins in a career
- National Hunt jockeys with most wins in a season
- Most National Hunt jockeys' titles
- National Hunt trainers

> It's the greatest achievement a jump jockey can have. It's always what you wanted ever since you started riding. I am only sorry I never won it twice.
>
> **Willie Robinson,** after winning the Grand National on Team Spirit, 1964

Top 10 Jockeys in the Grand National

	Jockey*	First/last win	Wins
1	George Stevens	1856–70	5
2	Tom Oliver	1838–53	4
3 =	Mr. Jack Anthony	1911–20	3
=	Mr. Tommy Beasley	1880–89	3
=	Brian Fletcher	1968–74	3
=	Arthur Nightingale	1890–1901	3
=	Mr. Tommy Pickernell	1860–75	3
=	Ernie Piggott	1912–19	3
9 =	Richard Dunwoody	1986–94	2
=	Mr. Alec Goodman	1852–66	2
=	Carl Llewellyn	1992–98	2
=	Bryan Marshall	1953–54	2
=	John Page	1867–72	2
=	Mr. Maunsell Richardson	1873–74	2
=	Pat Taaffe	1955–70	2
=	Arthur Thompson	1948–52	2
=	Mr. Ted Wilson	1884–85	2
=	Fred Winter	1957–62	2
=	Percy Woodland	1903–13	2

* Amateur riders are traditionally indicated by the prefix "Mr".

Ernie Piggott, Lester Piggott's grandfather, is the only man to ride Grand National winners at two different courses. He rode Poethlyn to victory in the substitute race at Gatwick in 1918, and again at Aintree the following year.

Top 10 Fastest winning times of the Grand National

	Horse	Year	Time (min:sec)
1	Mr. Frisk	1990	8:47.8
2	Rough Quest	1996	9:00.8
3	Red Rum	1973	9:01.9
4	Royal Athlete	1995	9:04.6
5	Lord Gwyllene	1997	9:05.8
6	Party Politics	1992	9:06.3
7	Bindaree	2002	9:08.6
8	Papillon	2000	9:09.7
9	Grittar	1982	9:12.6
10	Bobbyjo	1999	9:14.0

The times of the substitute races held at Gatwick in the years 1916–18 are not included.

◄ Richard Dunwoody after winning the 1994 Grand National on the Martin Pipe-trained Minnehoma.

Top 10 First 20th-century favourites to win the Grand National

	Horse	Odds	Year
1	Drumcree	13-2	1903
2	Lutteur III	100-9	1909
3	Jerry M	4-1	1912
4	Poethlyn	11-4	1919
5	Sprig	8-1	1927
6	Freebooter	10-1	1950
7	Merryman II	13-2	1960
8	Red Rum	9-1	1973
9	Grittar	7-1	1982
10	Rough Quest	7-1	1996

Earth Summit (7-1), in 1998, was the only other favourite in the 20th century to win the race. In complete contrast, there have been just four 100-1 winners of the Grand National; the last, and perhaps most famous, was Foinavon in 1967. There is now a fence at Aintree named after him.

Top 10 National Hunt jockeys with most wins in a career

	Jockey	Years	Wins
1	Richard Dunwoody	1983-99	1,699
2	Peter Scudamore	1978-95	1,678
3	Tony McCoy	1994-2002*	1,603
4	John Francome	1970-85	1,138
5	Stan Mellor	1952-72	1,035
6	Adrian Maguire	1991-2002*	1,024
7	Peter Niven	1984-2002*	1,002
8	Fred Winter	1939-64	923
9	Graham McCourt	1975-96	921
10	Bob Davies	1966-82	911

* As at end of 2001-02 season

Peter Niven and Adrian Maguire both passed the 1,000 winners mark in 2001 and, by coincidence, they are the only two members of the "1,000 Club" never to have won the National Hunt jockeys' title. Niven is also the first Scot to ride 1,000 National Hunt winners.

Top 10 National Hunt jockeys with most wins in a season*

	Jockey	Years	Wins
1	Tony McCoy	2001-02	289
2	Tony McCoy	1997-98	253
3	Tony McCoy	1999-2000	245
4	Peter Scudamore	1988-89	221
5	Richard Dunwoody	1993-94	197
6	Tony McCoy	2000-01	191
7	Tony McCoy	1996-97	190
8	Tony McCoy	1998-99	186
9 =	Tony McCoy	1995-96	175
=	Peter Scudamore	1991-92	175

* Based on wins by champion jockeys

Tony McCoy's rise to becoming one of the greatest National Hunt jockeys has been meteoric since riding his first winner at Thurles, Ireland, on 26 March 1991. He moved to England in 1994, and joined the Toby Balding stable. He won his first jockeys' title in 1995-96 and has won it every year since.

Top 10 Most National Hunt jockeys' titles*

	Jockey	First/last win#	Total
1	Peter Scudamore	1982-91	8
2 =	John Francome	1976-85	7
=	Tony McCoy	1996-2002	7
=	Gerry Wilson	1933-41	7
5	Tich Mason	1901-07	6
6 =	Tim Molony	1949-55	5
=	Bilbie Rees	1920-27	5
=	Billy Stott	1928-32	5
9 =	Josh Gifford	1963-68	4
=	Fred Rimmell	1939-46	4
=	Fred Winter	1953-58	4

* Since 1900

Where the season is over two years, the year indicates the second half of the season

Peter Scudamore never managed to win the Grand National or the Cheltenham Gold Cup despite winning a record eight jockeys' titles. He also won 1,678 races in his career and achieved 221 winners in the 1988-89 season, both records at the time of his retirement.

Top 10 National Hunt trainers*

	Trainer	Season	Prize money ($)
1	Martin Pipe	2001-02	2,692,177
2	Martin Pipe	1999-2000	1,677,604
3	Martin Pipe	1997-98	1,504,898
4	Martin Pipe	1996-97	1,399,510
5	Martin Pipe	2000-01	1,356,517
6	Martin Pipe	1998-99	1,257,034
7	Martin Pipe	1995-96	964,214
8	David Nicholson	1994-95	896,683
9	Martin Pipe	1992-93	808,012
10	David Nicholson	1993-94	754,069

* Based on money won by the leading trainers in a UK season

Martin Pipe broke Arthur Stephenson's all-time record for being the most successful trainer in Britain when he saddled Through the Rye to victory at Folkestone on 4 February 2000. It was the 2,989th winner of his training career and 25 years after his first winner, Hit Parade, at Taunton on 9 May 1975.

◄ Tony McCoy, the most successful National Hunt jockey of the last seven seasons, which in 2001-02 saw him break the all-time UK record for the most winners in a season.

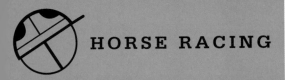
SHOW JUMPING & OTHER EQUESTRIAN SPORTS

- Riders winning both the Badminton and Burghley Horse Trials
- Olympic equestrian medallists
- Olympic three-day event medal-winning countries
- Olympic dressage medal-winning countries
- Olympic show jumping medal-winning countries

DEFYING THE ODDS

The dressage silver medallist of 1952 and 1956, Lis Hartel of Denmark, contracted polio in 1944 when she was 23 years old and pregnant. She gave birth to a baby daughter and, despite being paralyzed from the knees downwards, won two Olympic silver medals. The sight of gold medal winner Henri St. Cyr helping Lis onto the victory podium in 1952 was a moment that epitomized the true spirit of the Olympics.

Top 10 Riders winning both the Badminton and Burghley Horse Trials*

Rider/country#	Badminton	Burghley	Total
1 = Lucinda Green (née Prior-Palmer)	6	2	8
= Virginia Leng (née Holgate)	3	5	8
= Mark Todd, New Zealand	3	5	8
4 Mark Phillips	4	1	5
5 Sheila Waddington (née Wilcox)	3	1	4
6 = Jane Bullen	2	1	3
= Mary King (née Thomson)	2	1	3
= Richard Meade	2	1	3
9 = Bruce Davidson, USA	1	1	2
= Anneli Drummond-Hay	1	1	2
= James Templer	1	1	2

  * A rider must have won each event at least once to qualify for the list

  # All UK unless otherwise stated

Ian Stark also had three wins, but all were in the Badminton event. Lucinda Green was born in Hampshire in 1953 and has been riding since the age of four. Her record six Badminton wins came on six different horses: Be Fair (1973), Wideawake (1976), George (1977), Killaire (1979), Regal Realm (1983), and Beagle Bay (1984). A World and European champion, she never achieved Olympic gold, although she was the British team's flag bearer at the 1984 Los Angeles Games.

Top 10 Olympic equestrian medallists

Rider/country	Gold medals	Silver medals	Bronze medals	Total
1 Dr. Reiner Klimke, Germany	6	0	2	8
2 Hans-Günther Winkler, Germany	5	1	1	7
3 = Piero d'Inzeo, Italy	0	2	4	6
= Raimondo d'Inzeo, Italy	1	2	3	6
= Josef Neckerman, Germany	2	2	2	6
= Michael Plumb, USA	2	4	0	6
= Isabell Werth, Germany	4	2	0	6
8 = Henri Chammartin, Switzerland	1	2	2	5
= Gustav Fischer, Switzerland	0	3	2	5
= André Jousseaumé, France	2	2	1	5
= Liselott Linsenhoff, Germany	2	2	1	5
= Christine Stückelberger, Switzerland	1	3	1	5
= Earl Thomson, USA	2	3	0	5
= Mark Todd, New Zealand	2	1	2	5
= Anky van Grunsven, Netherlands	1	4	0	5

> Dressage may not strike the uninitiated as a very dramatic sport, but like so many of the really good things in life, it can become an acquired taste.
>
> **Sandy Pflueger,** US 1984 Olympic dressage competitor

Top 10 Olympic three-day event medal-winning countries

	Country	Gold medals	Silver medals	Bronze medals	Total
1	USA	6	9	6	21
2	Germany/West Germany	3	7	8	18
3 =	Sweden	7	3	3	13
=	UK	4	5	4	13
5	Australia	6	2	2	10
6	New Zealand	3	2	4	9
7	Italy	3	3	2	8
8	Netherlands	5	2	0	7
9	France	2	1	2	5
10	USSR	1	1	1	3

Although Helen Dupont of the United States did not win a medal at the 1964 Tokyo Olympics, she made history as the first female competitor in the history of three-day eventing at the Games. Three-day eventing dates from the 1912 Stockholm Olympics, when the United States won its first medal in the event in the team competition.

Top 10 Olympic dressage medal-winning countries

	Country	Gold medals	Silver medals	Bronze medals	Total
1	Germany/West Germany	17	7	7	31
2	Sweden	5	5	7	17
3	Switzerland	3	6	3	12
4 =	France	3	5	2	10
=	USSR	4	3	3	10
6 =	Netherlands	1	4	2	7
=	USA	0	1	6	7
8 =	Austria	1	0	1	2
=	Denmark	0	2	0	2
10 =	Bulgaria	0	1	0	1
=	Canada	0	0	1	1
=	Portugal	0	0	1	1
=	Romania	0	0	1	1

Dressage is notable for providing some of the oldest Olympic competitors. Arthur von Pongracz of Austria was 72 when he competed in Berlin in 1936, and in Munich in 1972. Maud Von Rosen of Sweden became the oldest female medallist in Olympic history at the age of 46.

Top 10 Olympic show jumping medal-winning countries

	Country	Gold medals	Silver medals	Bronze medals	Total
1	Germany/West Germany	13	3	5	21
2	France	5	4	5	14
3 =	Italy	3	5	5	13
=	USA	3	7	3	13
5	UK	1	3	5	9
6 =	Belgium	1	2	3	6
=	Sweden	3	0	3	6
=	Switzerland	1	3	2	6
9 =	Mexico	2	1	2	5
=	Netherlands	2	3	0	5

It is perhaps surprising that, with their record in the World and European championships, the UK has won only one gold medal in the show jumping event at the Olympics, in Helsinki in 1952, when Wilfred White, Douglas Stewart, and Harry Llewellyn won the team gold.

◀ One of eventing's leading exponents, Lucinda Green, who won Badminton a record six times between 1973 and 1984.

OTHER SPORTS

At the Start

Human ingenuity has given rise to an infinite variety of sporting activities devised with the purpose of pitting individuals and teams against each other. Some, such as Australian rules football, represent national variations on games played elsewhere, while others are simple innovations – for example, table tennis developed from impromptu indoor games. Many sports, including cycling, Paralympic events, and bobsleighing, have developed as new materials and technologies have been applied to established equipment. Yet others, such as darts, have been adapted from a form of self defence – the Pilgrim Fathers are known to have played darts aboard the *Mayflower* on their way to the New World in 1620.

CYCLING

- Most wins in the three major Tours
- Most medals in the World Road Race Championship
- Oldest cycling classic races
- Medal-winning cycling countries at the Olympics
- Countries providing the most winners of the three major Tours

HISTORY REPEATED

The result of the 2001 Tour de France was a repeat of the previous year's race, when Lance Armstrong (USA), Jan Ullrich (Germany), and Joseba Beloki (Spain) once again occupied first, second, and third places. The only other time this occurred was in 1978 and 1979, when Bernard Hinault (France), Joop Zoetemelk (Netherlands), and Joaquim Agostinho (Portugal) occupied the first three places in successive years.

Top 10 Most wins in the three major Tours*

	Cyclist/country	Tour	Giro	Vuelta	Years	Total
1	Eddy Merckx, Belguim	5	5	1	1968–74	11
2	Bernard Hinault, France	5	3	2	1978–85	10
3	Jacques Anquetil, France	5	2	1	1957–64	8
4 =	Fausto Coppi, Italy	2	5	0	1940–53	7
=	Miguel Induráin, Spain	5	2	0	1991–95	7
6 =	Gino Bartali, Italy	2	3	0	1938–48	5
=	Alfredo Binda, Italy	0	5	0	1925–33	5
=	Felice Gimondi, Italy	1	3	1	1965–76	5
9	Tony Rominger, Switzerland	0	1	3	1992–95	4
10 =	Lance Armstrong, USA	3	0	0	1999–2001	3
=	Louison Bobet, France	3	0	0	1953–55	3
=	Giovanni Brunero, Italy	0	3	0	1921–26	3
=	Pedro Delgado, Spain	1	0	2	1986–89	3
=	Laurent Fignon, France	2	1	0	1983–89	3
=	Charly Gaul, Luxembourg	1	2	0	1956–59	3
=	Greg LeMond, USA	3	0	0	1986–90	3
=	Fiorenzo Magni, Italy	0	3	0	1948–55	3
=	Philippe Thys, Belguim	3	0	0	1913–20	3

* The three major tours are: the Tour de France, launched in 1903 and won by Maurice Garin (France); the Tour of Italy (Giro d'Italia), first contested in 1909 and won by Luigi Ganna (Italy); the Tour of Spain (Vuelta de España), first held in 1935 and won by Gustave Deloor (Belgium)

Eddy Merckx won a record 33 stages in the Tour de France in 1969–75.

Top 10 Most medals in the World Road Race Championship*

	Cyclist/country	Years	G	S	B	Total
1 =	Jeannie Longo, France	1981–2001	5	2	1	8
=	Ketie von Oosten Hage, Holland	1966–78	2	3	3	8
3	Yvonne Reynders, Belgium	1959–76	4	2	1	7
4 =	Alfredo Binda, Italy	1927–32	3	0	1	4
=	André Darrigade, France	1957–60	1	1	2	4
=	Anna Konkina, Russia	1967–72	2	0	2	4
=	Greg LeMond, USA	1982–89	2	2	0	4
=	Catherine Marsal, France	1989–97	1	2	1	4
=	Rik van Steenbergen, Belgium	1946–57	3	0	1	4
=	Rik van Looy, Belgium	1956–63	2	2	0	4

* Men's and women's

G – gold medals, S – silver medals, B – bronze medals

◀ Lance Armstrong of the USA during the Prologue of the Tour De France 2001 in Dunkerque, France.

Top 10 Oldest cycling classic races

	Race	First held
1	Bordeaux–Paris	1891
2	Liège–Bastogne–Liège	1892
3	Paris–Brussels	1893
4	Paris–Roubaix	1896
5	Tour de France	1903
6	Tour of Lombardy	1905
7	Milan–San Remo	1907
8	Giro d'Italia (Tour of Italy)	1909
9	Tour of Flanders	1913
10	Grand Prix des Nations	1932

Regarded as the "Derby of Road Racing", the Bordeaux–Paris race lasted for around 16 hours, starting in darkness in the early hours of the morning. The first race, in 1891, was won by the UK's George Pilkington Mills. Originally for amateurs, it became a professional race and remained so until its last staging in 1989.

Top 10 Medal-winning cycling countries at the Olympics

	Country	G (men)	S (men)	B (men)	G (women)	S (women)	B (women)	Total
1	France	33	10	24	5	4	1	77
2	Italy	31	12	7	4	1	0	55
3	UK	10	22	17	0	0	1	50
4	Germany/West Germany	14	14	15	1	3	2	49
5	USA	11	6	13	1	2	3	36
6	Netherlands	9	11	4	4	2	3	33
7 =	Australia	6	9	10	1	3	1	30
=	USSR/Russia	11	5	9	2	1	2	30
9	Belgium	6	7	10	0	0	0	23
10	Denmark	6	4	7	0	0	0	17

G – gold medals, S – silver medals, B – bronze medals

Since riders were not allowed to have assistance from outsiders during the road race in 1932, it is reported that the champion, Attilio Pavesi (Italy), carried with him the following: a bowl of soup, a bottle of water, sandwiches, spaghetti, cinnammon rolls, jam, and two spare tyres.

Top 10 Countries providing the most winners of the three major Tours

	Country	Tour	Giro	Vuelta	Total
1	Italy	9	60	4	73
2	France	36	6	9	51
3	Spain	8	2	24	34
4	Belgium	18	7	7	32
5	Switzerland	2	2	5	9
6	USA	6	1	0	7
7	Luxembourg	4	2	0	6
8	Netherlands	2	0	2	4
9	Ireland	1	1	1	3
10 =	East Germany	0	0	2	2
=	Germany/West Germany	1	-	1	2
=	Russia	0	2	0	2

▶ Spain's Miguel Induráin, the only man to win the Tour de France five years in succession, from 1991–95.

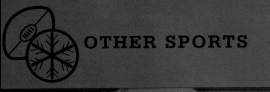
GYMNASTICS

- Olympic medals in men's gymnastics
- Olympic medals in women's gymnastics
- Medal-winning countries in men's events at the Olympics
- Medal-winning countries in women's events at the Olympics
- Most individual World gymnastic titles

MAKING A TRIBUTE

When gymnast Vera Cáslavská returned home to Czechoslovakia from the 1968 Mexico Olympics, she gave her four gold medals away to the four Czech leaders, Dubcek, Svoboda, Cernik, and Smrkorsky, who had been in power at the time of the Soviet invasion in 1967.

Top 10 Olympic medals in men's gymnastics

	Gymnast/country	Years	G	S	B	Total
1	Nikolai Andrianov, USSR	1972–80	7	5	3	15
2 =	Takashi Ono, Japan	1956–64	5	4	4	13
=	Boris Shakhlin, USSR	1956–64	7	4	2	13
4 =	Sawao Kato, Japan	1968–76	8	3	1	12
=	Alexei Nemov, Russia	1996–2000	4	2	6	12
6	Viktor Chukarin, USSR	1952–56	7	3	1	11
7 =	Aleksandr Ditiatin, USSR	1976–80	3	6	1	10
=	Akinori Nakayama, Japan	1968–72	6	2	2	10
=	Vitaly Scherbo, Unified Team/Belarus	1992–96	6	0	4	10
10 =	Eizo Kenmotsu, Japan	1968–76	3	3	3	9
=	Heikki Savolainen, Finland	1928–52	2	1	6	9
=	Yuri Titov, USSR	1956–64	1	5	3	9
=	Mitsuo Tsukahara, Japan	1968–76	5	1	3	9
=	Mikhail Voronin, USSR	1968–72	1	5	3	9

G – gold medals, S – silver medals, B – bronze medals

Aleksandr Ditiatin is the only gymnast to obtain medals in all eight events at one Olympiad, winning three golds, four silvers, and a bronze in Moscow in 1980.

Top 10 Olympic medals in women's gymnastics

	Gymnast/country	Years	G	S	B	Total
1	Larissa Latynina, USSR	1956–64	9	5	4	18
2	Vera Cáslavská, Czechoslovakia	1960–68	7	4	0	11
3 =	Polina Astahkova, USSR	1956–64	5	2	3	10
=	Ágnes Keleti, Hungary	1952–56	5	3	2	10
5 =	Nadia Comaneci, Romania	1976–80	5	3	1	9
=	Lyudmila Tourischeva, USSR	1968–76	4	3	2	9
7 =	Margit Korondi, Hungary	1952–56	2	2	4	8
=	Sofia Muratova, USSR	1956–60	2	2	4	8
9 =	Nelli Kim, USSR	1976–80	5	2	0	7
=	Olga Korbut, USSR	1972–76	4	2	0	7
=	Maria Goroshovskaya, USSR	1952	2	5	0	7
=	Karin Janz, East Germany	1968–72	2	3	2	7
=	Shannon Miller, USA	1992–96	2	2	3	7

G – gold medals, S – silver medals, B – bronze medals

With 18 medals, Larissa Latynina (USSR) holds the record for medals won by any athlete in any sport in Olympic history. Vera Cáslavská (1968) and Daniela Silivas, (Romania, 1988) are the only gymnasts to win medals in all six events at one Olympics.

◀ Vera Cáslavská (Czechoslovakia) in action during the vault competition at the 1968 Olympics in Mexico City. She won the gold medal for the event.

Top 10 Medal-winning countries in men's events at the Olympics

	Country	Gold medals	Silver medals	Bronze medals	Total
1	USSR/Unified Team/Russia	49	45	24	118
2	Japan	27	28	30	85
3	USA	22	17	19	58
4	Switzerland	16	19	13	48
5	Germany/West Germany	12	7	11	30
6	Italy	13	7	9	29
7	Finland	8	5	12	25
8	China	9	10	4	23
9	France	4	9	9	22
10	Czechoslovakia	3	7	9	19

Gymnastics was first seen at the inaugural Modern Olympics in 1896 and has been contested at every Games since. The United Kingdom has won just three gymnastics medals, one silver and two bronzes, the last being a bronze medal in 1928. Europeans dominated the first two Olympics in Athens in 1896 and Paris in 1900, but the St. Louis Games of 1904 were monopolized by the host country, who won 27 of the 33 gymnastics medals, including a clean sweep in nine of the 11 events. The other six medals were distributed evenly between Austria, Switzerland, and Germany.

Top 10 Medal-winning countries in women's events at the Olympics

	Country	Gold medals	Silver medals	Bronze medals	Total
1	USSR/Unified Team/Russia	42	34	32	108
2	Romania	18	15	19	52
3	Hungary	7	6	10	23
4	East Germany	3	10	7	20
5	USA	4	6	9	19
6	Czechoslovakia	9	6	1	16
7	China	3	4	4	11
8	Sweden	1	1	1	3
9 =	Bulgaria	0	1	1	2
=	Germany/West Germany	1	1	0	2
=	Ukraine	1	1	0	2

Women's gymnastics was first seen at the 1928 Amsterdam Games, but for a team competition in combined exercises only – individual events were not introduced until the 1952 Helsinki Games. Rhythmic Gymnastics was introduced in Los Angeles in 1984, and is for women gymnasts only. The leading country is USSR/Unified Team/Russia, which has won nine of the 21 medals contested up to 2000. Aleksandra Tymoshenko (USSR/Unified Team) is the only person to win two Rhythmic Gymnastics medals (one gold and one bronze).

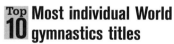

▶ Olga Korbut, the girl who reinvigorated the sport of gymnastics. She became the darling of the crowd at the 1972 Munich Games, and the judges liked her too – she won two individual gold medals.

Top 10 Most individual World gymnastics titles

	Gymnast/country	Years	Golds
1	Vitaliy Scherbo, Belarus	1993–96	14
2	Larissa Latynina*, USSR	1956–64	12
3 =	Vera Cáslavská*, Czechoslovakia	1962–68	10
=	Boris Shakhlin, USSR	1956–64	10
5 =	Nikolai Andrianov, USSR	1972–80	9
=	Dimitry Bilozerchev, USSR	1983–88	9
=	Akinori Nakayama, Japan	1966–72	9
=	Daniela Silivas*, Romania	1985–89	9
=	Leon Stukelj, Yugoslavia	1922–28	9
10	Joseph Martinez, France	1903–09	7

* Women's champion

The World Championships were first held in Antwerp in 1903. In Olympic years, the Olympic champion is also declared World Champion.

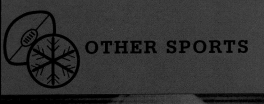

BADMINTON, TABLE TENNIS & SQUASH

- Most All-England badminton singles titles

- Most World table tennis titles

- Most World table tennis team titles

- Most British Open squash titles

ALL-ROUNDER

Kitty McKane, winner of four All-England badminton titles between 1920 and 1924, was also the women's singles champion at Wimbledon on two occasions, in 1924 and 1926 (as Kitty Godfrey in the latter year).

Top 10 Most All-England badminton singles titles

	Player/country	Male/female	Years	Wins
1	Rudy Hartono, Indonesia	M	1968–76	8
2	Erland Kops, Denmark	M	1958–67	7
3 =	Frank Devlin, Ireland	M	1925–31	6
=	Judy Hashman (née Devlin), USA	F	1961–67	6
5	Ralph Nicholls, England	M	1932–38	5
6 =	Eddy Choong, Malaysia	M	1953–57	4
=	Morten Frost, Denmark	M	1982–87	4
=	Wong Peng Soon, Malaysia	M	1950–55	4
=	Susi Susanti, Indonesia	F	1990–94	4
=	George Thomas, England	M	1920–23	4

First contested in 1899, the All-England Championships were the most prestigious badminton championships in the world prior to the launch of the World Championships in 1977. However, they have still retained their standing as a major event within the sport.

Top 10 Most World table tennis titles

	Country	Singles	Men's doubles	Women's doubles	Mixed doubles	Total
1	Maria Mednyánszky, Hungary	5	0	7	6	18
2	Viktor Barna, Hungary/England	5	8	0	2	15
3	Angelica Rozeanu, Romania	6	0	3	3	12
4	Anna Sipos, Hungary	2	0	6	3	11
5 =	Gizi Farkas, Hungary	3	0	3	4	10
=	Miklós Szabados, Hungary	1	6	0	3	10
7	Bohumil Vána, Czechoslovakia	2	3	0	3	8
8 =	Ichiro Ogimura, Japan	2	2	0	3	7
=	Ferenc Sidó, Hungary	1	2	0	4	7
10	Deng Yaping, China	3	0	3	0	6

Viktor Barna won five singles titles between 1930 and 1935. He was prevented from making it six in a row by his regular doubles partner Miklós Szabados, who beat Barna in the 1931 final. He captured all three titles at the 1935 Championships at Wembley, England. His singles career was ended shortly afterwards when his playing arm was severely injured in a car crash. He made a comeback, though, and, representing England with Richard Bergmann, won the doubles in 1939.

Top 10 Most World table tennis team titles*

	Country	Swaythling Cup	Corbillon Cup	Total
1	China	13	14	27
2	Japan	7	8	15
3	Hungary	12	0	12
4	Czechoslovakia	6	3	9
5 =	Romania	0	5	5
=	Sweden	5	0	5
7 =	England	1	2	3
=	USA	1	2	3
9 =	Germany	0	2	2
=	Korea/South Korea	0	2	2

* For the Swaythling Cup (men) and Corbillon Cup (women)

The Swaythling Cup was first contested in 1926 and is the men's team trophy at the World Championships, which is held every two years. It was donated by Lady Swaythling, the mother of the Hon. Ivor Montagu, the first president of the International Table Tennis Federation. The Corbillon Cup is the ladies' equivalent of the Swaythling Cup and was presented in 1934 by Marcel Corbillon, president of the French Table Tennis Association.

Top 10 Most British Open squash titles

	Player/country	Male/female	Years	Wins
1	Heather McKay (née Blundell), Australia	F	1962–77	16
2 =	Jahangir Khan, Pakistan	M	1982–91	10
=	Janet Morgan, UK	F	1950–59	10
4 =	Susan Devoy, New Zealand	F	1984–92	8
=	Geoff Hunt, Australia	M	1969–81	8
6	Hashim Khan, Pakistan	M	1951–58	7
7 =	Jonah Barrington, UK	M	1967–73	6
=	Abdelfattah Amr Bey, Egypt	M	1933–38	6
=	Jansher Khan, Pakistan	M	1992–97	6
=	Michelle Martin, Australia	F	1993–98	6

Until the launch of the World Amateur Championships in 1967, the British Open was regarded as the unofficial World Championship. It was first held for women at Queen's Club in 1922, and for men in 1930, when C. R. Read was designated as "champion", though in the first match for the championship, also at Queen's Club, in 1931, he was beaten by Don Butcher.

▶ Pakistan's Jahangir Khan was the British Open winner ten times, and won the World Open title six times.

WEIGHTLIFTING, WRESTLING & JUDO

- Olympic medal-winning countries in weightlifting
- Countries setting the most world weightlifting records
- Olympic medal-winning countries in freestyle wrestling
- Olympic medal-winning countries in men's judo
- Olympic medal-winning countries in women's judo

A STARRING ROLE

The silver medallist in the 82.5 kg class (now light-heavyweight) weightlifting competition at the 1948 London Olympics was Harold Sakata of the United States who played the part of Oddjob in the James Bond film, *Goldfinger*. He was also a one-time professional wrestler using the name Tosh Togo.

Top 10 Olympic medal-winning countries in weightlifting

	Country	Gold medals	Silver medals	Bronze medals	Total
1	USSR/Unified Team/Russia	46	26	5	77
2	USA	15	16	10	41
3	Bulgaria	11	16	7	34
4	Germany/West Germany	7	9	14	30
5	Poland	4	4	19	27
6	China	7	7	8	22
7	Hungary	2	7	10	19
8 =	France	9	2	4	15
=	Greece	7	5	3	15
=	Italy	5	5	5	15

Weightlifting made its debut in the first Modern Olympics in 1896. It appeared again in 1904, and also at the Intercalated Games of 1906, but it has not been a regular sport since 1920. Women's weightlifting was added in Sydney in 2000, when China won four of the seven gold medals.

Top 10 Countries setting the most world weightlifting records*

	Country	Men	Women	Total
1	USSR/Russia	648	9	657
2	China	42	445	487
3	Bulgaria	226	26	252
4	USA	60	7	67
5 =	France	51	0	51
=	Turkey	44	7	51
7	Poland	33	13	46
8	Germany/West Germany	44	0	44
9	Egypt	40	0	40
10	Japan	38	0	38

* Senior men's and women's world records only

Source: International Weightlifting Federation (IWF)

G – gold medals, S – silver medals, B – bronze medals

Vassily Alexeev (USSR) is one of the most prolific world record holders in any sport. Between 20 January 1970 and 1 November 1977 he set 80 world records. Weighing 148 kg (327 lb), he would have a 36-egg omelette for breakfast and half a dozen steaks for lunch.

Top 10 Olympic medal-winning countries in freestyle wrestling

	Country	G	S	B	Total
1	USA	45	34	24	103
2	USSR/Unified Team/Russia	38	19	15	72
3	Turkey	16	11	7	34
4	Japan	16	9	8	33
5	Bulgaria	7	16	9	32
6 =	Sweden	8	10	8	26
=	Iran	5	9	12	26
8	Finland	8	7	10	25
9	South Korea/Korea	4	8	7	19
10	UK	3	4	10	17

G – gold medals, S – silver medals, B – bronze medals

Freestyle wrestling was first seen at the 1904 St. Louis Games and has been featured ever since, with the exception of 1912. Wilfred Dietrich (West Germany) is the only man to have won five Olympic wrestling medals (all freestyle). He won one gold (1960), two silvers (1956, 1960), and two bronzes (1964, 1968).

▶ Vassily Alexeev of Russia on his way to winning the Super Heavyweight gold medal at the 1976 Montreal Olympics with a total lift of 640 kg – 30 kg more than the silver medallist.

Top 10 Olympic medal-winning countries in men's judo

	Country	Gold medals	Silver medals	Bronze medals	Total
1	Japan	21	6	8	35
2	USSR/Unified Team/Russia	7	5	16	28
3	France	6	4	14	24
4	South Korea/Korea	5	9	8	22
5	Germany/West Germany	2	5	9	16
6	UK	0	5	7	12
7	Brazil	2	3	5	10
8	East Germany	1	2	6	9
9 =	Netherlands	4	0	4	8
=	USA	0	3	5	8

Top 10 Olympic medal-winning countries in women's judo

	Country	Gold medals	Silver medals	Bronze medals	Total
1 =	Cuba	4	4	5	13
=	Japan	2	6	5	13
3	China	4	1	4	9
4 =	France	4	1	3	8
=	South Korea/Korea	2	2	4	8
6	Belgium	1	1	4	6
7	Spain	3	0	2	5
8 =	UK	0	2	2	4
=	Italy	0	1	3	4
10	Netherlands	0	0	3	3

Judo was first contested at the Tokyo Olympics in 1964. It was not included in 1968, but returned in 1972, and has been contested ever since.

Great Britain has always done well at judo, despite not having won an Olympic gold medal. Neil Adams won consecutive silver medals in 1980 and 1984. He was on course to win the UK's first judo gold in 1984, but with just three minutes to go in the final against Frank Wieneke of Germany, Adams glanced at the clock in the hall. Noticing his distraction, his opponent pounced and Adams was on the mat. He lost by an ippon for the first time in his career, and the gold medal slipped away.

Women's judo was first included as a demonstration sport at the 1988 Seoul Olympic Games, and became a full medal sport four years later.

Two of Spain's three gold medals came on home soil at the 1992 Barcelona Olympic Games. The judges were popular with the home crowd, particularly after the half-lightweight semi-final between local favourite Almundena Muñoz Martinez and tournament-favourite Sharon Rendle of the UK. The referee awarded the contest to Rendle, but the judges overruled and gave the match to the Spanish competitor, who went on to win the gold medal by beating Japan's Noriko Mizoguchi.

OTHER SPORTS

- Most men's World archery titles
- Olympic medal-winning countries in archery
- Men's individual Olympic shooting medal winners
- Individual Olympic fencing medal winners

LONG OLYMPIC CAREER

Danish fencer Ivan Osiier appeared in the Olympics before World War I and after World War II. He made his debut at London in 1908 and bowed out, also in the London Games, 40 years later. His medal haul consisted of just one silver, in 1912.

ARCHERY, FENCING & SHOOTING

Top 10 Most men's World archery titles

	Archer/country	Gold medals	Silver medals	Bronze medals	Total
1	Richard McKinney, USA	8	4	2	14
2	Einar Tang-Holbek, Denmark	3	7	3	13
3	Darrell Pace, USA	7	4	0	11
4	Hans Deutgen, Sweden	5	3	1	9
5	Georges De Rons, Belgium	2	5	1	8
6	Oscar Kessels, Belgium	1	3	3	7
7 =	Frantisek Hadas, Czechoslavakia	3	2	1	6
=	Emil Heilborn, Sweden	2	2	2	6
=	Henry Kjellson, Sweden	2	0	4	6
=	Kyosti Laasonen, Finland	1	4	1	6
=	Joe Thornton, USA	4	2	0	6

Source: FITA

Three of Richard McKinney's gold medals came in the individual event, and the others were as part of the US team, which dominated the team prize every year from 1959 to 1983. McKinney was in five of their winning teams. His individual titles were in 1977, 1983, and 1985, the first two being with Championship-best scores. McKinney never won an Olympic gold medal.

Top 10 Olympic medal-winning countries in archery

	Archer/country	Gold medals	Silver medals	Bronze medals	Total
1	USA	14	9	8	31
2	France	7	9	6	22
3	Korea/South Korea	11	6	4	21
4	Belgium	10	7	2	19
5	USSR/Unified Team	1	3	5	9
6	UK	2	2	4	8
7 =	China	0	3	0	4
=	Finland	1	1	2	4
=	Italy	0	1	3	4
10 =	Germany	0	1	1	2
=	Japan	0	1	1	2
=	Poland	0	1	1	2
=	Sweden	0	2	0	2
=	Ukraine	0	1	1	2

▶ The women's individual silver medal winner, Soo-Nyung Kim of Korea, in action during the 2000 Sydney Olympics.

> It is the very difficulty of hitting that round target with its bright and open countenance that makes archery so engrossing.
>
> **Alice B. Leigh,** on Ladies' Archery, 1894

Top 10 Men's individual Olympic shooting medal winners

	Competitor/country	Gold medals	Silver medals	Bronze medals	Total
1	Carl Osburn, USA	5	4	2	11
2	Alfred Swahn, Sweden	3	3	3	9
3 =	Vilhelm Carlberg, Sweden	3	4	1	8
=	Otto Olsen, Norway	4	3	1	8
5 =	Willis Lee, USA	5	1	1	7
=	Einar Liberg, Sweden	4	2	1	7
=	Léon Moreaux, France	2	2	3	7
8	Oscar Gomer Swahn, Sweden	3	1	2	6
=	Albert Helgerud, Norway	2	4	0	6
=	Johann Hübner von Holst, Sweden	2	3	1	6
=	Alfred Lane, USA	5	0	1	6
=	Maurice Lecoq, France	1	1	4	6
=	Ole Lillö-Olsen, Norway	5	1	0	6
=	Harald Natvig, Norway	3	2	1	6
=	Louis Richardet, Switzerland	5	1	0	6

Alfred Lane won one of his gold medals in the Military Revolver Team event at the 1920 Antwerp Games. One of his team-mates was veterinary professor James Howard Snook, who achieved notoriety when, in 1929, he was arrested for murdering his mistress, Theora Hix, by beating her to death with a hammer. On 28 February 1930, Snook went to his death in the Ohio Penitentiary electric chair.

Top 10 Individual Olympic fencing medal winners

	Competitor/country	Gold medals	Silver medals	Bronze medals	Total
1	Edoardo Mangiarotti, Italy	6	5	2	13
2	Aladár Gerevich, Hungary	7	1	2	10
3	Giulio Gaudini, Italy	3	4	2	9
4 =	Philippe Cattiau, France	3	4	1	8
=	Roger Ducret, France	3	4	1	8
6 =	Pál Kovács, Hungary	6	0	1	7
=	Gustavo Marzi, Italy	2	5	0	7
=	Ildikó Ságiné–Rejtö (née Uljaki-Rejtö)*, Hungary	2	3	2	7
9 =	Elena Belova-Novikova*, Belarus	4	1	1	6
=	Georges Buchard, France	2	3	1	6
=	Giuseppe Delfino, Italy	4	2	0	6
=	Christian d'Oriola, France	4	2	0	6
=	Lucien Gaudin, France	4	2	0	6
=	Rudolf Kárpáti, Hungary	6	0	0	6
=	Gyözö Kulcsár, Hungary	4	0	2	6
=	Nedo Nadi, Italy	6	0	0	6
=	Vladimir Nazlymow, Russia	3	2	1	6
=	Daniel Revenu, France	1	0	5	6
=	Philippe Riboud, France	2	2	2	6
=	Viktor Sidiak, Belarus	4	1	1	6
=	Giovanna Trillini*, Italy	4	0	2	6

*Women competitors

Fernand de Montigny (Belgium) won five fencing medals; he also won a bronze as a member of the Belgian hockey team in 1920.

SNOOKER, BILLIARDS, DARTS & BOWLS

- Most World professional snooker titles
- Most snooker ranking tournament wins
- Most World professional billiards titles
- Most World Darts Championship finals
- Countries in the men's Outdoor Bowls Championship

Top 10 Most World professional snooker titles

	Player/country	Years	Wins
1	Joe Davis, England	1927–40, 1946	15
2	Stephen Hendry, Scotland	1990, 1992–96, 1999	7
3 =	Steve Davis, England	1981, 1983–84, 1987–89	6
=	Ray Reardon, Wales	1970, 1973–76, 1978	6
5	John Spencer, England	1969, 1971, 1977	3
6 =	Fred Davis, England	1948–49	2
=	Walter Donaldson, Scotland	1947, 1950	2
=	Alex Higgins, Northern Ireland	1972, 1982	2
9 =	Ken Doherty, Ireland	1997	1
=	Terry Griffiths, Wales	1979	1
=	John Higgins, Scotland	1998	1
=	Joe Johnson, England	1986	1
=	Horace Lindrum, Australia	1952	1
=	Ronnie O'Sullivan, England	2001	1
=	John Parrott, England	1991	1
=	Dennis Taylor, Northern Ireland	1985	1
=	Cliff Thorburn, Canada	1980	1
=	Mark Williams, Wales	2000	1

Between 1964 and 1968, the World Championship was operated on a challenge system, and John Pullman (England) met and beat seven challengers. The World Championship was launched in 1926, and was won by Joe Davis who beat Tom Dennis 20–11, at Camkin's Hall, Birmingham. The event became known as the Embassy World Professional Championship in 1976 and, since 1977, it has been held at the Crucible Theatre, Sheffield.

DARTS CHAMPIONSHIPS

There are currently two world darts championships: the BDO (British Darts Organization) Embassy World Professional Championship and the Skol World Championship. Phil Taylor, Dennis Priestley, and John Part have appeared in both BDO and PDC finals. Taylor and Priestley are the only men to have won both finals.

▶ Scotland's Stephen Hendry, the most successful player of the modern era. He overtook Steve Davis' record of six Crucible World Championship wins in 1999 when he beat Mark Williams to win his seventh title.

Top 10 Most snooker ranking tournament wins*

	Player/country	Years	Wins
1	Stephen Hendry, Scotland	1987–2002	34
2	Steve Davis, England	1981–95	28
3	John Higgins, Scotland	1994–2002	16
4 =	Ronnie O'Sullivan, England	1993–2002	12
=	Mark Williams, Wales	1996–2002	12
6 =	John Parrott, England	1989–96	9
=	Jimmy White, England	1986–92	9
8 =	Ken Doherty, Ireland	1993–2001	5
=	Peter Ebdon, England	1993–2002	5
=	Ray Reardon, Wales	1974–82	5

* As end of 2001–02 season

A ranking system was first introduced in 1976 with the purpose of seeding players in the World Championship. The first rankings were calculated on a player's performance in the previous three World Championships, which effectively made the 1974 Championship the first ranking event. Until 1982, the only ranking tournament was the World Championship, but two other events were added in the 1982–83 season: the Jameson International and the Professional Players' Tournament. In the 2001–02 season, there were nine ranking tournaments.

Top 10 Most World professional billiards titles

	Player/country*	Years	Wins#
1	Tom Newman	1921–22, 1924–27	6
2 =	Melbourne Inman	1908, 1912–14, 1919	5
=	Mike Russell	1989, 1991, 1996–97, 1999	5
=	H. W. Stevenson	1901 (twice), 1909–11	5
5 =	Joe Davis	1928–30, 1932	4
=	John Roberts Jr.	1870–71, 1875, 1885	4
=	Geet Sethi, India	1992–93, 1995, 1997	4
=	Rex Williams	1968, 1971, 1982–83	4
9	Charles Dawson	1889, 1901, 1903	3
10 =	Joseph Bennett	1870, 1880	2
=	William Cook	1870–71	2
=	Fred Davis	1980 (twice)	2
=	Peter Gilchrist	1994, 2000	2
=	Walter Lindrum, Australia	1933–34	2
=	Willie Smith	1920, 1923	2

* All England unless otherwise stated

\# Number of times a player won the title; successful defences not included

First held in 1870, the World professional billiards championship was organized on a challenge basis until 1909, when it became a knockout tournament. It became dormant in 1934, but was revived in 1951, again on a challenge basis, until becoming a knockout event once more in 1980, when it was won by the 67-year-old Fred Davis.

Top 10 Most World Darts Championship finals

	Player/country	Wins	Finals
1	Phil Taylor, England	10	11
2	Eric Bristow, England	5	10
3	John Lowe, England	3	8
4	Dennis Priestley, England	2	6
5 =	Ray Barneveld, Holland	2	3
=	Richie Burnett, Wales	1	3
7 =	Ronnie Baxter, England	0	2
=	Bobby George, England	0	2
=	Ted Hankey, England	1	2
=	John Part, Canada	1	2
=	Leighton Rees, Wales	1	2
=	Dave Whitcombe, England	0	2
=	Jocky Wilson, Scotland	2	2

Top 10 Countries in the men's Outdoor Bowls Championship

	Country	Singles	Pairs	Triples	Fours	Team	Total
1	England	5	0	1	3	2	11
2	Scotland	0	2	0	1	4	7
3 =	Australia	0	2	1	0	2	5
=	New Zealand	1	1	2	1	0	5
=	South Africa	1	1	1	1	1	5
6	Northern Ireland	1	1	1	1	0	4
7 =	Hong Kong	0	1	0	1	0	2
=	Israel	0	0	2	0	0	2
=	USA	0	1	1	0	0	2
=	Wales	1	0	0	1	0	2

These are the only countries to have won titles in the nine Championships that have been contested since the first Championship in 1966. The winners of the team trophy at each Championship play for the Leonard Trophy. South Africa is the only nation to have won all five titles.

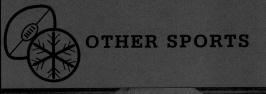

OTHER SPORTS

SKIING

- Men's alpine skiing World Cup titles
- Women's alpine skiing World Cup titles
- Medal-winning countries in men's alpine events at the Olympics
- Medal-winning countries in women's alpine events at the Olympics

> I'm not there to hear the crowd yelling or to achieve glory or to earn money. I'm there to ski a perfect race.
>
> Jean-Claude Killy

Top 10 Men's alpine skiing World Cup titles

	Skiier/country	O	D	GS	SG	S	C	Total
1	Ingemar Stenmark, Sweden	3	0	8	0	8	0	19
2 =	Marc Girardelli, Luxembourg	5	2	1	0	3	4	15
=	Pirmin Zurbriggen, Switzerland	4	2	3	4	0	2	15
4	Hermann Maier, Austria	3	2	3	4	0	0	12
5 =	Phil Mahre, USA	3	0	2	0	1	3	9
=	Alberto Tomba, Italy	1	0	4	0	4	0	9
7	Gustavo Thoeni, Italy	4	0	2	0	2	0	8
8	Kjetil Andre Aamodt, Norway	1	0	1	1	1	3	7
9	Jean-Claude Killy, France	2	1	2	0	1	0	6
10 =	Luc Alphand, France	1	3	0	1	0	0	5
=	Franz Klammer, Austria	0	5	0	0	0	0	5
=	Karl Schranz, Austria	2	2	1	0	0	0	5
=	Andreas Wenzel, Liechtenstein	1	0	0	0	0	4	5

O – Overall; D – Downhill; GS – Giant Slalom; SG – Super-G; S – Slalom; C – Combined

The World Cup was launched in the 1966–67 season. It is a winter-long series of races, with champions being declared in five categories in addition to an overall champion.

Top 10 Women's alpine skiing World Cup titles

	Skiier/country	O	D	GS	SG	S	C	Total
1	Annemarie Moser-Pröll, Austria	6	7	3	0	0	1	17
2	Vreni Schneider, Switzerland	3	0	5	0	6	0	14
3	Katja Seizinger, Germany	2	4	0	5	0	0	11
4	Erika Hess, Switzerland	2	0	1	0	5	1	9
5 =	Michela Figini, Switzerland	2	4	1	1	0	0	8
=	Hanni Wenzel, Liechtenstein	2	0	2	0	1	3	8
7	Maria Walliser, Switzerland	2	2	1	1	0	1	7
8 =	Renate Goetschl, Austria	1	2	0	1	0	2	6
=	Carole Merle, France	0	0	2	4	0	0	6
=	Lisa-Marie Morerord, Switzerland	1	0	3	0	2	0	6
=	Anita Wachter, Austria	1	0	2	0	0	3	6

O – Overall; D – Downhill; GS – Giant Slalom; SG – Super-G; S – Slalom; C – Combined

Annemarie Moser-Pröll won her seven downhill titles within a period of nine years (1971–79), including five in succession between 1971 and 1975. She won 62 World Cup races in her career. Her best season was in 1975, when she won the Downhill, Giant Slalom, and Overall titles.

▶ The greatest female slalom skier of all time, Vreni Schneider of Switzerland.

◄ Champion skier Ingemar Stenmark of Sweden. Stenmark has won a record 19 World Cup titles.

Top 10 Medal-winning countries in men's alpine events at the Olympics

	Country	Gold medals	Silver medals	Bronze medals	Total
1	Austria	17	15	20	52
2	Switzerland	6	11	9	26
3	France	19	5	7	22
4	Norway	7	7	6	20
5	Italy	7	5	2	14
6	USA	3	5	2	11
7	Germany/West Germany	3	3	1	7
8	Sweden	2	0	3	5
9	Liechtenstein	0	1	3	4
10 =	Canada	0	0	2	2
=	Luxembourg	0	2	0	2

Austria has produced some great champions over the years, including Toni Sailer, who won three golds at the 1956 Olympics, but none can match the renown of Franz Klammer. He may have won only one Olympic gold medal, in the downhill on home soil in Innsbruck in 1976, but such was the popularity of Klammer that when he was left out of the team in 1980, the Austrian coach had to appear on national television and publicly explain to the people of Austria his reasons for excluding their hero from the team.

Top 10 Medal-winning countries in women's alpine events at the Olympics

	Country	Gold medals	Silver medals	Bronze medals	Total
1	Austria	9	14	11	34
2	Germany/West Germany	10	9	8	27
3	Switzerland	10	7	7	24
4	USA	7	9	3	19
5	France	4	8	6	18
6	Italy	5	3	5	13
7	Canada	4	1	3	8
8 =	Liechtenstein	2	1	2	5
=	Sweden	2	2	1	5
10	Croatia	3	1	0	4

Two of Austria's gold medals were won by Petra Kronberger in 1992. She first won the Alpine Combined after coming from behind with a strong second run in the slalom section. She followed that victory with another gold, in the Slalom event, again having to come from behind after finishing third after the first run, to capture first place.

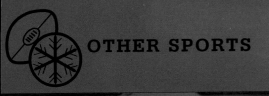

SKATING & BOBSLEIGHING

- ● Olympic figure skating medal winners

- ● Most World figure skating titles

- ● Olympic speed skating medal winners

- ● Olympic medal-winning countries in the bobsleigh

MULTI-TALENTED

Three members of the US gold-medal four-man bobsleigh team at the 1932 Winter Olympics each had a small claim to fame: Billy Fiske was the first American to join the British Royal Air Force, in 1939; Edward Eagan became the first and only man to win gold medals at both Summer and Winter Olympics – he was the light-heavyweight boxing champion in 1920; and Clifford "Tippy" Gray wrote over 3,000 songs, including "If You Were the Only Girl in the World".

Top 10 Olympic figure skating medal winners*

	Skater/country	Male/female	Years	Gold	Silver	Bronze	Total
1	Gillis Grafström, Sweden	M	1920–32	3	1	0	4
2 =	Andrée Brunet (née Joly), France	F	1924–32	2	0	1	3
=	Pierre Brunet, France	M	1924–32	2	0	1	3
=	Artur Dmitriev, USSR/Russia	M	1992–98	2	1	0	3
=	Sonja Henie, Norway	F	1928–36	3	0	0	3
=	Irina Rodnina, USSR	F	1972–80	3	0	0	3
7 =	Lyudmila Belousova, USSR	F	1964–68	2	0	0	2
=	Dick Button, USA	M	1948–52	2	0	0	2
=	Yekaterina Gordeyeva, USSR/Russia	F	1988–94	2	0	0	2
=	Sergei Grinkov, USSR/Russia	M	1988–94	2	0	0	2
=	Oksana Grishuk, Russia	F	1994–98	2	0	0	2
=	Yevgeny Platov, Russia	M	1994–98	2	0	0	2
=	Oleg Protopopov, USSR	M	1964–68	2	0	0	2
=	Karl Schäfer, Austria	M	1932–36	2	0	0	2
=	Katarina Witt, East Germany	F	1984–88	2	0	0	2
=	Aleksandr Zaitsev, USSR	M	1976–80	2	0	0	2

* Minimum qualification: 2 gold medals

Top 10 Most World figure skating titles

	Skater/country	Men	Women	Pairs	Dance	Total
1 =	Sonja Henie, Norway	0	10	0	0	10
=	Irina Rodnina, USSR	0	0	10	0	10
=	Ulrich Salchow, Sweden	10	0	0	0	10
4 =	Herma Planck (née Szabo), Austria	0	5	2	0	7
=	Karl Schäfer, Austria	7	0	0	0	7
6 =	Aleksandr Gorshkov, USSR	0	0	0	6	6
=	Lyudmila Pakhomova, USSR	0	0	0	6	6
=	Aleksandr Zaitsev, USSR	0	0	6	0	6
9 =	Dick Button, USA	5	0	0	0	5
=	Lawrence Demmy, UK	0	0	0	5	5
=	Carol Heiss, USA	0	5	0	0	5
=	Jean Westwood, UK	0	0	0	5	5

Top 10 Olympic speed skating medal winners

	Skater/country	Male/female	Gold	Silver	Bronze	Total
1 =	Karin Kania (née Enke), East Germany	F	3	4	1	8
=	Gunda Niemann-Stirnemann (formerly Niemann-Kleeman), Germany	F	3	4	1	8
3 =	Ivar Ballangrud, Norway	M	4	2	1	7
=	Andrea Ehrig (née Mitscherlich, formerly Schöne), East Germany	F	1	5	1	7
=	Claudia Pechstein, Germany	F	4	1	2	7
=	Clas Thunberg, Finland	M	5	1	1	7
7 =	Bonnie Blair, USA	F	5	0	1	6
=	Roald Larsen, Norway	M	0	2	4	6
=	Lydia Skoblikova, USSR	F	6	0	0	6
10 =	Marc Gagnon, Canada	M	3	0	2	5
=	Yevgeny Grischin, USSR	M	4	1	0	5
=	Eric Heiden, USA	M	5	0	0	5
=	Knut Johannesen, Norway	M	2	2	1	5
=	Johann-Olaf Koss, Norway	M	4	1	0	5
=	Chung Lee Kyung, Korea	F	4	0	1	5
=	Rintje Risma, Netherlands	M	0	2	3	5
=	Christa Rothenberger-Luding, East Germany	F	2	2	1	5

Eric Heiden's five gold medals all came at Lake Placid in 1980 and, because of the United States' boycott of the Moscow Summer Games, he can claim to be the only individual US Olympic champion of 1980. In addition to his Olympic golds, Heiden won seven World Championship gold medals and one silver. After ending his skating career, he turned to cycling and entered the 1986 Tour de France.

Top 10 Olympic medal-winning countries in the bobsleigh

	Country	G	S	B	Total
1	Switzerland	9	10	9	28
2	Germany/ West Germany	7	9	7	23
3	USA	6	4	6	16
4	East Germany	5	4	3	12
5	Italy	4	4	3	11
6	UK	1	1	2	4
7 =	Austria	1	2	0	3
=	USSR	2	0	1	3
9 =	Belgium	0	1	1	2
=	Canada	2	0	0	2

G – gold medals, S – silver medals, B – bronze medals

The four-man event made its debut at the 1924 Games. The two-man bobsleigh event was introduced at the 1932 Olympics, and has been held at every Games since then, with the exception of 1960 – there was no bob run at Squaw Valley. The two-woman bobsleigh event was held for the first time at the 2002 Olympics, and was won by the United States.

▶ The veteran Wolfgang Hoppe leading the Germany I four-man bobsleigh team during the 1987 World Championships in St. Moritz, Switzerland.

TEN-PIN BOWLING, TRIATHLON, FIELD HOCKEY, HURLING, GAELIC FOOTBALL & HANDBALL

- First PBA bowlers to roll a perfect 300 game on national television
- Fastest Hawaii Ironmans
- Olympic medal-winning countries in field hockey
- Hurling teams
- Gaelic football teams
- World Championship medal-winning countries in handball

The 10 First PBA bowlers to roll a perfect 300 game on national television

	Bowler	Opponent (score)	Venue	Year
1	Jack Biondolillo	Les Schissler (216)	Akron, Ohio	1967
2	John Guenther	Don Johnson (189)	San Jose, California	1969
3	Jim Stefanich	Glenn Carlson (243)	Alameda, California	1974
4	Pete McCordic	Wayne Webb (249)	Torrance, California	1987
5	Bob Benoit	Mark Roth (255)	Grand Prairie, Texas	1988
6	Mike Aulby	David Ozio (279)	Wichita, Kansas	1993
7	Johnny Petraglia	Walter Ray Williams Jr. (179)	Toledo, Ohio	1994
8	Butch Soper	Bob Benoit (236)	Reno, Nevada	1994
9	C. K. Moore	Parker Bohn III (192)	Austin, Texas	1996
10	Bob Learn Jr.	Johnny Petraglia (279)	Erie, Pennsylvania	1996

Source: PBA (Professional Bowlers' Association)

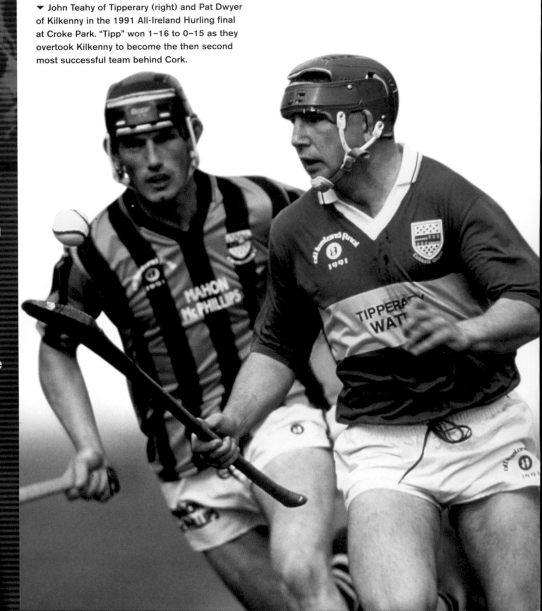

▼ John Teahy of Tipperary (right) and Pat Dwyer of Kilkenny in the 1991 All-Ireland Hurling final at Croke Park. "Tipp" won 1–16 to 0–15 as they overtook Kilkenny to become the then second most successful team behind Cork.

LUCKY ENTRY

The United Kingdom won a surprise field hockey bronze medal at the 1984 Los Angeles Olympics by beating one of the pre-tournament favourites, Australia, in their play-off match. The United Kingdomqualified for the Games only as a result of the Soviet boycott.

◀ American Mark Allen, who has set the fastest time for the Hawaii Ironman on three occasions.

Top 10 Fastest Hawaii Ironmans

	Triathlete/country	Year	Time (hr:min:sec)
1	Luc Van Lierde, Belgium	1996	8:04:08
2	Mark Allen, USA	1993	8:07:45
3	Mark Allen, USA	1992	8:09:08
4	Mark Allen, USA	1989	8:09:15
5	Luc Van Lierde, Belgium	1999	8:17:17
6	Mark Allen, USA	1991	8:18:32
7	Greg J. Welch, Australia	1994	8:20:27
8	Mark Allen, USA	1995	8:20:34
9	Peter Reid, Canada	2000	8:21:01
10	Peter Reid, Canada	1998	8:24:20

The most famous of all triathlons, the Hawaii Ironman was first held at Waikiki Beach, Hawaii, in 1978, but has been held at Kailua-Kona since 1981. The competitors have to complete, or attempt to complete, a 3.86-km (2.4-mile) swim, a 180-km (112-mile) cycle race, and a full marathon of 26 miles 385 yards. The fastest time for women is 8:55:28, by Paula Newby-Fraser of Zimbabwe, in 1992.

Top 10 Olympic medal-winning countries in field hockey*

	Country	G (men)	S (men)	B (men)	G (women)	S (women)	B (women)	Total
1 =	India	8	1	2	0	0	0	11
=	Netherlands	2	2	3	1	0	3	11
3 =	Australia	0	3	3	3	0	0	9
=	Germany/West Germany	2	3	2	0	2	0	9
5 =	UK	3	1	3	0	0	1	8
=	Pakistan	3	3	2	0	0	0	8
7	Spain	0	2	1	1	0	0	4
8	South Korea	0	1	0	0	2	0	3
9 =	USA	0	0	1	0	0	1	2
=	USSR	0	0	1	0	0	1	2

G – gold medals, S – silver medals, B – bronze medals

* Based on total medals won in the men's and women's events

Hockey made its Olympic debut in London in 1908, but was not seen again until 1920. The women's competition was introduced in 1980.

Between 1928 and 1960, India played 30 consecutive hockey matches in the Olympic Games without losing or drawing. In that time, they scored 197 goals and conceded just eight. Their run came to an end in the 1960 final, when they were beaten 1–0 by Pakistan, also ending their sequence of six consecutive titles. They regained the title four years later but had to wait until 1980 for their record eighth, and last, Olympic title.

Top 10 Hurling teams*

	Team	Years	Wins
1	Cork	1890–1999	28
2	Kilkenny	1904–2000	26
3	Tipperary	1887–2001	25
4	Limerick	1897–1973	7
5 =	Dublin	1889–1938	6
=	Wexford	1910–96	6
7 =	Galway	1923–88	4
=	Offaly	1981–98	4
9	Clare	1914–97	3
10	Waterford	1948–59	2

* Based on wins in the All-Ireland Final
Source: Gaelic Athletic Association

The All-Ireland Hurling Final is played at Croke Park, Dublin, on the first Sunday in September each year. It was first contested in 1887, and won by Tipperary. The winners play for the McCarthy Cup.

Top 10 Gaelic football teams*

	Team	Years	Wins
1	Kerry	1903–2000	32
2	Dublin	1891–1995	22
3	Galway	1925–2001	9
4	Meath	1949–99	7
5	Cork	1890–1990	6
6 =	Cavan	1933–52	5
=	Down	1960–94	5
=	Wexford	1893–1918	5
9 =	Kildare	1905–28	4
=	Tipperary	1889–1920	4

* Based on wins in the All-Ireland Final
Source: Gaelic Athletic Association

The All-Ireland Gaelic Football Final is played at Croke Park, Dublin on the third Sunday in September each year. It was first contested in 1887, when it was won by Limerick. The finalists play for the Sam Maguire Cup.

Top 10 World Championship medal-winning countries in handball*

	Country	G	S	B	Total
1 =	USSR/Russia	7	5	1	13
=	Yugoslavia	2	4	7	13
3	Sweden	4	3	4	11
4 =	Czechosloavkia	2	3	3	8
=	East Germany	3	2	3	8
=	Hungary	1	4	3	8
=	Romania	5	1	2	8
8	Germany/ West Germany	3	1	3	7
9 =	Denmark	1	3	1	5
=	France	2	2	1	5

G – gold medals, S – silver medals, B – bronze medals

* Based on medals won in the World Championships

The handball World Championship was first held for men in 1938 and for women in 1949. On both occasions, the events were played outdoors, but it is now chiefly an indoor sport.

OTHER SPORTS

AUSTRALIAN RULES FOOTBALL

- Most AFL Premierships
- Annual leading goal kickers with the most goals
- Most leading goal kicker medals
- Brownlow medal winners receiving the most votes
- Fewest seasons taken to win the AFL

AUSSIE RULES

"Aussie" Rules is the main code of football in Victoria, Western Australia, South Australia, Tasmania, and the Northern Territory, and also has a strong following in the Australian Capital Territory. It is also played in Queensland and New South Wales. Up to 1992, all winners of the AFL had come from Victoria, but that run was ended by the West Coast Eagles of Perth.

Top 10 Most AFL Premierships

	Club	First win	Last win	Total
1 =	Carlton	1906	1995	16
=	Essendon	1897	2000	16
3	Collingwood	1902	1990	14
4	Melbourne	1900	1964	12
5	Richmond	1920	1980	10
6	Hawthorn	1961	1991	9
7	Fitzroy	1898	1944	8
8	Geelong	1925	1963	6
9	North Melbourne/ Kangaroos	1975	1999	4
10	South Melbourne/ Sydney	1909	1933	3

The Victoria Football League (VFL) was formed on 2 October 1896 with eight clubs: Carlton, Collingwood, Essendon, Fitzroy, Geelong, Melbourne, South Melbourne, and St. Kilda. Over the years, non-Victorian State teams joined the League, and the inevitable change of name from the VFL to the Australian Football League (AFL) came about in 1990. Freemantle and Port Adelaide are the only current clubs not to have won the title.

Top 10 Annual leading goal kickers with the most goals*

	Player/club	Year	Goals
1	Peter Hudson, Hawthorn	1970	146
2	Peter Hudson, Hawthorn	1971	140
3	Jason Dunstall, Hawthorn	1992	139
4	Bob Pratt, South Melbourne	1934	138
5	Peter McKenna, Collingwood	1972	130
6	Jason Dunstall, Hawthorn	1989	128
7	Peter Hudson, Hawthorn	1968	125
8 =	Gary Ablett, Geelong	1993	124
=	Jason Dunstall, Hawthorn	1988	124
10	Doug Wade, Geelong	1969	122

* Based on goals scored by the season's leading goal kicker

Source: Australian Football League

Probably the greatest forward of all time, Peter Hudson averaged 5.64 goals per game, which is a League record. He was prevented from scoring in just five games throughout his career.

Top 10 Most leading goal kicker medals

	Player	Club(s)	Years	Wins
1	Dick Lee	Collingwood	1907–10, 1914, 1916–17, 1919	8
2	Gordon Coventry	Collingwood	1926–30, 1933	6
3	John Coleman	Essendon	1949–53	5
4 =	Peter Hudson	Hawthorn	1968, 1970–71, 1977	4
=	Tony Lockett	St. Kilda, Sydney	1987, 1991, 1996, 1998	4
=	Doug Wade	Geelong, North Melbourne	1962, 1967, 1969, 1974	4
7 =	Gary Ablett	Geelong	1993–95	3
=	Jason Dunstall	Hawthorn	1988–89, 1992	3
=	Fred Fanning	Melbourne	1944–45, 1947	3
=	John Peck	Hawthorn	1963–65	3

Source: Australian Football League

The player kicking the most goals in the home and away rounds receives the John Coleman medal, presented in honour of the former Essendon player and later coach, whose career was cut short by injury after 537 goals in just 98 games. It was first awarded in 1897 and won by Eddy James of Geelong with 22 goals.

◀ Veteran player Bob Pratt: he kicked 138 goals for South Melbourne in the 1934 season, a tally that was to stand as a record for 36 years.

▼ One of the best-known players in the 1980s and 1990s was Gary Ablett of Geelong, seen here in action against Essendon during the 1988 season.

Top 10 Brownlow medal winners receiving the most votes

	Player	Club	Year	Votes
1	Graham Teasdale	South Melbourne	1977	59
2	Graham Moss	Essendon	1976	48
3 =	Des Fothergill	Collingwood	1940*	32
=	Herbie Matthews	South Melbourne	1940*	32
=	Robert Harvey#	St. Kilda	1998	32
6	Greg Williams	Carlton	1994	30
7	Roy Wright	Richmond	1954	29
8 =	Shane Crawford#	Hawthorn	1999	28
=	Alistair Lord	Geelong	1962	28
10 =	Gordon Collis	Carlton	1964	27
=	Keith Greig	North Melbourne	1973	27
=	Keith Greig	North Melbourne	1974	27
=	Dick Reynolds	Essendon	1937	27

* Shared title

\# Active in 2001

The Charles Brownlow medal was instituted in 1924. It is awarded to the "fairest and best" player in the League's home and away series. The field umpires decide after each game who was the best player on the field, awarding him three points, two points to the second best, and one to the third. In 1976 and 1977, the voting was changed so that the two field judges were each allocated six points per game, which explains why the figures for numbers one and two are so high.

Top 10 Fewest seasons taken to win the AFL*

	Club	First year in League	First title	Span (seasons)
1	Essendon	1897	1897	1
2	Fitzroy	1897	1898	2
3	Melbourne	1897	1900	4
4 =	Brisbane#	1996	2001	6
=	Collingwood	1897	1902	6
=	West Coast	1987	1992	6
7	Adelaide	1991	1997	7
8	Carlton	1897	1906	10
9 =	Richmond	1908	1920	13
=	South Melbourne	1897	1909	13

* Previously the VFL

\# The Brisbane Lions were formed in 1996 following a merger of Fitzroy Lions and Brisbane Bears

Time taken is based on first season in the League and a team's first title. St. Kilda had to wait the longest for their first triumph. As founder members in 1897, they did not win their first title until 1966, after a wait of 70 seasons.

SPORTING WORLD

- Sport whose participants have the largest average heart
- Most popular participation activities in the UK
- Highest-earning sportsmen
- Most popular participation activities in the United States
- Highest-earning sports films

> Sport is the only entertainment where, no matter how many times you go back, you never know the ending.
> **Neil Simon,
> US playwright**

Top 10 Sport whose participants have the largest* average heart

	Sport
1	Tour de France cyclists
2	Marathon runners
3	Rowers
4	Boxers
5	Sprint cyclists
6	Middle-distance runners
7	Weightlifters
8	Swimmers
9	Sprinters
10	Decathletes

* Based on average medical measurements

The size of the heart of a person who engages regularly in a demanding sport enlarges according to the strenuousness of the sport.

Top 10 Most popular participation activities in the UK

	Sport/pastime	(%)*
1	Walking	65
2	Swimming	42
3	Snooker/pool/billiards	22
4	Aerobics/yoga	19
5	Cycling	17
6	Darts	13
7	Golf	12
8	Ten-pin bowling/skittles	11
9 =	Badminton	9
=	Running/jogging	9
=	Weightlifting/weight training	9

* Based on percentage of population participating in activity
Source: Office for National Statistics

Fishing, for many years regarded as the most popular participation sport in the UK is, in fact, enjoyed by only 6 per cent of the population and is down to joint 13th place.

Top 10 Highest-earning sportsmen

	Name*	Sport	Team	Income 2000 ($)
1	Michael Shumacher, Germany	Motor racing	Ferrari	59,000,000
2	Tiger Woods	Golf	–	53,000,000
3	Mike Tyson	Boxing	–	48,000,000
4	Michael Jordan	Basketball	Chicago Bulls	37,000,000
5	Grant Hill	Basketball	Detroit Pistons	26,000,000
6	Dale Earnhardt†	Stock car racing	–	24,500,000
7	Shaquille O'Neal	Basketball	LA Lakers	24,000,000
8 =	Oscar De La Hoya	Boxing	–	23,000,000
=	Lennox Lewis, UK	Boxing	–	23,000,000
10	Kevin Garnett	Basketball	Minnesota Timberwolves	21,000,000

* All USA unless otherwise stated
† Killed 18 February 2001 during the Daytona 500
Used with permission of Forbes magazine

Forbes' annual analysis of celebrity income includes many of the world's highest-earning athletes. Among those falling outside the Top 10 are boxers such as George Foreman ($20,100,000) and tennis player Andre Agassi ($17,500,000). The extended list includes several non-Americans, among them Australian golfer Greg Norman ($15,000,000) and Czech-born tennis player Martina Hingis ($11,000,000), the highest-earning woman among this elite group. She is closely followed by Anna Kournikova and Venus Williams (both on $10,000,000), Serena Williams ($7,500,000), and Lindsay Davenport ($6,000,000). The earnings of many represent their cumulative income from the sport itself and from sponsorship deals: Tiger Woods' contract with Nike, for example, is reported to be worth $40 million over five years.

Top 10 Most popular participation activities in the United States

	Activity	% change since previous year	Number participating (2000)
1	Exercise walking	+0.6	81,300,000
2	Swimming	+2.3	59,300,000
3	Camping	-2.3	49,900,000
4	Fishing	+4.5	48,800,000
5	Exercising with equipment	-4.4	43,200,000
6	Bicycle riding	+0.3	42,500,000
7	Bowling	+1.6	42,300,000
8	Billiards/pool	+0.1	32,200,000
9 =	Aerobics	+3.5	27,200,000
=	Basketball	-8.1	27,200,000

Source: National Sporting Goods Association

The annual NSGA survey includes people aged over seven who participated in each activity on more than one occasion. From 1995 to 2000, skateboarding experienced the greatest increase in the number of participants, while windsurfing sustained the sharpest decline.

Top 10 Highest earning sports films

	Film/year of release	Sport	World box office income ($)
1	Rocky IV (1985)	Boxing	300,500,000
2	Jerry Maguire (1996)	American football	273,600,000
3	Space Jam (1996)	Basketball	225,400,000
4	The Waterboy (1998)	American football	190,200,000
5	Days of Thunder (1990)	Stock car racing	165,900,000
6	Cool Runnings (1993)	Bobsleighing	154,900,000
7	A League of Their Own (1992)	Baseball	130,500,000
8	Remember the Titans (2000)	American football	130,000,000
9	Rocky III (1982)	Boxing	122,800,000
10	Rocky V (1990)	Boxing	120,000,000

While three of the hugely successful Rocky films appear in the Top 10, the original (made in 1976) and its sequel *Rocky II* (1979) failed to earn enough globally to merit an entry. Sylvester Stallone was paid a reported $16 million for acting, writing, and directing *Rocky IV* – more than half its total budget.

▼ Rocky Balboa (Sylvester Stallone) gunning for the Russian fighter Ivan Drago (Dolph Lundgren) in the sports film blockbuster *Rocky IV*.

AWARDS

- Most Associated Press Athlete of the Year Awards

- First back-to-back winners of the Associated Press Athlete of the Year Award

- Last BBC Sports Personality of the Year Award winners

- Latest winners of the Jesse Owens International Trophy

- Sports represented by the James E. Sullivan Award

- First Sullivan Award winners to become Olympic champions

ATHLETE OF THE YEAR

Pioneered in 1931 by the Associated Press, the annual Athlete of the Year Award, unlike the Sullivan Award, can be awarded to amateur or professional athletes, and a person can win it more than once. It also differs in that a separate award is made to women athletes. Babe Didrikson Zaharias, Maureen Connolly, and Michael Jordan all won the award three years in succession.

Top 10 Most Associated Press Athlete of the Year Awards

	Athlete	Sport	Years	Total
1	Babe Didrikson Zaharias	Track & field/Golf	1932, 1945–47, 1950, 1954	6
2	Chris Evert	Tennis	1974–75, 1977, 1980	4
3 =	Patty Berg	Golf	1938, 1943, 1955	3
=	Maureen Connolly	Tennis	1951–53	3
=	Michael Jordan	Basketball	1991–93	3
=	Tiger Woods	Golf	1997, 1999–2000	3
7 =	Tracy Austin	Tennis	1979, 1981	2
=	Donald Budge	Tennis	1937–38	2
=	Althea Gibson	Tennis	1957–58	2
=	Billy Jean King	Tennis	1967, 1973	2
=	Sandy Koufax	Baseball	1963, 1965	2
=	Carl Lewis	Track & field	1983–84	2
=	Nancy Lopez	Golf	1978, 1985	2
=	Alice Marble	Tennis	1939–40	2
=	Joe Montana	Football	1989–90	2
=	Martina Navratilova	Tennis	1983, 1986	2
=	Byron Nelson	Golf	1944–45	2
=	Wilma Rudolph	Track & field	1960–61	2
=	Monica Seles	Tennis	1991–92	2
=	Kathy Whitworth	Golf	1965–66	2
=	Mickey Wright	Golf	1963–64	2

The first winner of the men's award in 1931 was baseball player Peper Martin; the first women's winner was swimmer Helene Madison, also in 1931.

The 10 First back-to-back winners of the Associated Press Athlete of the Year Award

	Athlete	Sport	Years
1	Donald Budge	Tennis	1937–38
2	Alice Marble	Tennis	1939–40
3	Byron Nelson	Golf	1944–45
4	Babe Didrikson Zaharais	Golf	1945–46
5	Maureen Connolly	Tennis	1951–52
6	Althea Gibson	Tennis	1957–58
7	Wilma Rudolph	Track & field	1960–61
8	Mickey Wright	Golf	1963–64
9	Kathy Whitworth	Golf	1965–66
10	Chris Evert	Tennis	1974–75

> It's ironic; I used to ride my bike to make a living.
> Now I just want to live so that I can ride.
>
> **Lance Armstrong**

The 10 Last BBC Sports Personality of the Year Award winners

	Year	Winner/sport
1	2001	David Beckham, Football
2	2000	Steve Redgrave, Rowing
3	1999	Lennox Lewis, Boxing
4	1998	Michael Owen, Football
5	1997	Greg Rusedski, Tennis
6	1996	Damon Hill, Motor racing
7	1995	Jonathan Edwards, Athletics
8	1994	Damon Hill, Motor racing
9	1993	Linford Christie, Athletics
10	1992	Nigel Mansell, Motor racing

First presented in 1954, when it was won by athlete Chris Chataway, the annual award is based on a poll of BBC television viewers. Muhammed Ali was voted Sports Personality of the Century in 1999.

Top 10 Latest winners of the Jesse Owens International Trophy

	Year	Winner/sport
1	2001	Marion Jones, Athletics
2	2000	Lance Armstrong, Cycling
3	1999	Marion Jones, Athletics
4	1998	Haile Gebrselassie, Athletics
5	1997	Michael Johnson, Athletics
6	1996	Michael Johnson, Athletics
7	1995	Johann Olav Koss, Speed skating
8	1994	Wang Junxia, Athletics
9	1993	Vitaly Scherbo, Gymnastics
10	1992	Mike Powell, Athletics

The Jesse Owens International Trophy has been presented by the International Amateur Athletic Association since 1981, when it was won by speed skater Eric Heiden, and is named in honour of US athlete Jesse (James Cleveland) Owens (1913–80). Michael Johnson and Marion Jones are the only sports personalities to have won the award twice.

Top 10 Sports represented by the James E. Sullivan Award

	Sport	Awards
1	Track & field	37
2	Swimming	9
3	(American) Football	4
4	Diving	3
=	Speed skating	3
=	Wrestling	3
7	Basketball	2
=	Golf	2
=	Sculling	2
10 =	Baseball	1
=	Figure skating	1
=	Gymnastics	1
=	Tennis	1

Source: Amateur Athletic Union

The award is made annually to the sportsman or woman who has contributed most to good sportsmanship. The trophy is in memory of James E. Sullivan, the president of the Amateur Athletic Union (AAU) from 1906 to 1914.

The 10 First Sullivan Award winners to become Olympic champions

	Athlete	Award year	Sport	Event	Olympic year
1	Jim Bausch	1932	Track & field	Decathlon	1932
2	Glenn Morris	1936	Track & field	Decathlon	1936
3	Bob Mathias	1948	Track & field	Decathlon	1948
4	Ann Curtis	1944	Swimming	400 metres freestyle	1948
5	Bob Richards	1951	Track & field	Pole vault	1952
6	Horace Ashenfelter	1952	Track & field	Steeplechase	1952
7	Dick Button	1949	Ice skating	Men's figures	1952
8	Pat McCormick	1956	Swimming	Springboard diving	1956
9	Glenn Davis	1958	Track & field	400 metres hurdles	1960
10	Rafer Johnson	1960	Track & field	Decathlon	1960

Button, McCormick, and Davis, like several other athletes, also won Olympic golds prior to winning their Sullivan Awards.

◀ Lance Armstrong won the Tour de France three years in succession, from 1999–2001, after successfully combating cancer.

INDEX

ACKNOWLEDGEMENTS

Dorling Kindersley would like to thank the following for their contributions: Picture Research Franziska Marking, Carolyn Clerkin; Picture Library Hayley Smith; Jacket Editor Jane Oliver-Jedrzejak; Jacket Designer Dean Price.

Index by Indexing Specialists, Hove, Brighton

PICTURE CREDITS

The publisher would like to thank the following for their kind permission to reproduce their photographs: (Abbreviations key: t=top, b=bottom, r=right, l=left, c=centre)

2: Empics Ltd/Rob Tringali Jnr (cr), Getty Images/Tony Duffy (c), Getty Images/Gary M. Prior (l); 3: Empics Ltd/Neal Simpson (c), Getty Images/Mike Powell (l); 5: Getty Images/Clive Mason; 6: Getty Images/ Andrew Redington; 8–9: Getty Images/Scott Barbour; 11: Getty Images/Tony Duffy (bl); 12: Getty Images/Tony Duffy (br); 13: Getty Images/Andy Lyons (tl); 14: Getty Images/Clive Brunskill (bc); 15: Empics Ltd/Andy Heading; 16: Getty Images/Shaun Botterill (br); 17: Getty Images/Gary M Prior; 19: Empics Ltd; 21: Getty Images/Clive Brunskill (tl); 21: Empics Ltd/Alpha (bl); 23: Empics Ltd/Andy Heading; 24–25: Empics Ltd/Jon Buckle; 26: Empics Ltd/Tony Marshall; 27: Getty Images/Stephen Munday; 28: Empics Ltd/Tony Marshall; 29: Getty Images/Scott Halleran (r); 29: Empics Ltd/Don Morley (tl); 30: Empics Ltd/Tony Marshall (l); 30–31: Getty Images/Steve Munday (b); 31 Getty Images/ Hulton Getty Archive (tl); 32: Empics Ltd/Tony Marshall (l); 32–33: Getty Images/Andrew Redington (b); 34–35: Empics Ltd/Mike Egerton (b), Empics Litd/Tony Marshall (l); 35: Getty Images/Hulton Getty Archive (tl); 36–37: Getty Images/David Cannon (bc); 36: Empics Ltd/Tony Marshall (l); 38–39: Getty Images/Scott Halleran (bc); 38: Empics Ltd/Tony Marshall (l); 40–41: Empics Ltd/Tony Marshall; 42: Empics Ltd/Neal Simpson; 43: Empics Ltd/Topham Picturepoint; 44: Empics Ltd/Neal Simpson; 45: Action Plus (b), Empics Ltd/Nick Potts (tl); 46: Empics Ltd/Neal Simpson (l); 46–47: Empics Ltd/Bob Tringali; 48: Empics Ltd/Neal Simpson; 49: Getty Images/ Holly Stein (tl), Getty Images/John Gichigi (b); 50: Empics Ltd/Neal Simpson; 51: Empics Ltd/S&G; 52–53: Getty Images/Al Bello; 54: Getty Images/Gary M. Prior; 55: Empics Ltd/Alpha (tl), Getty Images/Gary M. Prior (bl); 56: Getty Images/Gary M. Prior; 57: Getty Images; 58: Getty Images/Gary M. Prior; 59: Action Images/Chris Barry (b), Getty Images (tl); 60: Getty Images/ Gary M. Prior; 61: Getty Images (br), Getty Images/Tony Duffy (tl); 62: Getty Images/ Gary M. Prior (l); 62–63: Getty Images/Clive Brunskill

(bc); 64: Getty Images/Gary M. Prior; 65: Empics Ltd/Mike Egerton (b), Getty Images (tl); 66–67: Getty Images/Al Bello; 68: Getty Images/Al Bello; 69: Getty Images/Brian Bahr (br), Getty Images/Matthew Stockman (tl); 70: Empics Ltd/Frank Peters (br), Getty Images/Al Bello; 71: Empics Ltd/ Matthew Ashton; 72: Getty Images/Al Bello, Getty Images/Matthew Stockman (br); 74: Getty Images/Al Bello (br); 75: Getty Images/Jed Jacobsohn; 76: Getty Images/ Al Bello; 77: Empics Ltd/Tony Tomsic (br), Getty Images/Brian Masck (tl); 78: Getty Images/Al Bello (l); 78–79: Empics Ltd/Rob TringaliJnr (b); 79: Getty Images/Tom Pidgeon (tl); 80: Getty Images/Al Bello; 81: Getty Images/Robert Laberge; 82–83: Empics Ltd/Rob Tringali Jnr; 84: Empics Ltd/Rob Tringali Jnr (l); 85: Getty Images/Hulton Getty Archive (tl), Empics Ltd/Rob Tringali Jnr (bl); 86: Getty Images/ Jeff Gross (br), Empics Ltd/Rob Tringali Jnr (l); 88: Empics Ltd/Rob Tringali, Jr. (l), Hulton Getty Archive/Howard Muller (br); 89: Empics Ltd/SportsChrome (tl); 90: Empics Ltd/Rob Tringali Jnr; 91: Getty Images/Doug Pensinger (bl); 92: Empics Ltd/Rob Tringali Jnr (l); 93: Getty Images/Jed Jacobsohn (bl); 94: Empics Ltd/Rob Tringali Jnr (l); 94–95: Corbis/Bettmann; 96: Empics Ltd/Rob Tringali Jnr; 97: Getty Images/Allsport/Hulton Getty (br), Empics Ltd/Michael Zito, Empics Ltd/SportsChrome (tl); 98–99: Getty Images/Rocky Widner/NBAE; 101: Empics Ltd/Steve Lipofsky (tl), Empics Ltd/Steve Lipofsky (br); 103: Corbis/Bettmann; 105: Empics Ltd/Steve Lipofsky; 107: Empics Ltd/Steve Lipofsky; 109: Empics Ltd/Steve Lipofsky (tl), Empics Ltd/Steve Lipofsky (br); 110: Getty Images/Todd Warshaw (br); 111: Getty Images/David Leah; 114–115: Empics Ltd/Aubrey Washington; 116: Getty Images/Mike Powell; 117: Empics Ltd/Rob Tringali Jr. (bc), Getty Images/Elsa (tl); 118: Getty Images/Mike Powell; 119: Empics Ltd/SportsChrome (tl), Getty Images/Mike Powell (bc); 120: Getty Images/Mike Powell; 121: Corbis/Bettmann; 122: Getty Images/Mike Powell; 123: Getty Images/Sylvia Pecota; 124: Getty Images/Brian Bahr, Getty Images/Mike Powell; 126: Getty Images/Mike Powell; 127: Getty Images; 128–129: Empics Ltd/John Marsh; 130: Empics Ltd/Steve Mitchell; 131: Getty Images/Allen Steele; 132: Empics Ltd/Steve Etherington (br), Empics Ltd/Steve Mitchell (l); 134: Empics Ltd/Steve Mitchell; 135: Getty Images/Mark Thompson; 136: Empics Ltd/Steve Mitchell; 137: Getty Images/Pascal Rondeau (tl); 138: Empics Ltd/Steve Mitchell; 138–139: Getty Images/Pascal Rondeau; 140: Empics Ltd/S&G (br), Empics/Steve Mitchell (l); 142–143: Getty Images/Adam Pretty; 145: Getty Images/Hulton Getty Archive (bl), Getty Images/SOCOG (tl); 147: Getty Images/IOC Olympic Museum; 149: Empics Ltd (tl), Empics (br); 151: Getty Images/Mike Powell (tl), Empics Ltd/Jon Buckle (br); 153: Getty Images/Clive Mason (b); Todd

Warshaw (tl); 154: Empics Ltd/Adam Pretty (br); 156–157: Getty Images/Bob Martin; 159: Getty Images/Hulton Getty Archive (tl); Getty Images/Mike Powell (b); 161: Empics Ltd/Topham Picturepoint (tl), Getty Images/Al Bello (bc); 163: Getty Images/Hamish Blair; 164: Getty Images/Darren England (r); 166–167: Empics Ltd/John Marsh; 168: Empics Ltd/Chris Turvey; 169: Getty Images/Doug Pensinger; 170: Empics Ltd/Chris Turvey; 171: Getty Images/Doug Pensinger; 172: Empics Ltd/Chris Turvey; 173: Getty Images/Mike Powell (b), Empics Ltd/S&G (tl); 174: Empics Ltd/Chris Turvey (l); 174–175: Getty Images/Julian Herbert; 175: Getty Images/Mike Cooper (tl); 176: Empics Ltd/Chris Turvey; 177: Empics Ltd/Hamish Blair; 178–179: Empics Ltd/Tony Marshall; 180: Getty Images/Mike Powell; 181: Getty Images/Pascal Rondeau (tl), Getty Images/Vandystadt (br); 182: Getty Images/Mike Powell; 183: Getty Images (tl), Getty Images (bl); 184: Getty Images/Mike Powell; 185: Action Plus; 186: Getty Images/Mike Powell; 187: Getty Images; 188: Getty Images/Mike Powell; 189: Empics Ltd/Tony Marshall; 190: Getty Images/Chris Cole (br), Getty Images/Mike Powell (l); 192: Getty Images/Mike Powell; 193: Empics Ltd/Alpha (bc), Getty Images/Hulton Getty Archive (tl); 194: Getty Images/Mike Powell; 195: Getty Images/Mike Hewitt; 196: Getty Images/Simon Bruty (br), Getty Images/Mike Powell; 197: Getty Images/Mike Powell; 198: Getty Images/Mike Powell; 199: Getty Images/Allsport Australia (r), Getty Images/Sean Garnsworthy tl; 200: Getty Images/Mike Powell; 201: Kobal Collection/MGM/UA; 202: Getty Images/Mike Powell; 203: Getty Images/Doug Pensinger.

Jacket photography: front: Getty Images/Clive Brunskill; back: Empics Ltd/Chris Cole (tl), Empics Ltd/Neal Simpson (tr), Empics Ltd/Steve Mitchell (br), Empics Ltd/Tony Marshall (bl).

All other images © Dorling Kindersley.
For further information see: www.dkimages.com

AUTHORS' ACKNOWLEDGEMENTS

Ian and Russell would like to thank the following for all their help:

Ray Fletcher
Aylla Macphail
David Middleton, National Rugby League, Australia
Ann Morrison
Dafydd Rees
Debbie Smiley, US Trotting Association
David Wright, Southport Sports Quiz League